Regional Inequality and Development

A Case Study of Kenya

ARNE BIGSTEN
University of Gothenburg, Sweden

Gower

Published by
Gower Publishing Co. Ltd, Westmead, Farnborough, Hampshire, England

BL Cataloguing in Publication Data

Bigsten, Arne
Regional inequality and development
1. Kenya - Economic conditions
2. Underdeveloped areas - Economic conditions - Case studies
3. Regional economics - Case studies
I. Title
330.9'676'204 HC517.K4

ISBN 0 566 00382 1

Contents

Preface

This book is a revised version of my thesis. The study was initiated about five years ago by Åke Andersson. Most of the time I have been working at the Department of Economics at the University of Gothenburg, but I have also spent a period of time as visiting research fellow at the Institute for Development Studies at the University of Nairobi.

During my work I have received help from many people. Åke Andersson and Harald Dickson have been my thesis advisers; I am most grateful to them for their efforts. I should also like to thank Bo Södersten and Mats Lundahl for their cooperation in the field of development economics. Lennart Hjalmarsson and Johan Lybeck have given me constructive criticism. Håkan Persson has helped me solve problems in relation to the regionalization algorithm. William Senga, Peter Hopcraft and Clay Wescott at the IDS in Nairobi all took great interest in my work and gave me considerable help. I should also like to thank Martin Godfrey at the IDS in Sussex, Richard Anker, James Knowles and Gerry Rodgers of the ILO, Jan Gunning of the World Bank, William House and Tony Killick of the Department of Economics at the University of Nairobi, Marianne Ouma at the Central Bureau of Statistics in Nairobi, and Gillis Herlitz of SIDA. The extensive programming work has been done by Conny Ivarsson of the Gothenburg Computer Central. The study has been translated from 'English' to English by Henrik Lutzen. Karin Hane and Greta Fridmar have very efficiently typed the text. I am very grateful to all these people.

The study has been financially supported by SAREC (the Swedish Agency for Research Cooperation with Developing Countries), SRS (the Swedish Social Science Research Council), Kungl Vetenskapsakademien (the Royal Swedish Academy of Science), funds at the University of Gothenburg, and by the Institute for Development Studies, University of Nairobi.

Nairobi, February 1980

Arne Bigsten

I Regional inequality and development

I.1 INTRODUCTION

During the sixties the overall growth figures of most underdeveloped countries were good. Per capita incomes rose faster than at any time before. Growth was, however, in most cases concentrated to the small modern sector and to certain regions, while the majority of the population was left on a very low standard of living; in other words, the distribution of income has become more unequal.

Because of these findings, criticism against development strategies aimed at maximizing growth without consideration for the distributional consequences has been growing. 'Redistribution with Growth' by Chenery et al. (1974) and ILO's 'Employment, Growth, and Basic Needs' (1976) are the most important examples of attempts to define a new strategy. The latter of these draws upon experiences from the numerous country-studies made by the ILO (e.g. the mission to Kenya, ILO, 1972). Both of the works focus on the needs of the poor and outline economic policies aimed at improving their lot. It is stressed that to be able to reach the target groups, planning and policies must be more disaggregated than what has been the case so far. In support of such a policy change there is need for research on the mechanisms determining the distribution of income among sectors, regions and individuals. To be able to analyse the distributional consequences of growth, we need comprehensive models for integrated analysis of growth and distribution.

In this study I shall focus on one aspect of the general problem of distribution, namely regional distribution of income. Policy makers in the Third World are growing more and more aware of the fact that large parts of their countries have been left more or less outside the process of development; this has lead to an increasing concern for regional problems as can be seen in plan documents.

Integration of all regions of a country in the process of development is one important prerequisite for a general equalization of incomes. It is very difficult to bring about interpersonal equalization of incomes when certain areas are stagnating. Theoretically, one might perhaps solve the regional part of the problem of inequality with a very large emigration from these areas, but poor countries have difficulties in coping with large migration flows; an indication of this is the growing slum areas around the big cities. Therefore, keeping migration within certain limits may be considered a goal in itself, and a balanced regional development pattern may contribute to this end. Finally, a balanced regional development pattern is important to stave off inter-regional - which in Africa usually means tribal - conflicts, which often have very disruptive consequences.

The purpose of this study is to analyse the process determining the development of regional incomes and employment in Kenya. I shall attempt to do three things: First, I shall attempt to show how large the regional differences are and how they are developing; secondly, I shall identify the factors that determine their development over time and simulate this development; and thirdly, I shall discuss how it is possible to influence regional inequality by economic policy. These tasks are difficult, and the analysis that is developed obviously has weaknesses; due to the paucity of data, I have to make a number of simplifications in the model. Some relations are thus of an illustrative rather than an analytical nature, which obviously leaves considerable scope for future improvements. Still, I hope that the analysis will make some contribution to the understanding of the development of regional inequality in underdeveloped countries.

The outline of the study is as follows. In Chapter One I present its general perspective, that is introduce the most important explanatory factors. In Chapter Two the historical background to regional inequality in Kenya is presented. In Chapter Three the choice of model is motivated and a summary description of the model is given. In Chapter Four I describe the sectoral structure used in the analysis, and in Chapter Five I explain how the regional disaggregation of the national input-output table is done. Chapters Six to Ten contain a discussion and detailed description of the various steps of the analysis. These chapters deal with, respectively, final demand, production, employment, population and migration, and incomes and inequality. In Chapter Eleven I present the results of the basic solution of the model, or the development alternative without policy changes, and compare this with actual development. In Chapter Twelve regional policy and the effects of various policy changes are analysed. In the final chapter I discuss limitations and possible extensions of this type of approach and summarize the main conclusions of the study.

I.2 A DISEQUALIZING DEVELOPMENT PATTERN

It is a typical feature of growth in low income countries that it is combined with increasing inequality. Kuznets (1955) was one of the first to advance the hypothesis that interpersonal inequality first increases and then decreases with development. The reason for this is that growth in the early stages of development tends to be concentrated to the modern part of the economy, which at that time is small in terms of employment. In preindustrial society, where agriculture predominated, there was little differentiation; with the introduction of capitalistic industries the degree of differentiation increases, causing an increase in inequality.

Kuznets' seminal contribution was followed by a number of studies dealing with this issue. One can mention those by Karvis (1960), Oshima (1962), Adelman and Morris (1971, 1973), Paukert (1973), Chenery and Syrquin (1975), and Ahluwalia (1976a, 1976b). These studies of the distributional consequences of growth are exploratory. They do not investigate dynamic processes in a historical context for any particular country, which should be done, if one is to be able to identify the causal mechanisms. What is needed at present therefore are country studies, in which a more careful analysis of the dynamics of development can be made.

The tentative conclusion that can be drawn from the studies mentioned is that there seems to be a tendency towards increasing inequality in early stages of development, followed by a period of convergence after a certain income level has been reached.

The inverted 'U' pattern has then been claimed to be valid for the development of regional per capita incomes as well. Myrdal (1963) first advanced the hypothesis that there is a general tendency towards increasing regional inequalities in underdeveloped countries, or - in his own terminology - for the backwash effects to outweigh the spread effects. He claims (p. 34) that in poor countries the free play of market forces tends to create regional inequalities and to widen those already existing.

Myrdal argues that once an area within an underdeveloped economy has developed ahead of the others, the imbalance tends to perpetuate itself through a cumulative process. Industries and handicrafts in the backward areas tend to succumb to the increased competition from industries in the advanced areas. Capital migration tends to be 'perverse', that is, capital moves out of the areas where there is little capital per capita to areas where there is plenty. This may be due to higher profitability, to more developed capital markets, or to smaller risks within industrialized areas. Also labour migration tends to be 'perverse' in so far as the most qualified individuals are the first ones to leave the backward areas. As the country develops, the spread effects may begin to assert themselves, but as long as the dual or disintegrated structure of the economy remains they will not be very effective.

Very few empirical studies of the relation between regional inequality and development have been made. In 1965, Williamson presented the first cross-country study of regional inequality covering twentyfour nations (unfortunately, it included relatively few underdeveloped countries). Williamson arranges the countries according to income per capita and finds (p. 115) that "the relationship between level of development and degree of regional inequality is in the form of an inverted 'U', reaching a peak in the middle income class". Williamson also uses what little evidence there is to study the development of regional inequality over time in now developed nations such as the USA and Sweden. He finds (p. 138) that the evidence 'seems to be at least consistent with the result of the cross-section analysis'.

The regional income inequality thus seems to follow the same pattern as personal income inequality, that is, it increases as economic growth starts in an economy with very low incomes and then reaches a turning point, after which it decreases.

The reasons for the early increase in regional inequality advanced by Williamson are: 'Perverse' capital and labour migration and a central government policy aimed at maximizing growth. He argues that eventually the economy will reach a turning point as 'the spread effects may begin to assert themselves from those islands of industrial growth as the economy fully integrates itself and commodity and factor markets become more efficient' (p. 107).

Another factor which is conducive to this situation is changes in the economic policy. Williamson feels that it may be more difficult to disregard large regional inequalities when the country has more resources to spend on regional policy. Recent experiences suggest that the increase in popular pressure for regional equalization comes at a very early stage of the development process and that it, if disregarded, may create tensions hindering national development and integration. In young nations 'nation-building' is an overriding objective, which to be successfully accomplished, requires all parts of the country to have a share in the benefits of development.

Gilbert and Goodman (1976) have pointed out several inherent weaknesses in Williamson's study, some of which Williamson himself has stressed. They particularly emphasize the fact that the results are very sensitive to whether the major city is included with a rural area or is considered as a separate region. In spite of these difficulties Gilbert and Goodman agree that there is at least a clear tendency towards convergence for developed countries. The divergence hypothesis, however, receives 'only flimsy support' (p. 117) by the evidence advanced by Williamson.

They agree that Williamson's hypothesis has received some supporting evidence from studies of other measures of economic activity, such as the provision of an infrastructure, which appears to become more spatially concentrated during the process of growth in low income countries. Still, more recently published, regional income data from fifteen low income countries do not show any marked tendency of regional income differentials to increase with rising per capita incomes. Tanzania and Kenya show the greatest regional income differentials despite the fact that their per capita incomes are among the lowest in the sample (p. 118). Obviously, it is rather difficult to clearly show that regional inequality increases with development by means of cross-section analyses. Time series analyses are necessary before anything definite can be said.

Still, for the poorly integrated African economies it seems plausible to hypothesize that there are strong economic forces working to maintain or further aggravate the imbalance.

However, before discussing the forces at work today I shall point to the historical background of regional inequality in Africa, which will help explain why regional problems are particularly severe in Africa. It will also explain the above mentioned high degree of regional inequality in Kenya and Tanzania.

I.3 THE COLONIAL BACKGROUND TO DEVELOPMENT IN AFRICA

Adelman and Morris (1973) found that dualistic economic development tends to reduce the income shares of the poorest groups. Most African economies can be characterised as dualistic, that is, they have a large (in terms of employment) and slow-growing traditional sector using simple production techniques, and a more rapidly growing modern sector. In most African countries the major part of modern sector production is located in one or a few regions, while semimonetary or subsistence production dominates in the remaining regions. These large differences among regions in sectoral structure explain a large part of regional differences in per capita income.

Almost all African countries have been under foreign domination and exposed to colonization by foreigners during most of the past century. The colonists superimposed an alien pattern of living and an alien pattern of production on a predominantly agricultural, rural and traditional economy. A biased structure of production was created to serve the needs of the mother country and the settlers. The attainment of independence meant that the systematic policy of discrimination was put to an end, but the economic structure has not changed drastically.

The urban and communication patterns that exist in African countries today were shaped according to the needs of the colonists. Most important was the establishment of efficient export channels. The communication system therefore usually centres on some port. The location of railways and colonial administrative centres determined the urban pattern, which in turn became an important determinant of the spatial distribution of industrial activity. However, also in rural areas large differences emerged between settler agriculture and traditional agriculture, which is still reflected in large differences in the size of production units, methods of production, crops, etc.

One of the reasons behind the concentration of production to certain 'enclaves' was, and still is, the fact that large parts of the so-called modern sector have very important relations with the industrialized countries. This is due to the fact that those countries often provide the capital, the technical know-how and the managerial skills used in this sector.

The point that I am trying to make in this section is that the process of growth in these countries led to particularly large regional differences due to the fact that it occurred in a colonial framework. The colonial policy reinforced the differences between a few areas integrated into the monetary economy and subsistence production, which continued to dominate in the rest of the country.

I.4 CUMULATIVE CAUSATION AND AGGLOMERATION ECONOMIES

It has been argued by many that the market mechanism is inefficient in achieving an efficient allocation of resources in underdeveloped countries, in which markets are far from perfect and in which externalities abound. Yet, in most of these countries resource allocation is left to the market, which is complemented with more or less 'development planning'. It is the workings of these market economies that are the object of this study.

Above, I have pointed to some evidence which indicates that growth in low income countries tends to increase interregional inequality. Now I shall try to identify the forces generating this pattern of development.

In the neoclassical models which have dominated regional growth theory, wage and capital yield differentials have been at the centre of the stage (Borts, 1960, Borts and Stein, 1964). According to analyses in this tradition the persistence of regional inequality is caused by lags in adjustment, due to the malfunctioning of the adjustment mechanisms. Imperfections are expected to decrease as the economy develops and factor as well as product markets become more integrated. Then factor transfers are supposed to bring about a process towards equalization of wages and capital yields, and there will be convergence in regional per capita incomes.

It seems reasonable to expect such a convergent pattern to emerge also in the now underdeveloped countries at some future time, but, historically, this tendency towards convergence has not occurred until fairly high income levels have been reached. The economies which I am considering are below this income level; in these economies the forces working to preserve income differentials are still strong. In neoclassical analyses the presumption usually is that the flow of capital from one region to another will tend to eliminate differences between marginal yields in the delivering region and those in the receiving region. In an underdeveloped economy, however, the equilibrating effect may be limited. An increasing capital stock in a region may even increase the marginal efficiency of investment there through external effects. This will subsequently attract even more capital into the rapidly growing and capital rich region. Even Borts (1960, p.329), who made a test on data for American states, found, for example, that the evidence shed 'considerable doubt on the hypothesis that low wages are a major influence on capital movements'.

Moreover, the usefulness of neoclassical models for regional analysis in general has been questioned by Richardson (1973, p. 23), who feels that many of the assumptions they rest upon are not applicable at the regional level. He claims that ' space is incompatible with perfect competition, complete certainty, marginal adjustments in prices, outputs and location, and the other background conditions of the neo-classical world'. He argues that to be realistic regional growth theory must take into account e.g. the effects of agglomeration economies and distances between economic agents.

At least for analysis of regional growth differences in low income countries it seems to be more fruitful to turn to the tradition of 'cumulative causation models', of which Myrdal (1963) was one of the earliest and most influential proponents. His main thesis was that once some areas in an underdeveloped economy have developed ahead of the others, the divergent pattern becomes self-sustaining because of the increasing advantages of producing in the fast growing regions. Myrdal argues (1963, p. 13) that changes in such an economy do not 'call forth countervailing changes, but, instead, supporting changes which move the system in the same direction as the first changes, but much further'. The favourable spread effects from the growing region(s), such as the expansion of markets for the lagging regions, are less than the negative backwash effects, such as the outflow of capital. The advantages that the lagging regions may have, for example a lower wage level, are, according to this view, insufficient to offset the advantages of the developed regions.

Similar arguments concerning regional growth have been advanced by Kaldor (1970, p. 340), who writes that he is sure that the "principle of cumulative causation - which explains the unequal regional incidence of industrial development by endogenous factors resulting from the process of historical development rather than by exogenous differences in 'resource endowments' - is an essential one for the understanding of the diverse trends of development between different regions".

Briefly outlined, Kaldor's argument is the following. First, he argues that the long-run growth rate of a region is determined by the growth of autonomous demand, and that for a region the main part of autonomous demand originates outside the region. His theory therefore, to some extent, resembles the export-base theory. The growth of export demand is then a function of the competitive position of the region, which primarily is determined by the movement of efficiency wages, that is the movement of money wages in relation to productivity, within the region compared to its development in other regions. Finally, he includes the so-called Verdoorn effect in his analysis. According to this, productivity growth is (at least partly) dependent on the growth of output itself. Rapidly growing regions can therefore improve their competitive position and continuously grow faster than the lagging regions. It is the Verdoorn effect that makes the model a cumulative causation model.

Dixon and Thirlwall (1975) have attempted to formalize the model along the lines sketched here. They must, however, satisfy themselves with a partial equilibrium approach where each region is considered in isolation. Interregional relationships are considered only implicitly. Because of the Verdoorn effect a region can sustain a high growth rate once it has got a growth advantage. This effect thus makes it difficult for the other regions to catch up.

Dixon and Thirlwall furthermore show that regional structure has important implications for regional growth in the model, a feature which Kaldor did not stress. They draw the conclusion that what the lagging regions need is to become more competitive and/or to change the industrial structure so that the regions get more industries producing goods with high income elasticities, or with high Verdoorn coefficients attached to them.

There are many other authors who have had more or less perfected ideas about the process working towards increasing regional inequality. One example is John Friedman, who emphasizes centre-periphery relations. He argues (1972) that the core regions dominate the periphery due to their higher capacity for innovative change. Another example is the discussion within the so-called dependency school (Frank, 1969, Amin, 1970, Sunkel, 1973), where the problem of underdevelopment is discussed in terms of centre-periphery or metropolis-satellite relations. The peripheral regions are linked to the centre by an exploitative relationship. Development at the centre is dependent on the periphery being drained of its surplus.

The common denominator of all of these analyses is that they identify cumulative forces working against equalization. Since the discussion, in most cases, has been kept in general terms, the concepts have proved to be difficult to operationalize. I shall here explicitly try to identify the most important agglomerative forces, and then to operationalize and use them in the model analysis.

One can distinguish between economies of scale which are internal to firms and external agglomeration economies. In the latter category one can distinguish at least three kinds of factors, namely input-output linkages, interactions between final demand and producers, and factors controlled by policy makers.

I.5 ECONOMIES OF SCALE

Internal economies of scale are due to technical and administrative factors (for a discussion, see e.g. Silberston, 1972). With economies of scale there are costs of decentralization; there will therefore be a tendency of concentration towards a few production units. The size distribution of firms producing some specific product can be explained by economies of scale (Hjalmarsson, 1974). In a small, underdeveloped economy the markets for many products are so small that there will be room for only one or a few firms.

One can, broadly, distinguish three types of industries in terms of location determining factors. First, there are the natural resource oriented industries, that is agriculture and mining; their location is basically determined by the location of the natural resources which they exploit; economies of scale are not so important for the locational decisions for this type of production. Secondly, there are industries where economies of scale are small and/or the distance elasticity of deliveries is high, that is construction, utilities, and tertiary activities; the location of these industries tends to reflect the distribution of demand for their output. Finally, there is the category which has considerable economies of scale as well as a low distance elasticity of deliveries, that is mainly manufacturing. It is primarily for this category that economies of scale will imply a tendency towards spatial concentration.

However, given that demand is spread out, the costs of transporting the products to the consumers or other communication costs will imply a tendency towards decentralization also for manufacturing. There will thus be a trade-off between reductions in production costs through concentration and reductions in transportation costs through decentralization. These problems have been analysed in market area analysis by e.g. Cristaller (1966) and Lösch (1954). Gunnarsson (1977) has analysed the formation of hierarchies of urban centres on the basis of assumptions of this type.

One may conclude that the locational choices of industries with economies of scale will tend to generate a more concentrated pattern of production than the choices of industries without economies of scale. Economies of scale alone cannot, however, explain the location of the factories. They cannot explain why manufacturing firms producing completely different products often locate together in a few geographical areas. Here the external relations of the firms must be taken into account. There may also be a tendency towards concentration by firms with no economies of scale, trying to minimize communication costs within the pattern of interregional input-output and final demand linkages. This will be discussed in the next section.

I.6 INPUT-OUTPUT AND FINAL DEMAND LINKAGES

In a market economy the critical factors in the pattern of regional growth are the location and output decisions of firms. Usually it is difficult for the government to influence the location decisions of private industries, even if there is a desire to do so (which is not always the case). Private firms locate according to their own preferences, that is, they choose the location that they believe to be the most profitable for the firm.

The idea that development implies structural change, and particularly that it is associated with divergent sectoral growth rates was advanced already by Schumpeter (1969). This idea then became central in the discussion of development theory starting with the classic articles by Rosenstein-Rodan (1943) and Lewis (1954). Since then, many theorists have analysed the course of structural transformation, but few have considered the spatial consequences of this transformation. I shall focus upon the latter aspect in this study.

My first point is that input-output linkages influence location decisions and thereby the development of regional incomes. Firms among which there is much interdependence tend to locate close together; this implies that there will be little stimulus to lagging regions from growth within such a cluster of firms. The secondary effects of growth within the lagging regions also tend to leak out to the more developed regions that can supply the intermediate inputs needed. These poor regions are in the same position vis à vis the more developed regions as an underdeveloped country is vis à vis the rest of the world. Domestic input-output linkages are weak, and much input has to be supplied from the outside.

In the development literature the importance of input-output linkages has been stressed particularly by Perroux (1955) and Hirschman (1958). Perroux introduced the concept of growth pole, and pointed out (1955, p. 94) that 'growth does not appear everywhere at the same time; it becomes manifest at points or poles of growth, with variable intensity; it spreads through different channels, with variable terminal effects on the whole of the economy'. A similar type of argument was advanced by Hirschman (1958, p. 195), who contended that what a lagging region needs is 'some ongoing and actively inducing economic activity of its own, in industry, agriculture, or services'.

In the wake of these early suggestions an extensive literature on 'growth pole theory' has cropped up. The early formulation of a theory of polarized development by Perroux was abstract, and it had little reference to geographical space. Boudeville (1966) and others have extended it to include this dimension as well.

Industrial complexes are central to this theory. By the concept of growth pole is meant a cluster of activities with high propulsive strength, that is, industries with high capacity to transmit growth impulses through backward as well as forward linkages to other industries.

To qualify as a development pole a centre must have a propulsive industry that belongs to the 'leading industry' category.

One thus tries to identify certain key industries within this theory. This is the central aspect of the theory, but there are also other features. There is, for example, much emphasis laid on the role of cities or systems of cities. In this context the importance of high-level amenities, such as hospitals, schools, cinemas, restaurants, etc. as well as a growth minded social structure is pointed out.

Still, I believe that much of the writings on growth pole theory is lacking in clarity; there are, for example, no criteria by which relevant centres may be identified (cfr. Alonso, 1968, p. 3, and Hansen, 1972). The theory does not show why a certain pole starts to grow at a certain location, nor what determines the spatial distribution of the induced growth effects.

It is argued by Hermansen (1972) that when the growth pole concept is applied to geographical space it has to rely on traditional theories of location, spatial organization, and external agglomeration, since it in itself is not a theory of location. It has been suggested that it should be viewed as a conditional theory explaining where growth <u>may</u> occur. 'The more intricate problem of establishing necessary and sufficient conditions for growth is left unresolved' (Hermansen, 1972, p. 174). The predictive power of the theory thus seems to be weak.

Even if the theory lacks in clarity, its emphasis on intersectoral linkages is commendable. They transmit growth impulses in a market economy. The gist of my first point therefore is that input-output linkages should be considered in the analysis of the development of interregional inequality.

The second main economic factor determining how growth impulses are transmitted is the interaction between final demand and production. Demand is the mediator of impulses from incomes to production. The location of demand depends on the location of incomes, but this, in turn, is determined by the location of production. Accordingly, it is important to consider the system in its entirety, that is, as an interdependent system.

Economic development may be looked upon as the result of a continued process of interaction between demand increases and increases in supply. If a decentralized economic system is to be able to keep up self-sustained growth, the interaction between demand and supply impulses must function smoothly. In an underdeveloped economy there are frictions and imperfections hindering the smooth functioning of this process, especially outside the most developed regions.

Both Richardson (1969, p. 343) and Kaldor (1970) emphasize the role of demand in the determination of regional growth, and also Borts (1960, p. 342) found in his study of the United States that demand appears to be a very important determinant of where growth will occur. Of course, there are supply restrictions on growth in an underdeveloped country, but within these the growth of markets undoubtedly is an important determinant of the regional pattern of growth.

We thus have interdependence between production and final demand. The concentration of production leads to a concentration of demand, which then tends to perpetuate or accentuate the agglomerative tendencies and regional inequalities in income. For industries producing consumer goods above a certain level of sophistication and for industries producing investment goods, a very large portion of the total market in most African economies is to be found in the main region(s).

It should be borne in mind that it is not only the location of demand that is important. We also know that the income elasticities differ, and that they are particularly low for agriculture, which usually dominates in the lagging regions.

The location and pattern of final demand is the second main force one should consider when analysing the development of regional incomes. I thus emphasize induced economic effects, which for most sectors are more important than differences in natural resource endowment. If one is interested mainly in the growth differentials in a situation where no new discoveries are made, this disregard of natural resources should be an acceptable simplification.

The rate of structural change is the central variable in the development process. What is of interest here is the differential impact of this change on different regions. The differences in the structure of production is the most important determinant of regional inequality in underdeveloped countries.

The pattern of development also has effects on the migration of people, which is the result of the totality of economic and social influencies. The fact that people move out of the lagging regions should counteract the tendency of increasing regional inequality. Migration is, however, to a large extent caused by the economic forces, which must be considered to be the driving force of the process. Therefore, attention should be concentrated on the allocation of capital.

In this section I have emphasized the role of input-output linkages and final demand in the transmission of growth impulses. There is, however, one set of factors relevant to this analysis which is controlled by the policy makers. These factors will be considered briefly in the next section.

I.7 REGIONAL POLICY

In the previous section the argument was that in an underdeveloped economy endogenous economic forces determine the development of regional incomes. In recent years the ambitions with regard to regional equity have been raised, and they are now often stated as one of the main policy objectives. A change of the development pattern in favour of the lagging regions implies an increase in the growth rates of the lagging regions relative to the more developed regions. To accomplish this one must find ways to influence the decisions on where to increase production.

In this section I shall discuss the role of the government and the regional effects of economic policy. The policy is controlled by the government, and it can be used to change the pattern of development outlined in the previous section in the direction desired by the government.

First, let us consider the policy makers, the institutional set up and the restrictions that the latter places on policy choices. The institutional problem has two sides: First, the possibility of lack of competence of the administrators or lack of resources to implement regional policy. It is a common observation that the planning machinery works better on plan formulation than on implementation. Administrative capacity is often a more pervasive constraint than lack of financial resources.

Furthermore, even if the resources and the administrative capacity needed for a regional policy do exist, it is not self evident that such a policy will be implemented. Influential pressure groups may work against shifting the distribution of public goods and the location of industry in the direction of the less developed regions.

There may be tribal interests which bias the allocation in favour of some regions. In Africa patron-client relationships often form the basis of politics, and politicians need to show results in their home areas to be able to retain their positions. It is possible for the powerful groups to influence the regional distribution in favour of their own areas, if power is unequally distributed among people from different regions or different tribes.

The type of government and the types of interests that it represents also places restrictions on the type of policies that will be proposed. One would expect the elite to be reluctant to suggest reforms that would eventually undermine its position. This is generally a strong force against redistributive policy in systems where the distribution of economic and political power coincide.

The factor most commonly referred to in connection with regional development policy is the development of infrastructure. Hirschman (1958) pointed to the construction of social overhead capital as one way of inducing private investment; the need to create a favourable investment climate in lagging regions through a build up of overhead capital has also been emphasized within the growth centre tradition. Investments in, for example, education and health facilities in themselves constitute a contribution to the welfare of the population, but in this context one usually only considers the induced effects on other investment. Investment in such amenities may increase worker productivity, but it may also make the location more attractive to people. Also Richardson (1973, pp. 232-3) believes that infrastructural investment is the best way for a government to create agglomeration economies.

We can distinguish two types of infrastructure. One is localized entirely within a region and affects it directly. The other type is an infrastructure which improves contacts with other parts of the country. The effects of the latter kind seem more difficult to predict, since there could be negative as well as positive effects associated with it. Competition from other regions would increase.

The communication system is of special interest in infrastructural development. In many African states (cfr. e.g. Mabogunje, 1965, 1971, on Nigeria) economic integration and production in the periphery is hampered by the inadequacy of the transport system. The transport networks developed by the colonial powers were intended to connect the areas of primary production with the export harbours or to secure political control.

> 'Export-orientated planning and imperially constituted frontiers have lead to transport systems throughout Africa, which are weirdly irrelevant to population patterns, potential market areas and natural sites for the development of industrial-agricultural complexes' (Green, Seidman, 1968, p. 66).

The transport networks were not designed to facilitate the flow of people, goods, or information between different parts of the nations of today. Improvements in the communication systems therefore are an important prerequisite for improved integration. This, in turn, would hopefully facilitate the spread of economic impulses outside the most developed areas, and make it possible for the peripheral regions to increase production for markets outside the region.

There are, of course, regional policies other than infrastructural investment. These may be of many kinds and more or less far reaching. First, of course, there is the possibility of using various taxes or subsidies to stimulate firms to behave in the manner desired by the government. It is also possible to use various ad hoc measures such as special funds, minimum wage differentials among regions, investment credit allowances, selective duty remission and tariff protection to influence investment decisions of firms. These measures may be combined with direct negotiations with the firms, which get certain benefits in return for the acceptance of a certain location.

Another possibility is to use demand policy. The easiest way, of course, is to change the allocation of the government's own demand in favour of the lagging regions. By transferring money to the poorest consumers demand should shift towards the poorer regions since there is a relatively larger fraction of poor people living there; this would increase the demand for food, the production of which often plays a relatively larger role in the economies of the poorer regions. One might also promote exports of goods produced mainly in the lagging regions, usually agricultural products.

If stimulus or negotiations are not effective enough, it is possible to go one step further and use direct regulation. The problem is, however, that in a free market system the producer may choose to abstain from making the investment alltogether, if he cannot make it at the location of his choice.

There is also the possibility of a more direct interference with or involvement in production by the government. It can pursue a structural policy either as a coordinator of independent producers, or in an owner capacity. The ultimate policy in this respect would, of course, be a fully planned economy, but then we have an economic system different from the one to which I originally restricted my analysis.

One should also consider the regional incidence of general economic policies. Because of the large differences in economic structure among regions one might expect varying regional effects of certain general policies, even if they are not regionally differentiated. An obvious example is the import substitution policy most underdeveloped countries have pursued - a policy which has worked against agriculture (Little, Scitovsky, Scott, 1970). As agriculture dominates in the lagging regions regional inequality increases. It is probably correct to say that no policies affect all regions equally. Policy makers should bear this in mind, if they consider regional equalization to be a vital objective.

I.8 A SUMMING UP

First, I have identified the regional problem as one part of the general problem of distribution. It has, however, one further dimension. If regional inequalities are allowed to grow, this might lead to tensions between different parts of a country. It is desirable to integrate all parts of a country in the process of development to get a stable base for long run development.

Of course, the policy objective of regional per capita income equalization is not an unproblematic one. Regional equalization does not necessarily imply reduced personal inequality or even a more efficient spatial organization of production. It is possible to create regional equalization and at the same time increase inequality within the regions. When choosing among the regional policy alternatives available, policy makers certainly need to make some qualifications of the objective in this respect.

I have emphasized two main types of influences. First, there are the endogenous economic forces. It was pointed out that economies of scale tend to generate concentration of production. Still, from this we cannot draw any conclusions about where these concentrations will be. The role of input-output linkages among producers and the links between final demand and producers in determining locational choice are emphasized. I have suggested that these forces tend to increase or preserve regional inequality in a poorly integrated, low income country. Secondly, the effects of economic policy on the pattern of development should be taken into account.

II A short historical background to regional inequality in Kenya

As a background to the analysis of regional inequality in Kenya today I shall briefly outline its recent economic history. I shall emphasize those aspects which are of relevance to the analysis of regional inequality.

The Swahili culture along the coast had for a long time been in contact with the outside world, but it was not until the 19th century that Europeans started to penetrate into the Kenyan inland. Until then life there had followed the same, traditional pattern as it had done for centuries. The agricultural societies were organized on a family or clan basis, among which power was evenly distributed. The ecological conditions vary among regions in Kenya with consequentially varying soil fertilities, but this was reflected in the settlement pattern. In low fertility areas the population density was low. At times, certain tribes, like the Masai, were powerful and controlled disproportionately large areas, but still one cannot talk about any significant land shortage for other groups. Therefore one can assume that the differences in standard of living among tribes were limited, that is, regional inequalities in per capita incomes at this time were relatively small. The large inequalities that existed in Kenya among regions and among groups of people at Independence were thus created during the period of colonial domination. The policy pursued by the British colonists aggravated the imbalances which tend to accompany economic growth.

The British were up to the 1870's content to rely on free trade to maintain their commercial interests in the area (Wolff, 1974, p. 32). From this time, however, they started to pursue a more active policy, partly due to the competition with Germany. The respective spheres of influence of Britain and Germany in East Africa were drawn up in negotiations in 1886 and 1890. First, the British government controlled the area indirectly through the British East Africa Company, but in 1895 the East Africa Protectorate was created.

During the period 1896-1901, a railway was built from Mombasa on the coast to Lake Victoria. It was financed by loans from the British Treasury. The British policy in the following years was determined by the need to make the colony pay its own administration and to pay back the loans for the railway. The way chosen to accomplish this was to try to establish a white settler agriculture which could produce for export.

The dominant concern of the authorities during the first decades of colonial rule was the provision of good and cheap agricultural land for the settlers. Large areas of land were alienated, and for example tribes like the Kikuyu, the Masai, and the Nandi had to give up land which previously had been under their control (Wolff, 1974, pp. 63-7). This land was sold to the settlers on favourable terms.

The White Higlands, comprising about twenty per cent of the best agricultural land in Kenya, was not legally demarcated until 1939, but in reality this land was exclusively European already from the beginning of the century (van Zwanenberg and King, 1975, p. 34).

Export production of primarily coffee and sisal but later also of wheat, maize, and tea gradually increased. Nevertheless, the settlers had continual difficulties in making the production profitable due to lack of knowledge and capital. They were chronically in debt, and insolvency was common (van Zwanenberg, 1975, p. xvi). This was the main cause of the enormous exploitation of labour that took place in Kenya; the settler farms had to have cheap wage labour to be economically viable.

A number of methods were used to guarantee a reliable and cheap supply of wage labour. (For an extensive discussion of this, see primarily van Zwanenberg, 1975, but also e.g. Brett, 1973, Wolff, 1974, Leys, 1975.) First, the fact that the Africans were restricted to their reserves meant that there was pressure on the land in many areas; this combined with the need to get money to be able to pay the Hut and Poll taxes, introduced by the colonial administration, forced many Africans to seek wage labour on European farms. However, these two factors by themselves were not enough to get a sufficient number of Africans to accept work at the going wages. A number of other measures were also necessary: notably force and, at a later stage, very 'active encouragement' by the authorities. The farmers used professional recruiters, or local chiefs or headmen, to recruit labour with methods of their own choice. The administration furthermore introduced laws concerning the terms of employment and pass laws to control the movements of the Africans, who had to have a registration certificate on which the periods of work were entered by their employers. It was a criminal offence to leave the employer before the contract period was at an end.

Since the Europeans had large unused areas of land, organized squatting was an increasingly common way of getting cheap labour. When land was scarce in the reserves, many Africans were willing to bring along their families and use some land on a European farm in return for their labour. In this fashion a considerable amount of African wage labour was created. It has been estimated that in the mid-twenties more than half of the able-bodied male Luos and Kikuyus were employed on European farms (Leys, 1975, p. 31), and in total about forty per cent of all eligible males were working on white farms (Wolff, 1974, p. 116).

The provision of cheap land and cheap labour were, however, not the only ingredients in the colonial policy of support of European agriculture. The settler colony managed to secure monopoly advantages in many other fields. They had exclusive control over the various marketing and regulatory boards, production committees etc. and used them to serve their interests.

African agriculture received practically no support (see e.g. van Zwanenberg and King, 1975, pp. 39-41). Apart from the fact that the Africans had little land, they had little access to extension services, which were geared to the needs of the white settlers. Furthermore, they were forbidden to grow various cash crops, and in most areas e.g. they were not allowed to grow coffee until sometime during the fifties.

The infrastructural development also favoured the settlers. The railway served the areas of white settlement. Education was primarily given to the children of the settlers. Brett (1973, p. 193) has pointed out that the tax system in fact transferred money from the poor African areas to the wealthy white areas.

The colonial administration thus actively contributed to the creation of enormous differences between different people and areas. The White Highlands were their concern, while the African areas were, more or less, regarded as a labour reserve. There was not much integration between the settler economy and the African economy apart from labour migration.

Still, some differences were created also among African areas. Those located within reach of the newly developed commercial links and centres could, to some extent, take advantage of this and sell some of their produce for cash. The outlying districts on the other hand could not sell anything; their only possibility to get cash was labour migration (van Zwanenberg, 1975, pp. 102-3).

Until the end of the thirties, industrialization in Kenya had not been actively encouraged. There was a general lack of interest, and in some cases even an active policy against the industrialization of East Africa (Brett, 1973, ch. 9). The colonies were primarily regarded as suppliers of raw materials and markets for British manufacturers.

Before the War the companies that existed in Kenya were devoted to agricultural production, ancillary services and food processing on a small scale (Swainson, 1975, p. 19). The market was too small to provide any stimulus for other industries. As the industries that existed at this time were devoeted to the processing of agricultural produce, they were located all over the country. They did not show the same pronounced pattern of concentration to urban centres, primarily Nairobi and Mombasa, which has emerged since then (van Zwanenberg and King, 1975, p. 139).

During the War there was a change in policy, as Britain no longer could supply the goods needed. The colony was stimulated to start producing consumer goods for the home market. A more active import substitution policy with tariffs, investment rebates, tax concessions, etc. was pursued (van Zwanenberg and King, 1975, p. 126).

The European farmers had started to do well in the forties, but the same cannot be said about African farmers. The increasing pressure on the land together with the lack of public support and even discrimination blocked progress. The African agriculture at this time was characterized by a very rapid deterioration of the land due to fragmentation, overstocking and erosion (Okoth-Ogendo, 1976, p. 157). The social system which had provided some controls of land use was also disintegrating. These factors lead to an increasing emigration from the African reserves.

The difficult situation in the reserves, primarily the Kikuyu area, led to the Mau Mau revolt and the Emergency in the fifties. This forced the government to concern themselves with the African agriculture, and in 1954 the Swynnerton plan was presented; it included the development of extension services in the African areas, permission to grow cash crops, access to credits, and land consolidation and registration: In short, it attempted to introduce capitalistic agriculture also within the African areas. The policies for small farm areas initiated at that time are still pursued (van Zwanenberg and King, 1975, p. 49).

Still, these policy changes could not halt the movement towards political independence. In the Lancaster House conferences in 1960 and 1962, the British and the African delegations worked out an agreement; the essence of that was that Africans buying land in the White Highlands should pay for it with loans from the Kenyan government, which in turn was to obtain considerable sums of money from the British for this purpose. The transfer of power could then take place in an orderly fashion, and the respect for private property would be upheld. The transfer of political power in 1963 did not bring about any radical changes in the economic structure (Wasserman, 1973a, 1973b, 1976, Leys, 1975).

About half a million Africans have been settled in the former White Highlands since independence (Leys, 1975, p. 63), but even so, considerable differences between large and small farm areas still remain. There is, however, not longer a clearcut division between European and African areas.

At independence, monetary production was concentrated to the White Highlands and a few urban agglomerations, while subsistence production dominated in the rest of the country. The infrastructural distribution reflected this pattern. Kenya thus inherited a disintegrated economic structure with enormous inequalities between different regions.

Since independence, Kenya has followed a policy of moderation and tried to preserve political stability. Politics are dominated by the civil service, which plays a crucial role. Frances Stewart (1976, p. 84) has summarized the development strategy followed by Kenya since independence as 'kenyanization and modernization (in particular industrialization) in a capitalist framework'. The kenyanization has been most far reaching in agriculture, but also within the administration and the private industry expatriate personnel has been replaced by Kenyans to a considerable degree.

To stimulate industrialization the government has pursued an import-substitution policy. This policy has resulted in an impressive growth in the national product (six-seven per cent per year until the 'oil crisis'). The fast growing, modern part of the economy has, however, not been able to absorb very much of the fast growing labour force, which is why small scale agriculture has had to absorb an increasing number of people. While the policy has benefited those who have been absorbed by the modern sector, the majority still earns very meagre incomes.

One important aspect of the industrialization policy has been the open door policy towards foreign investments. Kenya has striven to create a good investment climate offering foreign investors very favourable terms. This together with the fast economic growth has indeed attracted many foreign investors; in 1970-1973 foreign investment constituted ten to fifteen per cent of total investments in Kenya (Langdon, 1975, p. 84). The foreign influence is therefore very strong, particularly within manufacturing.

The policy of the government towards foreign investment is summarized by Leys (1975, p. 122) as 'Africanization of management posts; attempts at government control through regulation, taxation and exchange control; and measures to secure African participation in the equity of foreign firms'. These measures have not implied any serious restriction of the activities of foreign firms; they have the know-how and the capital which Kenya needs for its industrialization drive, and this together with their superior expertise gives them a very strong bargaining position.

The import substitution policy and the reliance on foreign capital has led to the use of a fairly capital intensive technology, which has created little employment. The benefits of the fast growth have been shared by relatively few. In the report of the World Bank mission to Kenya (1975, p. xi) it is pointed out that the performance of the Kenyan economy during the first decade of independence has been quite remarkable in many ways, but that it has been disappointing with respect to the growth of employment and its impact on the poverty of the lowest income groups.

It is argued that the 'rapid growth of the urban formal sector has not always been to the benefit of society as a whole'. The World Bank therefore argues for a change in the pattern of growth. Kenyan growth has been based on the growth of the market for Western consumer goods, and this market in turn has been created by the growth of the modern sector and the consequent creation of a wealthy middleclass. There is thus an interdependence between the type of production that expands and the type of demand that grows. The small modern sector creates its own demand, while the rest of the economy is of secondary importance. The dual economy is still a reality.

There are thus strong economic forces working to preserve the imbalances in the economy among sectors and thus also among regions. What is needed to change this pattern of development is an active government policy aimed at improving income distribution and integration of all parts of the economy into the monetary economy.

III Choice of approach

III.1 SCOPE OF THE STUDY

In almost every textbook on development economics, as well as in textbooks on development within other disciplines, there is a discussion of what development really is. E.g. one often tries to make a distinction between growth and development. Growth is then considered to be a purely quantitative phenomenon, namely the increase of total or per capita production. Economic development, on the other hand, is taken to mean qualitative changes such as structural transformation, technological improvements, and closing of sectoral and regional gaps. See e.g. Schumpeter (1969, p. 63), Myrdal (1968, pp. 1859-70), Georgescu-Roegen (1971, p. 292).

Much has been written on the subject, but all attempts to define development must have a more or less normative character. It is impossible to scientifically specify what development really is. In my opinion, one should therefore instead state, in an exact manner, what kinds of changes one intends to study. It is then possible to use one's own value judgements (and others can use theirs) to evaluate the changes, and to say whether the changes are for the better or for the worse.

A systems view is desirable when studying the evolution of a society. The strength of economics is its capacity to deal with interdependence within a system, that is to take a comprehensive view of the interrelations between different parts of the economy. The problem in relation to social change is that it is impossible to cover all relevant aspects of the social system consistently.

One alternative is then to try to cover all aspects, even if the analysis breaks down into a large number of partial analyses, the internal consistency of which cannot be checked effectively. Approaches of this kind are, for example, found in Myrdal's Asian Drama (1968) and the ILO-Report on Kenya (1972).

The other alternative is to retain some kind of equilibrium framework, within which checks of internal consistency are possible. This means that the scope of the study has to be somewhat narrower. It is not possible to determine once and for all which of these approaches is to be preferred. To a considerable extent it must be dependent on the purpose of the analysis.

Today there is a trend away from general models of development of the type which dominated the discussion during the fifties and the early sixties. For example, Higgins (1968, p. 347) believes that a general theory of development is beyond reach today, because of the difficulty in finding factors and relations which have been relatively invariant under different conditions in time and space. In relation to models of income distribution Chenery et al. (1974, p. XIX) write that 'because of the lack of an adequate theory of income distribution we do not put high priority upon the construction of more elaborate general-purpose models. Instead, the development of more limited models directed at particular problems appears more promising ...'.

A limited approach, which illustrates or explains a specific problem and thereby contributes to the solution of that problem, therefore seems justifiable. My ambition is to try to improve our understanding of the forces that create regional inequalities in per capita incomes and employment. Because interregional and intersectoral interdependencies are of fundamental importance to the development of regional inequality, I have chosen to use a kind of equilibrium framework for the analysis.

III.2 IN SEARCH OF A MODEL

The purpose of this study is to analyse the forces determining the development of regional inequalities in Kenya, and also to discuss what can be done about them. Thus, we need a model that can explain the growth of regional production and employment, and within which the effects of policy changes can be analysed. The main factors that should be taken into account were identified in Chapter I.

Since the model is to be implemented empirically in an underdeveloped economy, which has a limited data base, the scope for model-building is restricted. Still, the ambition must be to use a comprehensive approach. Partial analyses are unsatisfactory in this case, because interdependencies among sectors and regions are of great importance. Aggregate models are not satisfactory for an analysis of growth rate differences among regions with very different economic structures. For this purpose the advantages of a disaggregated model are obvious. Some checks of consistency must be provided to reach conclusions about the economic process which are not contradictory.

In this analysis of the development of a system of regions, I can either use a Keynes-Leontief model, which is demand-oriented, or a neoclassical model, which is supply-oriented.

There are two main reasons for preferring the Keynes-Leontief approach to the neoclassical approach. First, in Kenya it is not feasible to estimate production functions by regional sectors, which would be necessary to implement an interregional neoclassical model. Secondly, it is easier to incorporate the factors discussed in Chapter I in a Keynes-Leontief model.

Therefore, in order to determine where production will expand, the allocation of demand is used instead of the allocation of capital and labour (even if the allocation of the factors naturally must reflect the distribution of production). To be able to explain why certain regions are lagging behind, the interregional distances must be taken into account. The regional pattern of input-output and final demand linkages will therefore be modelled by means of a gravity approach.

The model that will be used is a recursive variant of the interregional input-output model. Compared to other regional models this type of model has the advantage that it is empirically applicable, but still disaggregated as well as general; it also takes into consideration the fact that the growth rate of a region is very much dependent on what is happening outside the region.

III.3 AN OVERVIEW OF THE MODEL

The model outlined here will be used to simulate the development of production and employment by region and sector in Kenya.

I am primarily interested in analysis rather than 'planning'. This type of analysis can furnish certain quantitative information on regional problems, but no precise answers. It brings out the structure of the economy in quantitative form and it may thereby serve an important pedagogical purpose. Datta-Chaudhuri (1975) has pointed out that on the basis of such a model one cannot, for example, make a detailed investment plan. What can be reached from the analysis are broad conclusions on how different forces determine the pattern of regional development and in what direction policy makers should try to influence these. Locational planning must thus be more specific, but the model can e.g. give some information on how investments should be allocated among regions to bring about a certain degree of equalization.

A forecasting or projection model can never give an exactly correct prediction of the future, but it should be able to suggest the general direction of change. On the basis of the best data available and on hypotheses about the critical relationships in the economy, the model generates production and employment projections for different sectors and regions of the economy. We get a basic scenario. Then, within the model, one can test the effects of changes in certain key parameters and the effects of various policy changes. The advantages as far as the policy analysis is concerned is that one is able to quantify the effects, and to study them systematically within a consistent framework. The model focuses on the monetary part of the economy, because it is the regional incidence of monetary production that is the main cause of regional inequalities in per capita incomes. In Kenya monetary production constitutes more than three quarters of GDP (Statistical Abstract).

One might ask what relevance this analysis has for the small scale farmers who constitute the majority of the population. In the model, they are mainly regarded as a pool of labour, but it should be borne in mind that more than fifty per cent of the production of modern agriculture emanates from the small scale farmers. Thus, many of the small farm families have one foot in the monetary economy.

From the study we can also see how fast the small farm population can be absorbed into modern employment, and also where this increase in employment will take place. The process of 'filtering down' would be facilitated with a more dispersed pattern of production. The commercialization of subsistence agriculture and also the growth of other economic activities in the peripheral regions would be stimulated by the establishment of modern production activities there.

Furthermore, through the extended family system incomes are redistributed outside the group of wage earners within the modern sector. Different types of wage employment already yield important extra incomes for small farmer households. It is therefore important also for family members who are not involved in the modern sector that some member of the family gets a job. Already twenty-one per cent of the male small farm population work outside the farm (Statistical Abstract, 1977, p. 134). The chances for someone in a particular area to get a modern sector job are better, if production is located nearby. Also, more of the earnings should flow back to the family, if the wage earner remains in the area. Equalization among regions is therefore important also for small farm families in the remote and poor areas, even if only one member of the family gets a modern sector job.

One limitation which ought to be pointed out is that the type of analysis presented here does not take cyclical phenomena into account. Shortrun problems and instruments are ignored. What I am trying to do is to give a reasonably accurate description of the long run development pattern.

Kenya experienced a steady growth of between six and seven per cent until the country was hit by the 'oil-crisis' and recession of 1974-75. These years are therefore atypical and their low growth rate due to exogenous foreign factors. Then in 1976-77, there was a commodity boom that increased incomes, particularly in agriculture. This type of change, of course, cannot be predicted by the model.

In the model, there is no distinction made between foreign owned firms and local firms. This is a drawback, if the behaviour of foreign and local firms differ significantly. However, according to the ILO-mission (Kaplinsky, 1978, p. 285) it is the sectoral differences that are significant rather than the differences in ownership. Gyllström (1977) on the other hand, found that the part of the Kenyan tea industry which is controlled by multinational corporations has a smaller impact on the local economy in terms purchases of inputs etc. than the locally owned firms. Yet, even if there exist differences that are due to nationality of ownership, there is, at present, no empirical basis for incorporating such factors in a model.

I have chosen to use an open, interregional input-output model for the analysis. Since it is difficult to apply a traditional dynamic input-output model, a stepwise recursive approach will be used. By choosing an open model it is easier to study the effects of variations in policy.

The sectoral structure of production within the regions play a central role. The pattern and growth of demand is the driving force of the model, which endogenously determines production and employment by sector and region, and migration.

Ideally, regional (supply) restrictions on economic growth should be taken into account, and the development of demand be allowed to determine the regional distribution of growth within these restrictions. However, I have not considered it feasible to incorporate such regionally specific restrictions. The fact that they may exist and are excluded should be kept in mind, when the results of the simulations are discussed.

In the first step, the model equates supply with demand for a number of aggregate commodities. In the production solution there then exists an equilibrium in the sense that there is no excess demand or supply in the product market. This result is taken as an input in the following submodels, in which no equilibrium is assumed to be reached. The employment model does not clear the labour market, and the migration flows are simply partial adjustments to regional differences.

This model is formulated in real terms, and ignores price changes and financial aspects - features which it shares with most economy wide models that have been applied in Third World countries. The model concentrates on structural change, and the simplification of constant prices means that the possible effects on structural change of long term trends in relative prices cannot be taken into account.

The simulation consists of five steps for each year:

STEP 1: Determination of final demand by sector and region
STEP 2: Determination of production by region and sector from the interregional input-output model and the final demand estimates
STEP 3: Determination of employment by region and sector
STEP 4: Determination of population size by region
STEP 5: Calculation of regional per capita incomes

III.3.1 Determination of final demand by region and sector (Step 1)

If there are r regions and i sectors one has to estimate ri items of each demand category, that is, private consumption (C), gross fixed capital investment by delivering sector (DI), government consumption (G), exports (E), and competitive imports (MC). (Final demand imports are assumed to be competitive.) Thus, in the model, one has to estimate as much as 5ri items of final demand. Since the model is solved in a sequential manner, consequetive periods must be linked together. Demand will therefore be dependent on incomes in the previous period.

The estimation of total final demand by delivering sector and region is complicated by the fact that consumption and investment demand generated within a region can be met also by deliveries from other regions. The procedure by which the demand directed towards each regional sector is computed is described in Chapter VI. Here it suffices to say that C and DI first are added together and that MC then is deducted. This gives us the vector of consumption and investment demand net of competitive imports by buying regional sector, which then is distributed among delivering regional sectors according to the procedure described in section VI.7. This procedure gives us the vector of demands of this category directed towards each regional sector (DCI). The estimated demand vectors E and G pose no similar problem.

The vector of net final demands (Z) then becomes

$$Z = DCI + G + E \qquad \text{(III.1)}$$

Thus, this is the vector of total final demands directed towards each regional sector, and one which must be met by production. The demand directed towards sector i in region r is denoted by Z_i^r.

III.3.2 Determination of regional production (Step 2)

The balance equations can in matrix form be written as follows:

$$X = AX + Z \tag{III.2}$$

X: Gross output vector, which here also includes imported intermediate goods, which are treated as non-competitive imports, as well as domestic intermediate inputs. X_i^r thus is gross output in sector i in region r.

A: Matrix of interregional input-output coefficients. The a_{ij}^{rs} - coefficient denotes delivery from sector i in region r to sector j in region s.

For illustrative purposes we can look at the balance equations for a two-region, two-sector case. The four equations then become

$$\begin{aligned}
X_1^1 &= a_{11}^{11} X_1^1 + a_{12}^{11} X_2^1 + a_{11}^{12} X_1^2 + a_{12}^{12} X_2^2 + Z_1^1 \\
X_2^1 &= a_{21}^{11} X_1^1 + a_{22}^{11} X_2^1 + a_{21}^{12} X_1^2 + a_{22}^{12} X_2^2 + Z_2^1 \\
X_1^2 &= a_{11}^{21} X_1^1 + a_{12}^{21} X_2^1 + a_{11}^{22} X_1^2 + a_{12}^{22} X_2^2 + Z_1^2 \\
X_2^2 &= a_{21}^{21} X_1^1 + a_{22}^{21} X_2^1 + a_{21}^{22} X_1^2 + a_{22}^{22} X_2^2 + Z_2^2
\end{aligned} \tag{III.3}$$

Each of these functions says that for a regional sector gross output shall be equal to the sum of intermediate demands in all regional sectors plus the sum of all final demand directed towards that regional sector.

When net final demand is known for all sectors in all regions gross output can easily be calculated by

$$X = (1 - A)^{-1} Z \tag{III.4}$$

For illustrative purposes we can also here look at a two-region, two-sector case. Formula (III.4) can be rewritten as

$$\begin{bmatrix} X_1^1 \\ X_2^1 \\ X_1^2 \\ X_2^2 \end{bmatrix} = \begin{bmatrix} 1-a_{11}^{11} & -a_{12}^{11} & -a_{11}^{12} & -a_{12}^{12} \\ -a_{21}^{11} & 1-a_{22}^{11} & -a_{21}^{12} & -a_{22}^{12} \\ -a_{11}^{21} & -a_{12}^{21} & 1-a_{11}^{22} & -a_{12}^{22} \\ -a_{21}^{21} & -a_{22}^{21} & -a_{21}^{22} & 1-a_{22}^{22} \end{bmatrix}^{-1} \begin{bmatrix} Z_1^1 \\ Z_2^1 \\ Z_1^2 \\ Z_2^2 \end{bmatrix} \tag{III.5}$$

Value added can then be calculated by region and sector from gross output by using valued added coefficients (the ratio value added/gross output) derived from the input-output table. The procedure is described in Chapter VII.

III.3.3 Determination of employment by region and sector (Step 3)

Estimation of employment can be made by different methods depending on what kind of data one has access to. What is known at this stage of the simulation is output by sector and region. One alternative would be to use a production function approach, but this would meet with serious problems. First, there are no data on capital stock by region and any estimate of this would rest on very shaky foundations. Secondly, shifts in the production functions are of great importance, and there exists very few time series data that can be used to estimate shift factors.

Since it is not feasible to use production functions here, I shall for modern sector employment use the simpler approach with labour productivity functions, that is, relations of the form

$$EMP_{i,t} = e_{i,t} \cdot VA_{i,t} \qquad (III.6)$$

where $EMP_{i,t}$ is employment in sector i at time t, VA is value added, and $e_{i,t}$ is a labour productivity ratio, which depends on time. The lower $e_{i,t}$ is, the higher the productivity. The methods of calculating other categories of employment are discussed in Chapter VIII.

III.3.4 Determination of population size by region (Step 4)

The growth of the population within a region is determined by two factors, namely the intrinsic rate of population growth and migration. For simplicity the first factor is taken as constant, which is defensible, if the analysis is not extended over too many periods.

A little more should be said about migration. Numerous papers have been written on urban-rural migration (the best known are Todaro, 1969, Harris and Todaro, 1970), and there is now widespread agreement that it, to a large extent, can be explained by economic factors. The data that we get from previous steps are data on output and employment. The employment and income situation may then be used to determine migration. This is discussed in Chapter IX.

III.3.5 Calculation of regional per capita incomes (Step 5)

Various aspects of the solution can be focused upon when one is to evaluate the outcome of the calculations. Of course, since the focusing point here is the development of regional inequality, regional per capita incomes are of great interest. These are naturally obtained if one divides regional value added (from Step 2) by regional population (from Step 4). To get some idea about whether inequality is increasing or decreasing over time, some inequality measures must be applied. This and some other aspects of inequality will be dealt with in Chapter X.

III.3.6 Concluding remarks

A large deficit in the balance of payments may make a realisation of the final demand impossible. This will make some kinds of economic adjustments necessary,but such a situation cannot be analysed within this model, as it is outlined here. This model generates only a series of external balances, and as long as the deficits are not too large, one may assume that they are covered by capital inflow. Kenya has so far been very successful in attracting foreign capital, wherefore this deficiency of the model may not be too serious.

Thus, the model used here differs from the traditional two-gap model in so far as no explicit balance of payments restriction limits growth, and, as was mentioned earlier, there is no explicit investment restriction either. The growth rate of the economy is therefore basically exogenously determined. What is studied in this model is the regional impact of the growth.

IV The structure of production

IV.I AN OVERVIEW OF THE ECONOMIC STRUCTURE

The Kenyan economy is characterized by considerable differences between different types of production, and is still far from being completely integrated. Because of the type of approach chosen I must take my starting point in the published input-output table. In this the economy is divided into two main categories: a) the non-monetary sector, and b) the monetary sector. It should be pointed out that this division is problematic, since there are certain production units which cannot be classified as belonging completely to one or the other category.

If we examine agricultural production, we find that the input-output table distinguishes between modern and subsistence agriculture. The large mixed farms, plantations and ranches pose no problems in this regard, since their production is marketed and registered as output from modern agriculture. Within small farm agriculture, however, there is production both for subsistence needs and for the market. These production units are in the middle of a process of commercialization; cash crops are playing an increasingly important role for the small farmers. The problem here is that the part of small farm produce which is marketed outside local markets is registered as output from modern agriculture, while that which is consumed on the farm or sold on local markets is registered as subsistence production. (It is pointed out in the input-output table for 1971 (p. 6) that this distinction is empirical. It is almost impossible to find a farmer who does not sell at least a small part of his output or buy a small part of his inputs.) At present more than half of marketed agricultural products is produced by small farmers (Economic Survey, 1977, p. 84), who are here, somewhat incorrectly, called subsistence farmers. The line of demarcation thus cuts right through many small farm production units. The analytical distinction between traditional and modern agriculture becomes blurred, and it would be more correct to say that there exists a continuum ranging from pure subsistence to fully commercialized farms.

The monetization of small scale agriculture has really gone further than the fifty per cent figure of output indicates, since part of what is registered as subsistence output, is actually marketed through the 'thriving system of local markets' (Heyer, 1976, p. 316). This village market trade is ignored in official statistics, and the produce thus classified as subsistence. If this fact were taken into account, the share of subsistence production in agricultural output would be even less. In the integrated rural survey (Economic Survey, 1977, p. 87) it was estimated that forty-five per cent of the output of small farms is consumed at home. Since I use the input-output table in the analysis, I must, however, be content to use the division between subsistence and modern agriculture as shown in the input-output table.

The non-agricultural part of the economy also poses certain problems. The production sectors within this part are by no means homogenous. One can primarily distinguish between two types of production, namely formal and informal. This terminology, introduced by the ILO-mission, focuses on one of the reasons for the lack of integration in under-developed economies, i.e. the fact that the formal private sector is recognized by the government, while the informal sector receives no support and is even being actively opposed.

Mazumdar(1975) argues that the informal sector has a dependency relationship to the formal sector. It is the growth of the latter which makes it possible for the informal activities to flourish. Also Child (1976, p. 52) emphasizes the fact that the market limitation restricts the growth of the sector. The scope for this type of activities is determined by the growth of formal production. Thus, it cannot play an independent role in development but can certainly offer ways of making a living for some people, who would otherwise be unemployed or have very small incomes.

Most statistics gathered in Kenya cover what is called the 'modern' sector. If an activity has a fixed location or a postal address, it is included in the regular survey of the 'modern' sector. Enterprises within this sector usually recruit labour on a permanent basis and for fixed rewards.

In the input-output table there is no distinction between formal and informal production. Since the distinguishing characteristic of informal production is that it largely takes place outside government control, it is self-evident that informal activities are poorly reflected in the table as well as in the national accounts. GDP is therefore slightly underestimated.

Thus, one can identify three basic types of production activities in the Kenyan economy:

1. Formal (or modern) production
2. Informal production
3. Subsistence production

It should also be pointed out that Kenya is still an overwhelmingly agricultural country, even if industrialization and diversification have taken place. Moreover, most of the people in the agricultural sector still live on small farms. Around one million people live as pastoralists in the Masai area in the south and in the arid north and north-east. These people (that is people of Turkana, Somali, Masai, Tugen, Elgeyo, Pokot, and parts of Kipsigis and Nandi tribes) earn their living from their livestock and are integrated with the rest of Kenya to a very small degree. Manufacturing industry is practically non-existent in these areas. For the pastoral areas the model analysis is practically irrelevant.

IV.2 THE INPUT-OUTPUT TABLE

The Central Bureau of Statistics has published two input-output tables for Kenya, the first for 1967 and the second for 1971. The latter will be used in the analysis. The simulations will thus have 1971 as the starting year. I shall use the table expressed in producer's prices, that is, the distribution charges are treated as payments for services rendered by the distribution sector.

The table contains 30 sectors, 2 non-monetary and 28 monetary. I aggregate this table to 1 non-monetary and 8 monetary sectors. This is done for several reasons. First, much of the regional data that are published concern only one-digit (ISIC) sectors. Secondly, this table will be disaggregated by regions and if I were to keep all thirty sectors I would get a table that would be too large to handle. Thirdly, the stability of coefficients is enhanced by the aggregation. The procedures by which the aggregation is done are discussed in detail in Bigsten (1978).

IV.3 THE STABILITY OF TECHNICAL COEFFICIENTS

Of course, input-output coefficients can never be completely insensitive to changes in endogenous and exogenous variables, but the question here is whether or not they are sufficiently stable to make the use of an input-output table meaningful.

In this study I use highly aggregated sectors. This may, theoretically influence the stability of the coefficients in both directions. On the one hand close substitutes are combined, and this should enhance stability of the coefficients compared to the more disaggregated ones; on the other hand, the fact that the coefficients represent the average for the constituent industries makes them sensitive to changes in product mix. Sevaldson (1970, p. 211) argues that it is plausible that aggregation improves stability, and in his study of Norwegian data he also finds a considerable increase of stability with aggregation (p. 236). From this one might guess that the fact that I reduce the input-output table to a few aggregated sectors improves the stability of coefficients.

Since Kenya has published two input-output tables it is possible to make some comparisons and to draw some highly tentative conclusions about the stability of coefficients. However, four years is too short a period on which to base any firm conclusions, particularly if one considers the many changes due to improvements in data and computational procedures. Information from the Central Bureau of Statistics indicates that the latter cause of change may be the most important one. Another fact that should be pointed out is that the two tables in some cases are based on the same surveys (with extrapolations), as many sectoral surveys in this type of countries are held very seldom. This fact implies that, probably, changes have been underestimated instead, and that some coefficients may seem to be more stable than they are in reality.

By comparing the 1967 and 1971 input-output tables one finds that the share of intermediate goods in gross output increased by 2.5 percentage points between 1967 and 1971. This is what one might expect in a developing economy. In Kenya, the share is still some ten percentage points below what it is in developed countries. It therefore seems likely that the trend will continue. The domestic economy provided only twenty-eight per cent of the increase, while seventy-two

Table IV:1

Basic (domestic) input-output table at producer's prices, 1971

	Subsist.	Modern Agricult.	Mining	Manu-fact.	Con-struct.	El & water	Com-merce	Trans-port	Ser-vices	Total
Subsistence	4,349	0	0	0	0	0	0	0	0	4,349
Modern agriculture	854	782	0	43,146	0	0	0	11	1,283	46,076
Mining	0	0	458	354	2,740	21	0	0	0	3,573
Manufacturing	2,485	4,878	1,113	25,597	17,458	1,113	6,172	14,701	24,037	97,554
Construction	0	0	85	789	5,000	0	72	15	7,663	13,624
El & water	0	425	153	3,389	485	684	968	945	3,017	10,066
Commerce	502	3,154	421	20,306	5,594	610	8,219	4,587	5,864	49,257
Transport	0	322	436	4,884	1,008	216	12,836	12,593	8,451	40,746
Services	5	1,783	234	3,210	875	312	1,910	1,171	4,259	13,759
Domestic input	8,195	11,344	2,900	101,675	33,160	2,956	30,177	34,023	54,574	279,004
Imported input	646	6,223	567	81,828	9,586	1,242	6,969	8,144	10,437	125,642
Depreciation	0	6,588	536	8,167	3,036	1,398	3,702	6,100	1,994	31,521
Wages & salaries	3,061	22,901	1,178	36,777	18,983	2,286	32,856	28,211	114,192	260,445
Profits	120,488	48,002	1,202	23,293	679	3,291	27,163	6,147	29,735	260,000
Interest paid	0	0	14	2,661	491	1,230	11,036	2,682	523	18,637
Value added	123,549	77,491	2,930	70,898	23,189	8,205	74,757	43,140	146,444	570,603
Indirect taxes	0	711	99	21,846	253	41	2,432	804	4,240	30,426
Subsidies	0	-997	0	0	-9	0	-14	-19	0	-1,039
Gross value added	123,549	77,205	3,029	92,744	23,433	8,246	77,175	43,925	150,684	599,990
Gross output	132,390	94,772	6,496	276,247	66,179	12,444	114,321	86,092	215,695	1004,636
Imports	0	8,286	13,727	165,302	326	621	3,630	8,817	11,941	212,650
Import duties	0	387	7,060	27,787	0	0	0	0	31	35,265
Total supply of resources	132,390	103,445	27,283	469,336	66,505	13,065	117,951	94,909	227,667	1252,551

Table IV:1 (cont.)

	Imported interme-diate use	Export	Govern-ment	Consumpt. & changes in stocks	Invest-ment	Total use of resources
Subsistence	0	0		115,923	12,118	132,390
Modern agriculture	5,162	26,195		23,208	2,804	103,445
Mining	20,787	2,748		175	0	27,283
Manufacturing	87,867	74,635		151,659	57,621	469,336
Construction	0	46		10	52,825	66,505
El & water	581	594		1,824	0	13,065
Commerce	2,509	19,547		35,824	10,814	117,951
Transport	3,825	29,264		21,074	0	94,909
Services	4,911	17,919	114,121	76,957	0	227,667
Domestic input	125,642	170,948	114,121	426,654	136,182	1252,551

per cent of the increase in intermediate inputs was imported. The domestic coefficients thus seem to be more stable than the total coefficients for the time being.

It is also possible to compare changes in total input requirements by sector for the disaggregated and the aggregated tables, both for domestic and total inputs.

We then find that for the domestic coefficients stability increased with aggregation from an average change in input-coefficients of sixteen per cent to ten per cent. For the total input coefficients the picture is less clear. I also checked the fifteen most important intermediate flows (according to the aggregated 1971 input-output table), which together constitute seventy-eight per cent of the total intermediate flows. Two of these were almost insignificant in 1967 (building-building, building-services), but had, by 1971, increased considerably in importance; these (five per cent of total intermediate flows) therefore showed extreme percentage changes. The remaining thirteen items had, on the average, changed thirteen per cent between these years.

What conclusions is it possible to draw from these observations? First of all, it is difficult to say how much of the change that is due to changes or improvements in the data base or construction procedures. If we assume that this is not important, single coefficients seem to have changed significantly, even if the changes for total domestic intermediate input by aggregate sector are moderate.

It is essential to get some idea about how important these changes are. To check this effect in terms of projections of intermediate deliveries I calculated output for 1971 using the 1967 input-output coefficients and compared total intermediate deliveries by sector.

There is a drastic change in deliveries from building; this trend cannot, however, be expected to continue. Of the important sectors mainly modern agriculture shows a significant change. The rest shows a considerable stability.

Four years and two observations are too short a period on which to base predictions of changes in input-output coefficients. I have therefore concluded that to assume fixed technical coefficients is the most reasonable alternative under existing conditions. Another argument in defense of the use of fixed coefficients is that I am primarily interested in the analysis of tendencies and qualitative results, rather than planning, or exact predictions.

V Regionalization of the national input-output table

V.I THE REGIONAL STRUCTURE OF KENYA

Before we go on to a discussion of the construction of the interregional input-output table, I should like to provide some basic facts about the geography of Kenya. I also need to explain why the provinces are chosen as units of analysis.

Kenya can be subdivided into four physical geographical regions: (1) the Coastal Plains, (2) the Arid Low Plateau, (3) the Kenya Highlands, and (4) the Lake Region. The Coastal Plain is relatively narrow, and the climate hot and wet with the greatest rainfall near Mombasa. The Arid Low Plateau covers most of the country; much of this area is desert, or semi-desert, which is fit for nothing else but pastoral agriculture. Nearly all of the Highlands have a reliable rainfall and a pleasant climate; the soil is among the most fertile in Africa. The Lake Region, a densely populated agricultural region, is warm and wet.

Of course, these great climatic differences have had a profound influence on the distribution of people within the country. They are concentrated to the south-west quarter and to the area around Mombasa, whereas the rest of the country is relatively sparsely populated.

When choosing geographical units of analysis one should ideally choose units that have maximum homogeneity in terms of production structure, climatic conditions etc. However, in reality, there is little choice, since data are collected on the basis of decentralized administrative units. For Kenya one might consider arranging districts in a way that differs from the provincial division, but since relatively little data are available on a district basis, this would further reduce the data base. Furthermore, most of the provinces are reasonably homogeneous(Nairobi, Western, Nyanza, Central, North Eastern). In the Coast province there are great economic differences between Mombasa and the rest of the area, but it is geographically well demarcated.

The Rift Valley and the Eastern provinces are the most problematic ones. Both provinces have an oblong shape, but most of the population is concentrated in the centrally located areas west and east of the Central province. The districts that are located peripherally in Rift Valley are Turkana, Samburu, Narok, and Kajiado, but they contain only twenty per cent of the population of the entire province. In the Eastern province the districts of Marsabit and Isiolo are remotely situated, but, on the other hand, they contain only four per cent of the population. The inclusion of these areas should not bias the estimates too much.

In this context it should be mentioned that the specific problems of the pastoral areas cannot be reasonably analysed in this model. These problems require special analysis, which will not be provided here.

Map 1: DISTRICTS AND PROVINCES

RV RIFT VALLEY
E EASTERN
NE NORTH EASTERN
W WESTERN
Ny NYANZA
C CENTRAL
N NAIROBI
C COAST

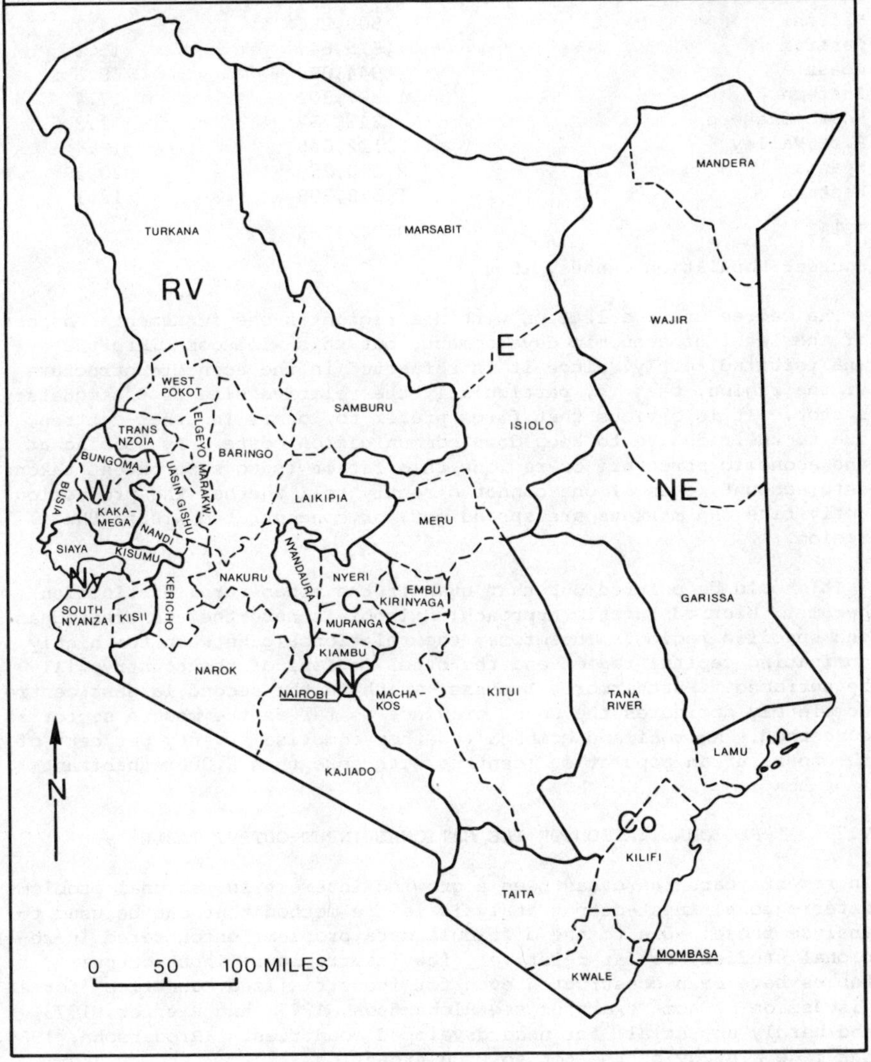

Thus, I will use the administrative areas as units of analysis, even if there are some problems connected with this approach. Kenya has eight provinces (including Nairobi) subdivided into forty-one districts with a population ranging from around 25,000 to three quarters of a million. (See table V.1 and map 1.) These districts are ethnically fairly homogeneous, but some of the areas comprise a wide variety of physical conditions.

Table V.I
Provinces and their population in 1969

Province	Population	Percentage of population
Nairobi	509,286	4.7
Central	1,675,647	15.3
Coast	944,082	8.6
Eastern	1,907,301	17.4
North Eastern	245,757	2.2
Rift Valley	2,122,045	19.4
Nyanza	2,210,289	20.2
Western	1,328,298	12.1
TOTAL	10,942,705	

Source: Population census, 1969

The degree of urbanization within a region is one fundamental aspect of the level of economic development, but this will come into the analysis indirectly, since it is reflected in the economic structure of the region, that is, particularly the relative size of the monetary sector. It is obvious that firms prefer to locate in urban centres, due to their desire to keep down communication costs. By looking at the economic structure of regions this factor is to some extent taken into account, even if one cannot directly tell whether the production activities and markets are spread out, or concentrated within the region.

It should be pointed out that even if the urban-rural distinction becomes blurred in this approach, Nairobi is nevertheless treated as one specific region. Therefore, the relationship between the highly dominating capital region and the other regions of the country will be surfaced. Furthermore, Mombasa, which is the second largest centre, completely dominates the Coast province as far as the modern sector is concerned. Nairobi and Mombasa together comprise seventy per cent of the total urban population (centres with more than 2,000 inhabitants).

V.2 REGIONALIZATION OF THE NATIONAL INPUT-OUTPUT TABLE

In recent years there has been a growing interest in regional problems; interregional input-output analysis is one method that can be used to analyse these. Due to the difficult data problems encountered in regional studies, so far relatively few interregional input-output tables have been constructed even for industrialized countries (for a discussion of some examples see Richardson, 1972, and Riefler, 1973) and hardly any at all for underdeveloped countries. (Brodersohn, 1965, has made a study of the not so rich Argentina.)

To estimate interregional input-output coefficients by survey techniques as is done with the national input-output coefficients is far too expensive and time consuming even for the industrialized countries; to try to use such a method for an underdeveloped country would be even more problematic. Some kind of non-survey technique must therefore be used. However, before discussing the choice of approach, a discussion of the factors determining the size of the flows is in place.

V.2.1 Determinants of flows of intermediate goods

There are two main types of influences determining the size of interregional flows of intermediate goods and services, i.e. the size of interregional input-output coefficients: First, there is the intersectoral interdependence, reflected in the technical input-output coefficients. Secondly, there is a group of factors that determine how the flows which are the result of the production technology are distributed in space.

Since no estimates of regional input-output coefficients exist in Kenya, I have to assume that the intersectoral interdependencies are similar in all regions, that is, the input-output coefficients are the same in all regions. Thus, the national coefficients are used throughout to characterize the technical relationships.

The assumption that national technical coefficients are valid also for regions has been discussed in a number of articles (see e.g. Morrison and Smith, 1974, McMenamin and Haring, 1974, Kipnis, 1976). These articles contain discussions on the construction of regional input-output tables for relatively small areas.

The article by Kipnis is of most interest in this context. He compares the Israeli national coefficients with regional coefficients obtained in a comprehensive field survey in one small area. He finds a considerable divergence when he compares the national coefficients with those of the town in the area studied. However, when rural as well as urban areas are included the divergence diminishes, even if it is still fairly large. He also finds that the divergence diminishes, as one moves from more to less regionally specific activities. The conclusion from this study seems to be that national coefficients give the best approximation in regions which include both urban and rural areas and where the level of aggregation is high. This is the case in my study.

The input-output coefficient together with the size of production determine the amount of input bought in each region and sector; however, a way must be found to determine from what regions the given amount of input is delivered. The theory of international trade has, for a long time, concerned itself with this type of problem; it is not unreasonable to believe that the theories within this tradition should have relevance also for analyses of trade flows within nations. Olsen (1971) also discusses this problem, and he constructs a model in which he tries to integrate different aspects of the theories discussed. However, he fails to apply and estimate his model in a meaningful manner due to the data requirements of his analysis.

In spite of these difficulties the theory of international trade should provide a good starting point; it has a number of alternative explanations, which stress different factors: According to Heckscher and Ohlin, trade is due to differences in factor endowments, according to Burenstam-Linder similarities in preferences and incomes are vital, and according to Linneman and others trade flows are functions of population, income and distance.

Even if comparative advantage is a prerequisite for trade, the theory of comparative cost cannot be used to determine the network of interregional trade flows, if we have more than two countries, except in very special instances. Leontief (1973, pp. 153-4) points out that

> 'Only to the extent to which transportation costs, custom tariffs or any other differential transfer costs between the individual trading countries can actually be taken into account and happen to be of decisive importance, will the comparative cost theory be capable to explain the magnitude and the composition of all the observed export-import flows. In case such differential transfer costs do not exist, or if they exist but cannot be accounted for, the magnitude and composition of the flows of goods and services from any other country remains within the framework of such theory entirely indeterminate.'

As long as transport or transfer costs are not introduced the theory cannot explain why a particular amount of some good is exported from a particular country (or region) to another particular country (or region).

Transfer costs must therefore be introduced in some way, if reasonable estimates of interregional trade flows are to be obtained. The problem then is: What measure of transfer costs should one use? What is needed is some kind of measure of economic or social distance, which reflects the real cost of transferring a good or a service between two regions.

Ghosh (1973) finds that transport costs are not 'sufficiently sensitive to all implications of the transportation problem arising in long distance flows'. He points out that these are not just more expensive but also more uncertain and time-consuming, and that the knowledge about trading opportunities is imperfect.

Fortune (1971) has made a statistical test of Linder's hypothesis concerning the determinants of trade intensities; his results support the hypothesis that distance is a powerful trade-braking force in international trade. This result should be valid for intracountry trade as well. Distance, which is easy to measure, can therefore be used as a proxy for transfer costs, as is often done for example in gravity type models. Since different products are affected differently by distance, a parameter will be introduced which takes this into account. Transfer costs will therefore be measured by distance adjusted for type of goods.

To sum up: The determinants of flows of intermediate goods are (1) the technical relationships, (2) the transfer costs, and, of course (3) the location of producers, and (4) the location of users of intermediate goods. If these four factors are taken into account, one should be able to get reasonably realistic estimates of the interregional flows of intermediate goods and services and thus of the interregional input-output coefficients.

In formula form the flow from sector i in region r to sector j in region s, called X_{ij}^{rs}, can be expressed as

$$X_{ij}^{rs} = a_{ij}^{rs} \cdot X_{j}^{s} \qquad (V.1)$$

where a_{ij}^{rs} is the interregional input-output coefficients representing the flow from sector i in region r to sector j in region s, and X_{j}^{s} is gross output of sector j in region s. The latter is known so the problem is to find an estimate of X_{ij}^{rs} and thus a_{ij}^{rs}.

The conclusion from the discussion above was that there were four factors determining the interregional flows of intermediate goods. The effect of the size of production in the user region is already taken into account, since X_{j}^{s} is introduced separately, but the remaining factors, that is the technical relation, the transfer costs, and the location of producers of intermediate goods, must in some way be reflected by the a_{ij}^{rs} coefficients.

It is assumed that the technical relation is adequately described by the national input-output coefficient a_{ij}. The product $a_{ij} \cdot X_{j}^{s}$ then determines how much sector j in region s needs of input i in total. The problem is now reduced to an estimate of the proportions, which can be called t_{ij}^{rs}, in which the delivering regions deliver good i to sector j in region s. This is assumed to be a function of the transfer costs and the location of the input producers. Formula (V.1) can be rewritten

$$X_{ij}^{rs} = t_{ij}^{rs} \cdot a_{ij} \cdot X_{j}^{s} \qquad (V.2)$$

To accept that the national input-output coefficients are valid also for the regions implies that the sum of deliveries from all regions to region s must add up to $a_{ij} \cdot X_{j}^{s}$, that is that

$$\sum_{r} t_{ij}^{rs} = 1 \qquad (V.3)$$

Thus the trade coefficients t_{ij}^{rs} should reflect the effect of the location of producers of input and transfer costs. The ways in which the four above mentioned factors can be introduced in the estimation of the interregional flows will now be discussed.

V.2.2 Some comments on methods of estimating interregional input-output coefficients

The 'ideal' model for estimation of interregional input-output coefficients presented by Isard (1951) requires information about flows of intermediate goods by industry and region of origin and destination. Since such information is very seldom available, various attempts have been made to construct simplified variants of this model, which make as efficient use as possible of the information available. In Riefler's survey (1973) four of the most well-known variants are presented; they are in falling order of data requirements due to Riefler and Tiebout, Moses and Chenery, Leontief and Moses, and Leontief and Strout.

The Leontief and Strout model does not require differentiation between national and local industries, it does allow for cross-hauling of goods between different regions, and the friction of distance is explicitly considered in the calculation of coefficients. Of these four alternatives this approach therefore seems to be the most suitable one in this case, where estimates or proxies are available only on technical coefficients, transfer costs, and the size of intermediate production and intermediate use by region and sector.

However, there are some problems with the Leontief-Strout approach: First, the intraregional flows have to be prespecified, which may be a problem. A procedure which solves these flows simultaneously with the interregional flows is to be preferred, when there is no a priori information about the actual size of intraregional flows. Secondly, the flows of the model are derived without being based on any assumption about optimizing behaviour. Finally, there is the practical problem of the approach requiring quite a lot of manipulation before the estimates can be obtained.

The question is: Is it possible to find some alternative method which combines the advantages of this model with some type of optimization and which, at the same time, is easy to handle?

The transportation model is an optimization model, which is sometimes used to predict interregional trade flows. The problem with this model is that it is necessary to have a very fine commodity classification to circumvent the cross-hauling problem. The problems associated with this model were actually the reason for Leontief's and Strout's decision to try to introduce behavioural relationships, that is, the gravity formulation in determining the trade flows.

The Leontief and Strout approach is probabilistic, and this is a useful feature. In recent years, a method has come into use which makes it possible to combine optimization with the behavioural restrictions of the gravity approach: The entropy maximization model, which is what I shall be using in this study. This approach generates cross-hauls like the model of Leontief and Strout, but unlike their model, no prespecification of intraregional flows is required.

V.2.3 The entropy maximization model

The entropy model is a special type of optimization model (for a more comprehensive presentation, see e.g. Paelinck and Nijkamp, 1975, pp.

371-7). By its probabilistic approach, it gives the most probable spatial configuration of a system that may adopt many different spatial states consistent with certain partial macroinformation. In this study the model is used to generate the most probable spatial flows of intermediate inputs, given a certain set of macrorestrictions.

It can be shown that the most probable pattern of flows, given a certain set of restrictions, is obtained if one maximizes the entropy, which can be written approximately as follows:

$$F = - \sum_i \sum_j \sum_r \sum_s (X_{ij}^{rs} \ln X_{ij}^{rs} - X_{ij}^{rs}) \qquad (V.4)$$

This formulation is based on the assumption that all flows are a priori equally probable. In the case of input-output flows, however, it is not so. There is certain a priori information relating to the microlevel (here individual intersectoral flows) available. For example, a flow from sector 1 to sector 2 is not equally as probable as one from 1 to 3, if we, a priori, know that $a_{12} = 0.2$ and $a_{13} = 0.02$. In the case where $a_{ij} = 0$, it is even more necessary that this technical specification is taken into account, since otherwise the entropy approach would generate flows from i to j which we, a priori, know are impossible.

A priori information about the location of production and about technical relationships should therefore be taken into account. At this stage, the effect of distance is left out; instead it will be determined by the transport restriction in the optimization procedure. Here intermediate deliveries of i from region r, $\bar{X}_{i\cdot}^{r\cdot}$, are considered, and $a_{ij}X_j^s$ determines the input needs of sector j in region s.

The a priori estimate of the flows can be written

$$\hat{X}_{ij}^{rs} = \frac{\bar{X}_{i\cdot}^{r\cdot} a_{ij} X_j^s}{\bar{X}_{i\cdot}} \qquad (V.5)$$

$\bar{X}_{i\cdot}^{r\cdot}/\bar{X}_{i\cdot}$ is the share of total intermediate production of i $(\bar{X}_{i\cdot})$ produced in region r; this prespecification of the flows says that, a priori, each region is expected to deliver a share of total input of good i in sector j in region s, which is equal to its share in total production of that intermediate good.

With the prespecification (V.5) the objective function becomes (see Snickars and Weibull, 1977, p. 143)

$$F' = - \sum_i \sum_j \sum_r \sum_s \left(X_{ij}^{rs} \ln \frac{X_{ij}^{rs}}{\hat{X}_{ij}^{rs}} - X_{ij}^{rs}\right) \qquad (V.6)$$

It is possible to obtain solutions for a number of different sets of macrorestrictions; in order to choose the best set one must determine what properties it is desirable for the estimates to have.

First, I do not have any information on regional input-output coefficients here, and have therefore assumed that they are equal to the national coefficients. This implies that we want total deliveries of i into sector j in region s to be equal to $a_{ij} X_j^s$. One restriction guaranteeing the fulfillment of this condition must therefore be introduced. This restriction is formulated as follows:

$$\sum_r X_{ij}^{rs} = a_{ij} X_j^s \qquad (V.7)$$

which says that the sum of deliveries from all regions to sector j in region s shall be equal to the technologically determined level. By imposing this restriction the correct amount of every input into sector j in region s is obtained; this also implies that the whole column of inputs meets the only consistency requirement that is reasonable for columns - namely that it is equal to the technologically determined total intermediate use of sector j in region s.

Next, it is necessary to introduce a restriction on the row sums. If this is not done, the allocation of intermediate production by regions is left to take a more or less arbitrary level. If information about the distribution of intermediate production by region and sector $\bar{X}_{i\cdot}^{r\cdot}$ is available this restriction should be imposed. (In this study no information is available separately for intermediate production, which is why I make the simplifying assumption that intermediate production is distributed as total production.) Restriction (V.8) is therefore introduced, i.e. total deliveries to all regions and sectors from sector i in region r shall be equal to the a priori determined level of intermediate production there.

$$\sum_j \sum_s X_{ij}^{rs} = \bar{X}_{i\cdot}^{r\cdot} \qquad (V.8)$$

Finally, in this type of approach, there must be a restriction on transport capacity (here regarding the transportation of intermediate goods) within the system (T). This can be formulated as

$$\sum_i \sum_j \sum_r \sum_s c_{ij}^{rs} X_{ij}^{rs} = T \qquad (V.9)$$

where c_{ij}^{rs} is a representation of the cost of transferring good i from region r to sector j in region s. Here it is assumed that the transfer cost does not vary among different sectoral destinations, wherefore the index j in c_{ij}^{rs} could be suppressed.

Now, let us take a closer look at the objective function. Derivation of (V.6) gives

$$\frac{\partial F'}{\partial X_{ij}^{rs}} = - \ln \frac{X_{ij}^{rs}}{\hat{X}_{ij}^{rs}} \qquad (V.10)$$

and from this we see that F' is a concave function with its maximum for

$$X_{ij}^{rs} = \hat{X}_{ij}^{rs} \quad (V.11)$$

Maximization of F' with not restrictions imposed yields the a priori estimate. The role of the restrictions in the optimization is therefore to adjust the crude a priori estimate so that the macrorestrictions are met.

Thus the problem is to maximize the objective function (V.6) subject to restrictions (V.7), (V.8) and (V.9).

The Langrangian for this problem is

$$L = - \sum_i \sum_j \sum_r \sum_s (X_{ij}^{rs} \ln \frac{X_{ij}^{rs}}{\hat{X}_{ij}^{rs}} - X_{ij}^{rs}) - \sum_i \sum_j \sum_s \lambda_{ij}^{s} (\sum_r X_{ij}^{rs} - a_{ij} X_j^{s}) -$$

$$- \sum_i \sum_r \mu_i^{r} (\sum_j \sum_s X_{ij}^{rs} - \bar{X}_{i\cdot}^{r\cdot}) - \gamma (\sum_i \sum_j \sum_r \sum_s c_{ij}^{rs} X_{ij}^{rs} - T) \quad (V.12)$$

The following conditions are necessary for an optimum:

$$\frac{\partial L}{\partial X_{ij}^{rs}} = - \ln \frac{X_{ij}^{rs}}{\hat{X}_{ij}^{rs}} - \lambda_{ij}^{s} - \mu_i^{r} - \gamma c_{ij}^{rs} = 0 \quad (V.13)$$

which can also be written as

$$X_{ij}^{rs} = \hat{X}_{ij}^{rs} \, e^{-\lambda_{ij}^{s}} \, e^{-\mu_i^{r}} \, e^{-\gamma c_{ij}^{rs}} \quad (V.14)$$

To solve the problem numerically I use the technique described by Paelinck and Nijkamp (1975, pp. 371-7).

First, set

$$e^{-\mu_i^{r}} = A_i^{r} \quad (V.15)$$

and

$$e^{-\lambda_{ij}^{s}} = B_{ij}^{s} \quad (V.16)$$

By inserting the a priori estimate (V.5) and expressions (V.15) and (V.16) into (V.14) we get

$$X_{ij}^{rs} = \frac{\bar{X}_{i\cdot}^{r\cdot} a_{ij} X_j^{s}}{\bar{X}_{i\cdot}} A_i^{r} B_{ij}^{s} e^{-\gamma c_{ij}^{rs}} \quad (V.17)$$

and by combining (V.8) and (V.17) we obtain

$$\sum_j \sum_s X_{ij}^{rs} = \sum_j \sum_s \frac{\bar{X}_{i\cdot}^{r\cdot}}{\bar{X}_{i\cdot}} a_{ij} X_j^s A_i^r B_{ij}^s e^{-\gamma c_{ij}^{rs}} = \tag{V.18}$$

$$= \bar{X}_{i\cdot}^{r\cdot} A_i^r \sum_j \sum_s \frac{a_{ij} X_j^s}{\bar{X}_{i\cdot}} B_{ij}^s e^{-\gamma c_{ij}^{rs}} = \bar{X}_{i\cdot}^{r\cdot}$$

and finally

$$A_i^r = \left(\sum_j \sum_s \frac{a_{ij} X_j^s}{\bar{X}_{i\cdot}} B_{ij}^s e^{-\gamma c_{ij}^{rs}}\right)^{-1} \tag{V.19}$$

In the same manner by using (V.7) and (V.17) we obtain

$$B_{ij}^s = \left(\sum_r \bar{X}_{i\cdot}^{r\cdot} A_i^r e^{-\gamma c_{ij}^{rs}} / \bar{X}_{i\cdot}\right)^{-1} \tag{V.20}$$

We see here that if c_{ij}^{rs} does not vary with j (as we assumed above) B_{ij}^s does not vary with j either.

To solve A_i^r and B_{ij}^s I first give initial values to all A_i^r; these are inserted in (V.20); a set of B_{ij}^s values can then be calculated. These, in turn are inserted in (V.19), and a new set of A_i^r values are obtained. This iteration continues until an equilibrium is reached. γ can be calibrated by calculating the left hand side of (V.9) together with (V.17). Changes in γ can be made as a function of the difference in (V.9) so that one approaches the limit set by the transport capacity restriction. Finally, the values of A_i^r, B_{ij}^s and γ are inserted in (V.17), and we obtain an estimate of the flows.

When the solution is reached the interregional input-output coefficients are easily obtained by

$$a_{ij}^{rs} = X_{ij}^{rs} / X_j^s \tag{V.21}$$

When $X_j^s = 0$, a_{ij}^{rs} is set to equal to zero.

These estimates are the most likely, given the assumptions in the model. Still, this is no guarantee that they correctly reflect reality. The assumptions may be too crude. Therefore, sensitivity analysis of the results should be made to see how great the effects of changes in the restrictions are. The most interesting check would of course be to compare the estimated flows with actually observed flows. The crux of the matter and the raison d'être of the approach is, however, that such information is not available. Therefore, at least in this case, no such check can be made.

V.2.4 Application in Kenya

The entropy maximization approach has thus been used to estimate the Kenyan interregional input-output table. First, the known a_{ij} - coefficients are taken as the basis for the a priori estimates. Then it has to be assumed that intermediate production is distributed among provinces in the same proportions as total production. Since there is no separate information on the distribution of intermediate production, this gives estimates of $\bar{X}_{i\cdot}^{r\cdot}$ and $\bar{X}_{\cdot j}^{\cdot s}$ $(= \sum_i \sum_j X_{ij}^{rs})$. Total production X_i is known from the input-output table.

To get a proxy for the transfer costs the following formula is used:

$$c_{ij}^{rs} = D^{rs} \cdot \alpha_i \qquad (V.22)$$

D^{rs} is the distance in km between region r and region s, and α_i is a sector specific parameter which indicates how sensitive the flows of the output of sector i is to distance or how much transport capacity it requires.

The distance measures are calculated as follows: First, the population weightedaverage of distances from the district centres in province A to the main town of province B is calculated, and then vice versa. The average of these two calculations is then used. Since distances are introduced in an exponential expression one can use zero intraregional distances (since $e^0 = 1$), which is natural. The following matrix is obtained:

Table V.2
Distances among provinces in kilometers

	Nairobi	Central	Coast	East.	North East.	Nyanza	Rift Valley	Western
Nairobi	0							
Central	103	0						
Coast	522	576	0					
Eastern	165	173	669	0				
North Eastern	707	631	792	524	0			
Nyanza	376	400	865	472	766	0		
Rift Valley	291	273	729	327	664	211	0	
Western	426	386	909	482	971	114	219	0

The α_i-coefficients must be determined exogenously. In this formulation it is their relative size that is of interest. First, α_i is set so high that no interregional trade is possible with subsistence products (products consumed by the producer himself or other locals). It is then assumed that sectors 2-4 are relatively insensitive to distance, while sectors 5-9 are assumed to be more sensitive. No differentiation is made within these groups. In the basic simulation it is assumed that $\alpha_{2-4}/\alpha_{5-9} = 1/4$. This is in accordance with estimates of distance elasticities made in developed countries (Black, 1972, Andersson and Ohlsson, 1974); it implies that sectors 2-4 trade extensively all over the country, while sectors 5-9 trade less outside the region of origin.

One can compare the use of α_i-coefficients with Tinbergen's approach (see Mennes, Tinbergen, and Wardenburg, 1969), where sectors are divided into national and regional sectors. The national sectors sell on the national or international market, while the regional ones are assumed to sell only within regions. In the approach suggested here, no such clearcut division is made. Still, by setting the α_i-values high for sectors which Tinbergen considers to be regional, the result will be that the sales of these industries is concentrated primarily to their own region and to some extent to the neighbouring regions.

Total capacity of the system to transport intermediate goods T is set at twenty million, and is assumed to grow by five per cent per year in the basic solution. Different figures were tried and this one was chosen simply because it gave what seems to be 'reasonable' estimates of the flows.

VI Estimation of final demand by sector and region

In Chapter III an overview of the approach was given. In this and the following chapters (VI-X) I shall describe the formulation of the model in greater detail.

In the two previous chapters I described how the national input-output table was first aggregated to nine sectors and then disaggregated by eight regions. The result of this procedure is an interregional input-output table of the size 72x72, that is with eight regions and nine sectors (eight monetary and one non-monetary). This table, together with estimates of final demand by regional sectors, will be used to estimate output by regional sectors. The procedures by which final demand is estimated in the basic solution will be presented in this chapter. In the basic solution the most likely pattern of development (excluding fluctuations) will be simulated. Alternative demand configurations will be tried in the policy analysis.

VI.1 CATEGORIES OF FINAL DEMAND

The first step in the analysis is thus to calculate demand by region and sector. In accordance with the division in the input-output table final demand is divided into

- private consumption plus increases in stock C. (The inclusion of increases in stock is due to the fact that private consumption is residually determined in the Kenyan input-output table. This is the normal procedure in underdeveloped countries.)
- gross fixed capital investment I
- government consumption G
- exports E
- competitive imports MC (which are here assumed to include import of consumption and investment goods, but not intermediate imports)

Import of intermediate goods are thus assumed to be non-competitive. This is, of course, not absolutely true, but the check made in Chapter V indicates that there has been relatively little substitution of domestic deliveries of intermediate goods for imported intermediate goods. On the other hand, imported intermediate inputs have increased their share in gross output; it would therefore be desirable to introduce this effect in some way. However, the future trend is dependent on the course of technical change (among other things), and this is difficult to predict. In accordance with my assumption of constant input-output coefficients I therefore simply assume that the share of imported intermediate input in gross output of each sector stays constant.

I have thus to estimate seventy-two items of each of the above mentioned demand categories, which makes a total of 360 items. In this chapter I shall describe how the calculations are done for each category.

It should be pointed out at once, that 'final demand for subsistence production' does not represent demand on a market in the way demand for the output of the other sectors does. Subsistence production goes directly to consumption and capital formation within the subsistence sector. (Part of it is actually sold through local markets, but this part cannot be separated due to lack of data.) Since there is little quantitative information about this sector, I can only assume that production grows according to the historical trend as described by the national accounts. Furthermore, in most underdeveloped countries, this trend is assumed to be equal to the population growth rate, possibly with some minor corrections according to information about crop failures etc.

The demand of one region is not in all cases met by production in the same region. There is interregional trade. The manner in which the demand generated in the various regions is distributed among delivering regions is dealt with in the last section of this chapter.

Producer's prices for 1971 are used when not otherwise is stated. Regional incomes are given in terms of value added, i.e. gross domestic product at factor cost. This is the best measure of the real level of production. However, the data on the final demand components are in market prices. To be able to estimate functions determining the development of final demand, I also need an estimate of modern sector GDP at market prices (YMODMP). This is equal to modern sector value added (or GDP at factor cost) plus indirect taxes and import duties less subsidies.

VI.2 CONSUMPTION DEMAND

Consumption by sector and region is determined in three steps. First, total modern consumption is determined as a function of income with a one period lag. Then the distribution of consumption among sectors in the initial year is taken as the starting point, and consumption of each category of modern sector goods is assumed to grow with income according to Engel elasticities. Subsistence consumption is assumed to be a constant share of subsistence production. Finally, it is assumed that the modern sector goods are consumed in the same proportions in all regions, which means that consumption demand for the output of each sector can be distributed among regions according to each region's share in income adjusted for interregional income transfers.

The input-output table contains data on consumption by the relevant sectors for the initial year, 1971. What remains to be done for this year is to distribute these figures by region. This directly gives us the vector of consumption demand by region and sector for the initial year. To start with, consumption is divided into two categories: Subsistence consumption and consumption of modern sector goods. Demand for consumption of the first kind will be related to regional subsistence income (YTRAD), and demand for the second category will be related to regional modern sector income (YMOD).

These income measures indicate how much income is generated in the different provinces. Consumption should, however, preferably be related to some measure of disposable income. Because financial variables are not included in the model, the possible differential regional incidence of taxes cannot be taken into account. One factor that will be taken into account is the large amounts of money that are remitted between different areas in Kenya, where 'cash migration' is prevalent. Johnson and Whitelaw (1974) have estimated that twenty-one per cent of the wage bill of Nairobi is remitted out of Nairobi. This, of course, reduces consumption demand in Nairobi and increases it in other areas; this should therefore be considered when determining the location of final consumption demand.

We do not have any estimates of transfers from cities other than Nairobi, but it seems reasonable to guess that approximately the same proportion is transmitted from the other cities. I therefore assume that, generally, twenty-one per cent of the urban wage bill is transmitted.

Unfortunately, there are no data on how the transfers are distributed across provinces. A reasonable hypothesis is that the outflow of money from a province is distributed in the same way as the immigrants to the province, since the money is remitted mainly within the extended family system.

Of course, there are also some transfers between rural areas located in different provinces. Compared to the urban remittances, however, the net flows between provinces should be smaller. Little is known about them, so I have chosen to disregard them.

I assume that twenty-one per cent of urban earnings are remitted from the towns to other areas. The money must be distributed across provinces. To do this I use the 1969 census migration data. I use figures for males because they dominate migration and, even more so, the remittance of money. There are no separate data on urban migrants, so I assume that the remittances from a province are distributed as the immigrants to the entire province. Since some of the migrants move between districts within their province of origin, the inter-provincial remittances from provinces other than Nairobi together become less than twenty-one per cent of earnings.

I compute net remittances of earnings to region r (REM^r) as the difference between remittances to province r and remittances from the same province. The formula used is

$$REM^r = \sum_q (EARN^q \cdot REMPROP^{qr}) \cdot 0.21 - \sum_s (EARN^r \cdot REMPROP^{rs}) \cdot 0.21 \qquad \text{(VI.1)}$$

$EARN^r$ - urban earnings in province r

$REMPROP^{qr}$ - coefficient for remittances of earnings from province q to province r

It would have been desirable to include estimates of remittances of capital income (that is, operating surplus or the sum of profits, depreciation and interest paid as specified in the input-output table) as well as earnings, but unfortunately, there exists no direct information on this. It may be assumed that the location of investments is the major determining factor for flows of capital income. An estimate made in Bigsten (1978) shows that investments are distributed approximately as capital incomes in 1971. This gives some support to the assumption that there are no interregional net remittances of capital incomes.

Net remittances estimated as in formula (VI.1) must be added to modern incomes generated within the regions to get adjusted regional income for each region.

$$ADJYMOD^r = YMOD^r + REM^r \qquad (VI.2)$$

As mentioned in the previous section, it is assumed that the structure of modern sector consumption is the same in all regions. Consumption shares (CSH_i) for sectors 2 to 9 are calculated from national data in the input-output table for 1971 and are assumed to be valid for all regions.

Subsistence consumption is not disaggregated in any way. It is simply assumed to stand in a constant relation to subsistence income. The constant is calculated from the input-output table.

$$C_1^r = 0.9383 \cdot YTRAD^r \qquad (VI.3)$$

Consumption by sector and region for the remaining sectors for 1971 is obtained by

$$C_i^r = 0.6951 \cdot ADJYMOD^r \cdot CSH_i \qquad i=2,\dots,9 \qquad (VI.4)$$

where the constant is calculated directly from the input-output table. About seventy per cent of the adjusted regional income is thus assumed to be consumed in all regions. It should be noted that taxes are not deducted from adjusted regional income; thus function VI.4 implies that the tax level is assumed to be approximately the same in different regions.

Consumption by regional sectors from t=1 (1972) and onwards then need to be determined. For the subsistence sector this is simple, since I have assumed that there are no interregional differences in the subsistence consumption function. This is therefore

$$C_{1,t}^r = 0.9383 \cdot YTRAD_t^r \qquad (VI.5)$$

Next, we must formulate consumption function for the modern sector. Modern sector GDP less government consumption will be used as a proxy for disposable income. The model requires that demand must be calculated on the basis of the income of the previous period, since no estimate of modern income has been obtained for the present period at this stage of the analysis.

It is problematic to estimate a consumption function directly on the basis of the national accounts data. During the first years after Independence, a considerable restructuring of the economy took place (particularly a large increase in the share of investments in GDP), and from 1974 Kenya was hit by the oil crisis and world recession. Disregarding these years we are left with too few observations to estimate a consumption function statistically. Instead, I have calculated the average growth rates of modern sector GDP at market prices (YMODMP), modern consumption (CMOD) and government consumption (G) for the relatively stable five years 1969-73. I have then directly calculated a function that corresponds to these growth rates, where $CMOD_t$ depends on $(YMODMP - G)_{t-1}$ and t.

The consumption function then becomes

$$CMOD_t = (0.8404 - 0.0013t)(YMODMP-G)_{t-1} \quad \text{(VI.6)}$$

When aggregate modern sector consumption has been determined, the next step is to distribute this total among different sectors or categories of goods. The procedure chosen must be such that there is consistency between the aggregate consumption estimate and the sum of the sectoral estimates. A simple linear expenditure system that meets the consistency requirement will be used. The utility function underlying this model is additive. Additivity implies independence among goods, which makes sense when applied to aggregate commodities as is done here.

As has already been pointed out, I let the sector distribution of consumption growth be determined by Engel elasticities. There are no time-series data available for the aggregate categories used in the analysis; estimates of income elasticities made on the basis of the two input-output tables and data on the development of incomes between 1967 and 1971 provide results which in some cases appear to be dubious. Instead of using these, I choose the alternative of borrowing income elasticities from an analysis of Columbia by Thorbecke and Sengupta (1972). I have taken the average of their two calculations and then scaled the elasticities down to make them meet the Engel aggregation criterion, which says that the sum of income elasticities weighted by shares in consumption (CSH_i) shall be equal to one, that is

$$\sum_i CSH_i \cdot \varepsilon_i = 1 \quad \text{(VI.7)}$$

In this case I had to scale the elasticities down by just three per cent, which may be compared with twenty-seven per cent for the elasticities calculated from the Kenyan input-output tables. The elasticities used were for agriculture 0.48, manufacturing 1.08, utilities 1.16, commerce 1.00, transport 1.12, and services 0.96.

A normal procedure to obtain sector consumption is to use a formula such as

$$C_{i,t} = f(\sum_i (C_{i,t})^{\varepsilon_i}) \quad \text{(VI.8)}$$

where ε_i is the Engel elasticity for good i. If such a constant elasticity model is used for projection purposes, however, one faces increasing adding up problems. To avoid this, the formula may be linearized around the base year consumption levels for the various sectors; in that case the following formula is obtained

$$C_{i,t} = C_{i,1971} + CSH_i \cdot \varepsilon_i \cdot (\sum_i C_{i,t} - \sum_i C_{i,1971})$$

$$i = 2,4,6,7,8,9 \qquad (VI.9)$$

The vector $C_{i,1971}$ thus has a role similar to the subsistence bundle of goods in Stone's linear expenditure system.

Since I want to obtain an estimate of the consumption by region and since I assume that a) the structure of consumption is the same in all regions and b) the level is determined simply by the level of modern regional income adjusted for interregional income transfers, the formula finally becomes

$$C^r_{i,t} = C^r_{i,1971} + CSH_i \cdot \varepsilon_i \cdot (\sum_{i,r} C^r_{i,t} - \sum_{i,r} C^r_{i,1971}) \cdot (ADJYMOD^r/YMOD)_{t-1} \qquad i = 2,4,6,7,8,9 \qquad (VI.10)$$

By applying this formula I get estimates for modern sector consumption demand by region and sector which are consistent with the estimate of total consumption.

The demand for consumption goods within a region is, however, not directed only towards goods produced within the same region, but also towards goods from other regions. This problem will be discussed in section VI.7, and a procedure by which demand can be distributed among regions will be devised.

VI.3 INVESTMENT DEMAND

The size of investment demand by region and sector will be determined in a stepwise procedure. First, total investments are determined; these are then distributed among sectors and regions.

One may assume that in Kenya it is the availability of investment resources that constrains investment rather than the lack of investment opportunities or deficient absorptive capacity. The total amount of domestic savings and the amount of foreign capital inflow can to some extent be controlled by the government through its economic policy. Therefore, one might regard total investment as an exogenous policy variable. In the basic solution, however, I will relate total investment demand to the level of income. This is admittedly a very simplistic way of determining total modern investment, which really is the outcome of a large number of decisions by the government and private firms. Yet, the development of incomes gives an indication of how the availability of investment resources is developing, and the estimated relation may also be regarded as a reflection of the preferences of the government with regard to the share of investments in GDP.

Investment in the subsistence sector is assumed to stand in a constant relation to subsistence income.

$$I_i = 0.0981 \cdot YTRAD \qquad (VI.11)$$

No lag needs to be introduced here, because subsistence income is assumed to grow according to a predetermined trend, and is thus known for each year.

Modern sector investment will simply be related to GDP at market price with a one year lag.

For reasons discussed above, it is not appropriate to estimate the investment function statistically on the basis of the data for 1964-76. As is done in the consumption function, I here simply calculate the average growth rate of investment for the five years 1969-73, and then calculate the investment function corresponding to this growth rate

$$IMOD_t = (0.2615 + 0.0074t)\ YMODMP_{t-1} \qquad (VI.12)$$

When the overall size of investments has been determined according to this formula, it must be distributed among sectors and regions.

As I argued in Chapter I, there are strong forces at work to preserve the concentrated pattern of production. To locate outside the established industrial areas often implies higher costs, and this tends to make the regional allocation of investment similar to the existing distribution of production. Even if production costs were not higher outside the established areas, one must assume that there are considerable costs of obtaining information on the relative attractiveness of investment opportunities in different regions; together with the risks and uncertainties associated with locational change this makes the investors follow a conservative location policy. Wescott (1976, p. 51) concludes in his study that personal considerations are of overriding importance. Many locally owned firms did not consider any location other than the one chosen. This indicates that an accelerator type of investment function, which says that investment takes place where growth already has occurred, gives a reasonably realistic description of investment behaviour. Foreign firms were found to be less restricted by personal considerations, but like domestic firms they did not make any extensive comparisons of different locations. They tended to choose the first location that satisfied certain criteria. This kind of search behaviour makes it likely that they will choose to locate in areas in which there already is industrial activity and in which there, historically, has been growth. This also implies that an accelerator formulation may be regarded as an acceptable simplification.

Political considerations also influence the distribution of investment among sectors and regions, but given that there are no great political changes, it may be a reasonable approximation to let investment be distributed according to incremental capital output ratios and production growth. In a situation with poor integration and immobile investors the accelerator should give a reasonably good description of conservative investors' behaviour.

Sector investment demands by region will be determined on the basis of the estimated national figures. For the subsistence sector this is simple. It is assumed that the same relation between subsistence production and subsistence investment holds for all regions. This implies that function VI.11 is simply changed to

$$I_1^r = 0.0981 \cdot YTRAD^r \qquad \text{(VI.13)}$$

The determination of the distribution among sectors and regions of modern sector investment is somewhat more complicated. I suggested above that it makes economic sense to use some accelerator mechanism to do this. Such a procedure also has the advantage, from a statistical point of view, that it does not require any information on the size of capital stock by region and sector. Some attempts have been made to estimate the size of the Kenyan capital stock by adding up investment figures and depreciating them (Powell, 1973, Tobin, 1974), but these estimates are very sensitive to the choice of assumptions. Moreover, a complete regional and sectoral breakdown made from these estimates would rest on very shaky foundations. To use some procedure that relies on these data therefore does not seem to be a good alternative. It is better to accept the fact that the statistical circumstances are such that one has to be content with some simplified approach.

I choose to let regional production increases by sector multiplied by gross incremental capital output ratios (ICOR) determine the distribution of the predetermined modern sector investment demand among sectors and regions. The following formula is adopted.

$$I_{i,t}^r = \frac{ICOR_i\ (VA_{i,t-1}^r - VA_{i,t-2}^r)\ IMOD_t}{\sum_{i=2}^{9}\sum_{r=1}^{8} ICOR_i\ (VA_{i,t-1}^r - VA_{i,t-2}^r)} \qquad i=2,\ldots,9 \qquad \text{(VI.14)}$$

Note, however, that the ICOR's are scaled equally to retain the consistency between the exogenously determined total investment and the sum of sectoral investments. To give the system a smooth start all VA_i^r for 1970 are assumed to be 94 per cent of VA_i^r for 1971 and for 1969 they are assumed to be 88 per cent.

It is well known that there are numerous problems connected with the use of capital-output ratios. In this case, it might be defensible to use them on the grounds that I do not actually use the ICOR's to calculate investment, but only to determine the distribution of a given total among sectors (and regions); only their relative size is therefore of interest.

I choose to use the gross ICOR's estimated by the World Bank (1975, p. 136) which are for modern agriculture 2.59, mining 2,90, manufacturing 2.58, construction 3.90, el & water 7.88, commerce 1.06, transport 5.75, and services 6.08.

To distribute investments according to production increases in the previous period is, of course, not ideal. Instead, one would like to relate to expected production increases in the coming period; yet, if the economy experiences a stable pattern of growth, it is not unrealistic to assume that the relative size of growth by region and sector in the previous period approximately reflects the expectations for the coming period.

I therefore think that it can be argued that formula VI.14 gives a distribution of investment demand that is sufficiently accurate for the present purpose. It should be pointed out that, in the model, it is demand which determines where growth occurs, not the growth of the capital stock. But, of course, one must assume that the capital stock is growing where production is growing.

The result of the calculations with formula VI.14 is a matrix of investment demand by using sector and region. These demands must be distributed among delivering sectors.

The structure of demand is not differentiated by buying sector, and it is assumed to be the same in all regions. The coefficients describing the origin of investment goods of the modern sector are calculated from the 1971 input-output table. The share of sector i in investment expenditures is called ISH_i.

Manufacturing and building are, of course, dominating. Their shares stayed approximately constant between 1967 and 1971. The share of manufacturing decreased by about two percentage points to forty-six per cent, while building increased by the same figure to forty-three per cent.

To obtain investment demand by delivering sector in each region DI_i^r I simply take the regional sums of investment demand (I_t^r) and distribute them across sectors according to the estimated ISH_i - coefficients. We then get

$$DI_{i,t}^r = I_t^r \cdot ISH_i \qquad i=2,\ldots,9 \qquad \text{(VI.15)}$$

These investment demands must, however, like consumption demand be distributed across regions. The manner in which this is done is discussed in section VI.7.

There is, of course, one obvious problem related to the assumptions used here. The capital-output ratios may well be (and probably are) different in different regions, and the structure of investment demand may also differ (the ISH_i - coefficients). It is, for example, obvious that demand for building investment in Nairobi is considerably higher than these assumptions imply. To correct this anomaly here would require a considerably more detailed analysis of the investment pattern. I abstain from this and simply make the adjustments of the demand distribution that are necessary by the procedure described in section VI.7.

VI.4 GOVERNMENT CONSUMPTION DEMAND

The level of government consumption demand is, of course, determined by the policy makers, and it may thus be regarded as a policy variable. I shall not make any attempt to analyse in detail how the policy makers come to a decision about the size of government consumption, but I need some function for the basic solution which determines the size of government consumption demand.

A reasonable assumption is that the expansion of government consumption is constrained by the size of total production. This influences the possibilities of financing the expenditures through taxes, import duties etc. These financial variables are not explicitly included in the model, but it may be assumed that the level of total government consumption is in some way related to the size of modern sector GDP, which constitutes the 'tax base'. To specify such a relationship I have used the same procedure as for consumption and investment, which gives the following relationship:

$$G_t = (0.2405 + 0.0025t)\ YMODMP_{t-1} \qquad \text{(VI.16)}$$

This function is used to determine the size of total government consumption from year 1 (1972) and onwards. For the first year (1971) the figure is taken directly from the input-output table.

Government consumption demand by region might, for example, be assumed to depend on the distribution of population, but such factors as political considerations (or political power) and level of economic development also play an important role. It is not possible here to analyse what factors determine the regional distribution of government consumption. It will be discussed more extensively in Chapter XII, but behavioural functions will not be introduced into the model. I use a set of exogenous parameters ($GRSH^r$) for the share of each region in total government consumption. These have been calculated from the district development plans published in the mid-seventies. (The figures, the sources, and the assumptions are presented in the following chapter in table VII.1.9:4.)

The size of regional government consumption demand then becomes

$$G^r_{9,t} = G_{9,t} \cdot GRSH^r \qquad \text{(VI.17)}$$

Thus, total government consumption demand is first calculated; then this total is distributed among provinces according to the fixed coefficients. These can be changed by policy makers, and this is actually what much of the political debate in Kenya is about. Here it is reasonable to assume that all government consumption demand is met from within the region.

VI.5 EXPORT DEMAND

An analysis of the factors determining the export prospects of Kenya would lead too far. I simply assume that exports grow at an exogenously determined rate, which is set by among other things demand factors abroad. This is a common assumption in models of this kind (cf. e.g. Johansen, 1974, p. 31). As above, I have here chosen to use the development over the period 1969-73 as my estimate of the export growth rate. Growth of total exports (ETOT) is then determined by the relation

$$ETOT_t = 170948 \cdot (1 + 0.0646)^t \qquad (VI.18)$$

The export structure in 1971 from the 1971 input-output table is used to estimate the share of each sector in total exports (ESH_i).

The shares for 1971 are not much different from those for 1967. The largest change was that manufacturing decreased by about four per cent, while transport increased by two and agriculture and services by one per cent respectively. It therefore does not seem unreasonable to assume that the sectoral shares remain constant over time.

Sectoral exports E_i are then obtained from total exports by

$$E_{i,t} = ESH_i \cdot ETOT_t \qquad (VI.19)$$

The final step is then to distribute the export of each sector among regions. No detailed analysis is done here. For sectors 3-8 it is simply assumed that the share of exports in output is the same in all regions. Export from each regional sector can then be estimated by formula

$$E^r_{i,t} = E_{i,t} \cdot v^r_{i,t-1} \qquad i=3,\ldots,8 \qquad (VI.20)$$

where v^r_i is the share of region r in the value added of sector i. The lag must be introduced since $v^r_{i,t}$ is not known at this stage of the model analysis.

For sectors 2 and 9 it was possible and also desirable to choose a slightly more ambitious approach to the calculation of the regional shares in sectoral export. The breakdown of agricultural export was calculcated from trade statistics for 1971 (Statistical Abstract, 1976, p. 68). Then each category was distributed among regions according to its share in national production of that product (table VII.1). Finally, the weighted average of these shares was calculated. Of course, coffee was the most important export crop, and its weight was almost two-thirds.

Export from the service sector is made up of export from all four different subcategories. Also here export of each type is distributed as the shares of the subsectors in national production (see table VII.1). The service export from each region is also here the weighted average of export of these four types. Here, of course, tourism is the most important foreign exchange earner.

The formula for export from these two sectors by region then becomes

$$E^r_{i,t} = E_{i,t} \cdot Vi^r \qquad i=2,9 \qquad (VI.21)$$

With formulas (VI.20-VI.21) we thus finally obtain estimates of export by region for all sectors.

VI.6 COMPETITIVE IMPORT DEMAND

In the analysis of import demand I differentiate between two categories, import of intermediate goods and import of final demand goods.

It is assumed that the first category grows in line with the growth of production. It is thus treated as non-competitive import (MNC). Import for consumption and investment are treated as competitive (MC), which implies that they are subtracted from the sum of the final demand components, C, I, G, and E (see Chapter III). In principle only goods which could be produced within the country in the short run and at competitive prices should be considered to be competitive, but it is not necessary to try to make such a distinction for the present purpose.

For the initial year, competitive imports are taken directly from the input-output table. One must, however, also have some relation, which determines how competitive imports grow over time. I here choose the simple approach of relating competitive imports to consumption and investment demand with fixed coefficients (even if fixed coefficients better reflect a situation where imports are non-competitive) and they are not differentiated by region. One could, of course, let the coefficients vary in some manner, or treat them as targets that are altered in accordance with the import-substitution policy of the government. In the basic solution, however, they are assumed to be fixed.

The size of competitive imports by region and sector can then be determined by the formula

$$MC^r_{i,t} = MSHC_i \cdot C^r_{i,t} + MSHI_i \cdot DI^r_{i,t} \qquad \text{(VI.22)}$$

I thus regard the regions as demand points, whose sectoral demands are lessened by the import leakage.

Here it need to be pointed out that imports, relative to GDP, were unusually high in 1971 compared to other years. Since the coefficients above had to be estimated on the basis of the input-output table for this year, one unfortunately must expect imports to be overestimated in the following years of the simulation.

VI.7 DISTRIBUTION OF DEMAND AMONG REGIONS

What remains to be done now is to distribute what remains of consumption and investment demand after the import leakage has been deducted.

I assume that consumption and investment demand are distributed in the same manner. This is not a particularly unrealistic or restrictive assumption, and besides there is no information available which could make a differentiation possible. What is to be distributed then is the sum of consumption and investment demand net of competitive imports (CDIN).

$$CDIN = C + DI - MC \qquad (VI.23)$$

The problem here is the same as for intermediate goods, namely that there is no direct information about interregional flows available. For subsistence production there is no problem, since all production within that sector may be assumed to be consumed within the region of production. For the other sectors, however, we must find a procedure which distributes the CDIN demand over all regions. This problem is similar to the problem of distributing intermediate deliveries, and therefore the entropy maximization approach can and will be used also here.

To obtain estimates of how much demand from region r that is directed to region s for each sector ($CDIN_i^{rs}$) I shall look at the situation in the initial year. For this year I have already estimated all $CDIN_i^r$, that is, the amount of consumption plus investment demand net of competitive imports for i that originates in region r. So far, however, I have no estimate of how much demand is directed to the various regions. The total demand of i directed towards region s is called DCI_i^s. I need an estimate of the DCI-vector to be able to apply the entropy maximization approach.

To obtain an estimate of this vector for the initial year, I calculate how much CDIN-demand each region and sector must get to make the main model give the a priori known output figures for the initial year, when the estimated DCI-values are inserted. To find these demand estimates, I start from the known output figures by region and sector and run the model in reverse, that is subtract intermediate inputs, export, and government consumption demand. The residual which then remains is the demand that must be directed to each regional sector to make total demand equal to production and the solution consistent. Thus, this estimated demand vector is the DCI-vector. It does not indicate how this demand is made up of demand from the different regions.

The estimation of the pattern of interregional flows of CDIN-demand will have to be made on the basis of the information available for the initial year of the analysis. For this year, we now know both how much demand that originates in each region (CDIN) and how much demand that is directed to each region (DCI). What remains to be determined is how the CDIN-vector is transformed to the DCI-vector, that is, how the demand of each region is distributed over all eight regions. The problem is to fill an 8x8-quadrant of $CDIN_i^{rs}$ for each sector i = 2,4-9, where $CDIN_i^{rs}$ indicates how much of the demand for good i generated in region r directed to region s.

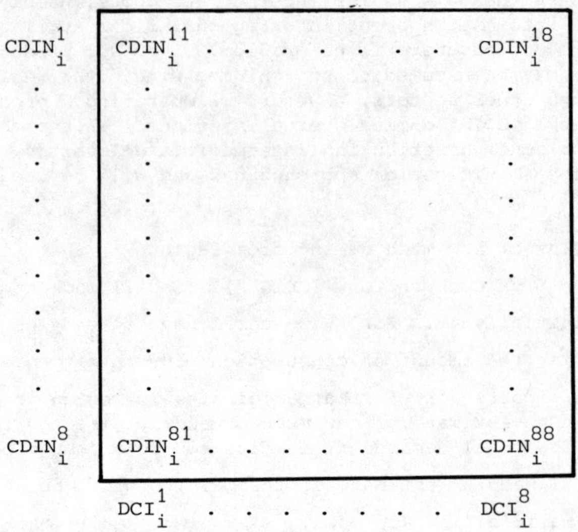

Figure VI.1

The solution must, of course, be such that the row and column restrictions are met.

$$\sum_{s} CDIN_i^{rs} = CDIN_i^{r} \qquad \text{(VI.24)}$$

$$\sum_{r} CDIN_i^{rs} = DCI_i^{s} \qquad \text{(VI.25)}$$

It should be mentioned that the row and column totals are calculated by me and not directly estimated, and that there therefore may be extra biases in these estimates. As far as the CDIN-vector is concerned there may be faults in the C, DI , and/or MC estimates, and the estimate of the DCI-vector is dependent on the assumption regarding G , E , and intermediate production. Still, the magnitudes should in most cases be about right.

As a first check of the direction of demand for different categories of goods I have simply calculated the ratios $DCI_i^r/CDIN_i^r$, which shows whether there is a net inflow or a net outflow of demand for each sector and region.

Table VI.1

Index of demand flows by region and sector
(Coefficients above one indicate a net inflow of demand)

Sector	Nairobi	Central	Coast	Eastern	North Eastern	Nyanza	Rift Valley	Western
Modern agriculture	0.08(-)	1.84(+)	0.39(-)	2.69(+)	1.70(+)	4.73(+)	1.13(+)	3.60(+)
Manufacturing	1.34(+)	0.68(-)	1.33(+)	0.96(-)	- (-)	0.65(-)	0.60(-)	0.05(-)
Building	2.07(+)	0.20(-)	0.24(-)	0.03(-)	0.05(-)	0.04(-)	0.24(-)	0.04(-)
El & water	1.50(+)	0.40(-)	1.16(+)	0.61(-)	-	0.69(-)	0.57(-)	0.32(-)
Commerce	1.45(+)	0.53(-)	1.07(+)	0.51(-)	0.06(-)	0.76(-)	0.55(-)	0.63(-)
Transport	1.21(+)	0.12(-)	2.42(+)	0.35(-)	0.26(-)	0.53(-)	0.47(-)	0.15(-)
Services	1.34(+)	0.58(-)	1.05(+)	0.68(-)	0.32(-)	0.85(-)	0.74(-)	0.71(-)

We see a very clear pattern here. The dominant urban areas, Nairobi and Mombasa (Coast), are net exporters of the outputs of all sectors except for agriculture (and for building in the Coast), while the remaining regions are net importers of everything except agricultural goods. This is an interesting observation because it supports the hypothesis that there are advantages of producing in the main centres of the economy. More of output is produced there than what is needed to satisfy the demand within the centres themselves. The nearness to the market as well as the superior infrastructure that is available in these regions makes it advantageous to produce there. The only industry (except the mining industry which is not included here) that is unable to take advantage of this is agriculture, which is bound in its location by the availability of land.

Another interesting observation that can be made is that these figures seem to indicate that there is a considerable interregional trade with goods and services from all sectors. Of course, this may, to some extent, be a reflection of unsatisfactory demand and/or production estimates. This is, for example, certainly the case for the building sector, where the estimates indicate a large interregional trade that is obviously not correct. This is mainly due to the crudeness of my procedure for determination of investment demand. Some other figures may also be the reflection of anomalies in the data or the procedures, but on the whole I think the figures correctly indicate that there is considerable interregional trade in most sectors in Kenya. When a country is on a very low level of development, some types of production can only be found in one or a few places, and the entire national market must then be fed from these few producers.

We shall now go back to the problem of determining the $CDIN^{rs}$ flows from the information available. Within the discipline of regional economics the market area analysis has traditionally been one of the corner stones. To determine how demand for consumption and investment (less competitive imports) is distributed across the system of regions, a starting point may therefore be found in this tradition.

It is usually assumed that each firm acts as a monopolist within its own market area, which, in many cases, is an unrealistic assumption. A more flexible approach has been put forward by Beckerman (1971), who uses dominating sales as a criterion for market areas. In his analysis, he assumes that each firm has to share each market with other firms. He assumes that the market share of each firm is a function of the economic distance to the market compared with that of the other firms and possibly some variable reflecting the relative attractiveness of the firm.

Here, I am not interested in determining the extent of market areas, but to find some way according to which I can distribute $CDIN_i^r$ over delivering regions. The problem is to find a reasonable way of determining the $CDIN_i^{rs}$ at the same time as both the row and the column restrictions are met. As has already been mentioned, I shall use the entropy approach to estimate the interregional flows, but I shall not reiterate the arguments for this (see Chapter V). One difference from the above is that I shall not use any a priori estimate of the type used in the estimation of interregional flows of intermediate goods (see Formula V. 5). Here, there is no information comparable to the a_{ij}'s that can be used as a basis for such an a priori estimate. The entropy approach without prespecification will therefore be used.

One solution for each sector $i=2,4,\ldots,9$ must be found. (There is no CDIN-deliveries in mining.) This means that an objective function for each of these sectors has to be maximized.

$$F_i = - \sum_r \sum_s (CDIN_i^{rs} \ln CDIN_i^{rs} - CDIN_i^{rs}) \qquad i=2,4,\ldots,9 \tag{VI.26}$$

The maximization must be made subject to restrictions (VI.24-VI.25). As before, also a restriction on the transport capacity is introduced.

$$\sum_r \sum_s c_i^{rs} \, CDIN_i^{rs} = T_i \tag{VI.27}$$

If T_i is now specified, the problem may be solved in the manner described in Chapter V. That means that the flow function becomes

$$CDIN_i^{rs} = e^{-\lambda_i^r} e^{-\mu_i^s} e^{-\gamma c_i^{rs}} \tag{VI.28}$$

By setting

$$A_i^r = \frac{e^{-\lambda_i^r}}{CDIN_i^r} \tag{VI.29}$$

$$B_i^s = \frac{e^{-\mu_i^s}}{DCI_i^s} \tag{VI.30}$$

function (VI.28) can be written as

$$CDIN_i^{rs} = A_i^r B_i^s CDIN_i^r DCI_i^s e^{-\gamma_i^{rs}} \tag{VI.31}$$

Then by the procedures shown in Chapter V we get

$$A_i^r = \{\sum_s B_i^s DCI_i^s e^{-\gamma c_i^{rs}}\}^{-1} \tag{VI.32}$$

$$B_i^s = \{\sum_r A_i^r CDIN_i^r e^{-\gamma c_i^{rs}}\}^{-1} \tag{VI.33}$$

A solution might now be obtained by iteration between A_i^r and B_i^s

and adjustment of γ to meet the transport restriction.

However, it seems more realistic to let the transport restriction cover all deliveries of CDIN . Therefore, instead of specifying T_i's for the respective sectors, I consider only one transport restriction T. A difference compared to the previous application is that here I do not specify T , but instead I specify that γ shall be equal to the γ in the solution to the input-output flows. This means that I assume that the distance friction is the same for final demand goods as for intermediate goods. Since the flows here are net flows, the transport requirement actually is larger than what the resulting T indicates.

I thus iterate between A_i^r and B_i^s for the sectors (i=2,4,...,9) until the resulting flows give a transport cost for the entire system.

$$\sum_{i=2,4}^{9} \sum_r \sum_s c_i^{rs}\, CDIN_i^{rs} = T \qquad \text{(VI.34)}$$

that is such that the desired γ is obtained.

The transport coefficient is, as before, expressed as

$$c_i^{rs} = d^{rs}\, \alpha_i \qquad \text{(VI.35)}$$

where the relation between the α_i for sectors 2-4 and 5-9 as before is assumed to be 1:4.

When all $CDIN_i^{rs}$ have been estimated by the procedure described here, the following coefficients are calculated.

$$\delta_i^{rs} = \frac{CDIN_i^{rs}}{CDIN_i^{r}} \qquad \text{(VI.36)}$$

These coefficients show how much of the $CDIN_i^r$-demand is directed to region s in the initial year. I assume for the basic solution that these coefficients remain constant over the period of analysis. It is not possible to let them change with time within the model like the coefficients for intermediate goods do. To be able to do so one would need an independent estimate of the DCI-vector for t=1 and onwards. To get such an estimate one would have to go outside the model. The new DCI-vector that is calculated in the model for each year is the result of the application of the δ_i^{rs}-coefficients, and can thus not be used as a basis for an estimate of the same coefficients. On the assumption that there are no drastic changes in the communication system or the distribution of other infrastructure, it seems likely that the trade pattern will not change very much.

What is done for each year is then that the interregional spread of $CDIN_i^r$-demand is calculated according to the formula

$$CDIN_i^{rs} = \delta_i^{rs} \; CDIN_i^r \qquad (VI.37)$$

Then the CDIN-demand directed towards each regional sector is obtained from

$$DCI_i^s = \sum_r CDIN_i^{rs} \qquad (VI.38)$$

When this final step has been taken, the total final demand vector net of competitive imports can be calculated as

$$Z = DCI + G + E \qquad (VI.39)$$

From this, production is then estimated as described in the following chapter.

VII Production by sector and region

The procedure for calculating demand by region and sector was described in the previous chapter. The next step in the model analysis is to use this information and the interregional input-output table (see Chapter V) to calculate production by region and sector. Before discussing how this is done (see section VII.2), I shall, however, describe how the production estimate for the initial year 1971 is made.

VII.1 PRODUCTION BY REGION AND SECTOR, 1971

Calculations of production by province and sector have been made for each year between 1967 and 1976 (Bigsten, 1977). The most detailed calculations were made for 1971 since this is the initial year of the model. The fact that the last Kenyan input-output table was constructed for this year also implies that there is quite a lot of data available. The results of the calculations as well as the sources and assumptions used are presented in detail in table VII.1. Figures on the absolute provincial production levels and per capita incomes as well as an index comparing provincial per capita incomes to Nairobi's (=100) are shown in table VII.2. The estimates for the other years will be presented in Chapter XI, where they will be compared with the pattern generated by the model.

Value added or gross domestic product at factor cost is used throughout as the measure of output. A detailed discussion of the assumptions and sources used and of the reliability of the data may be found in the tables.

The procedure followed has been to start from data on national production for each sector. For 1971, sector value added is taken from the input-output table (Chapter IV); then the provincial shares in the output of each sector are calculated from the best information available, after which the total is distributed among provinces according to these.

Table VII.1
Production by province and sector, 1971

Table VII.1.1
Subsistence production - value added by province (K£'000)

	Agri-culture	Building & owner-ship of huts etc.	Total	Per cent
Central	20,857	4,635	25,492	20.63
Coast	3,182	1,391	4,573	3.70
Eastern	18,499	4,172	22,671	18.35
North Eastern	652	695	1,347	1.09
Nyanza	30,031	4,172	34,203	27.69
Rift Valley	17,455	4,635	22,090	17.88
Western	9,696	3,477	13,173	10.66
TOTAL	100,372	23,177	123,549	100

Sources and assumptions

Agriculture: The percentage distribution of subsistence agricultural production (i.e. small farm production for home consumption or for sale in local markets) is calculated from the Integrated Rural Survey (IRS) for 1974/75. No similar data are available for 1971. Even if there may have been some changes between those two periods, this is probably the best estimate than can be obtained.

First, the average value of subsistence output per holding is calculated (IRS, p. 66), that is, output used on the farm, crops sold on local markets, and sales of cattle and milk. In the last category are included some sales to e.g. Kenya Meat Commission, which should be excluded. There is, however, no data on this in the IRS. Therefore the entire small farm output of cattle is included in the estimates. This may give some bias, but since only about twenty-five per cent of all cattle is sold through KMC one can assume that most of this does not come from the small farm areas. From the estimates of production value must be drawn farm costs relating to intermediate inputs (not labour costs); total intermediate cost per farm is therefore calculated for each province. The cost is then split up between commercial output and subsistence output in proportion to their respective percentages in total farm production. Then subsistence farm costs are deducted from subsistence output, which gives value added in subsistence production by farm in the sample area for each province.

To find total provincial production one must then know how many farms there are in each province. The population estimates made in the IRS differ considerably from estimates made on the basis of the population censuses (estimates for urban and rural population 1975 are presented in Kenya Statistical Digest, Sep. 1976, p.9). The latter should be more reliable, which is why I use these (the IRS estimate is about 700,000 people greater than the census estimate for the Central, Eastern, and Western provinces).

To start with, I thus calculate the rural population in the areas included in the IRS sample frame (district estimates for 1975 taken from Kenya Statistical Digest, Sep. 1972). The provincial estimates thus obtained are divided by the household sizes for each province shown in the IRS (p.32), which gives an estimate of the number of farms within the sample area for each province. The rural population in small farm and ranching areas outside the sample area also has to be calculated (the large farm areas of Trans Nzoia, Uasin Gishu, and Nakuru are excluded, even if there are some small farmers there). The rural population by province in the areas outside the sample area (West Pokot, Narok, Kajidado, Turkana, Samburu, Marsabit, Isiolo, Tana River, Lamu, Mandera, Wajir, Garissa) was then calculated as the district population minus estimates of their urban populations. The population (totalling 1,017,000) was then divided, for each province, by the same figures on household size as the population within the sample area, which thus gives an estimate of the number of households in the area. Since these are low potential areas and because a considerable part of what is produced is sold to the Kenya Meat Commission and thus is registered as modern agriculture, I assume that subsistence production within these areas is fifty per cent of what it is in the Coast, which has the lowest per capita subsistence production. I then multiply the estimates of average subsistence production and the estimated number of 'farms' for each province. The estimate of total national subsistence production obtained by this procedure is K£ 155 million. This is consistent with the estimates in the national accounts, which were K£ 131 million for 1974 and K£ 165 million for 1975. Using the estimates I have obtained, I calculate the percentage of each province in total subsistence production. These estimates are then applied to the value added figure for 1971 in subsistence agricultural production, which gives me my estimates of value added by province for 1971.

The production estimates presented here differ quite considerably from what the Central Bureau of Statistics have thought. My estimates for the Coast, Eastern, and Western provinces are higher. A note of caution about these figures is therefore in place. Later rounds of the IRS may make it possible to make more reliable estimates.

Building and ownership of huts: The percentage distribution among provinces is made according to estimates made by the Central Bureau of Statistics.

Table VII.1.2
Modern agricultural production

The value of gross marketed production for 1971 is distributed by province. The categories of output are:

	Value (K£'000)
Cereals	10,746
Wheat	5,206
Maize	4,276
Rice	725
Barley and others	539
Temporary industrial crops	7,481
Pyrethrum	2,423
Sugar	3,457
Cotton	878
Castor and other oil seeds	400

	Value (K£'000)
Tobacco	28
Pineapples	295
Other temporary crops	3,497
Pulses	303
Potatoes	1,652
Other temporary crops	1,542
Permanent crops	35,181
Coffee	18,922
Sisal	1,519
Tea	11,803
Cashew nuts	944
Wattle	423
Coconuts	545
Fruit and other permanent crops	1,025
Livestock and related products	26,049
Cattle and calves for slaughter	13,330
Sheep, goats and lambs for slaughter	733
Pigs for slaughter	593
Poultry and eggs	1,032
Wool	220
Hides and skin	841
Dairy products	9,300
Unrecorded marketed production	3,741
Total gross marketed agricultural production	86,695
Forestry GDP	4,470
Fishing GDP	1,220

Table VII.1.2:1

Cereals - gross marketed production by province (K£'000)

	Wheat	Maize	Rice	Sum	Barley etc	Total	Per cent
Central	572	74	612	1,258	66	1,324	12.32
Coast	-	-	-	-	-	-	-
Eastern	559	2	-	561	30	591	5.50
North Eastern	-	-	-	-	-	-	-
Nyanza	-	268	57	325	17	342	3.18
Rift Valley	4,075	2,329	-	6,404	338	6,742	62.74
Western	-	1,603	56	1,659	88	1,747	16.26
TOTAL	5,206	4,276	725	10,207	539	10,746	100

Sources and assumptions

Wheat: Report of the Kenya Wheat Board for 1.7.1971-30.6.1972, app. 5, 1972.

Maize: Monthly Statistics from the Maize and Produce Board, 70/71 and 71/72.

Rice: Annual reports from the Maize and Produce Board 70/71 and 71/72. The value given is a weighted average of the periods Aug. 70 - July 71 and Aug. 71 - July 72. The weights are 7/12 and 5/12 respectively.

Barley etc: Production of the remaining cereals (five per cent of total production) is distributed among provisions in the same proportion as the sum of wheat, maize and rice.

Table VII.1.2:2
Temporary industrial crops
Gross marketed production by province (K£'000)

	Pyre-thrum	Sugar	Cotton	Castor	To-bacco	Pine-apples	Total	Per cent
Central	605	-	87	13	4	295	1,004	13.42
Coast	-	387	186	76	-	-	649	8.68
Eastern	18	-	33	295	20	-	366	4.89
North Eastern	-	-	-	-	-	-	-	-
Nyanza	1,446	3,070	183	7	4	-	4,710	62.96
Rift Valley	354	-	-	2	-	-	356	4.76
Western	-	-	389	7	-	-	396	5.29
TOTAL	2,423	3,457	878	400	28	295	7,481	100

Sources and assumptions

Pyrethrum: Data from the Pyrethrum Board. Average for 1970/71 and 1971/72.

Sugar: Economic Review of Agriculture, Vol. 3, No 4, 1971, p. 45.

Cotton: Data from the Cotton Lint and Seed Marketing Board.

Castor etc: Maize and Produce Board Annual Reports 70/71 and 71/72. The two crop years are weighted together according to the number of months that refer to 1971, that is, the weights are 7/12 and 5/12 respectively.

Tobacco: Economic Review of Agriculture, Vol. 3, No 4, 1971, p.46.

Pineapples: Kenya Canners handle all industrial processing of pineapples and they get all their deliveries from the Central province. Pineapples are also grown elsewhere, but the marketed part of this is insignificant.

Table VII.1.2:3
Other temporary crops
Gross marketed production by province (K£'000)

	Pulses	Potatoes & other temp.	Total	Per cent
Nairobi	-	22	22	0.63
Central	47	685	732	20.93
Coast	7	608	615	17.59
Eastern	225	766	991	28.34
North Eastern	-	-	-	-
Nyanza	5	403	408	11.67
Rift Valley	7	385	392	11.21
Western	12	325	337	9.63
TOTAL	303	3,194	3,497	100

Sources and assumptions

Pulses: Annual reports of the Maize and Produce Board 70/71 and 71/72. The figures are weighted as earlier with 7/12 and 5/12 respectively. Price data for 1971/72 are used to weight the various crops together.

Potatoes and other temporary crops: No data on production by province are available. I have therefore calculated the area under these crops on small farms and large farms (small farm survey 1969/70 and large farm survey 1971. See Statistical Abstract, 1976). The acreage on large farms constituted only 1.4 per cent of the total area under these crops, but an informed guess from the Horticultural Crops Development Authorities says that its share in marketed production would be about fifteen per cent. I therefore distribute eighty-five per cent of total production between provinces according to small farm acreage and fifteen per cent according to large farm acreage. This unfortunately does not take into account the differences in market orientation between different provinces.

Table VII.1.2:4
Permanent crops
Gross marketed production by province (K£'000)

	Coffee	Sisal	Tea	Cashew	Wattle	Coco-nuts	Fruits	Total	Per cent
Nairobi	-	-	-	-	-	-	2	2	0.01
Central	14,120	411	1,825	-	185	-	303	16,844	47.87
Coast	16	563	-	944	238	545	297	2,603	7.40
Eastern	2,911	103	524	-	-	-	191	3,729	10.60
North Eastern	-	-	-	-	-	-	-	-	-
Nyanza	771	-	451	-	-	-	60	1,282	3.64
Rift Valley	891	442	9.003	-	-	-	91	10,427	29.64
Western	213	-	-	-	-	-	81	294	0.84
TOTAL	18,922	1,519	11,803	944	423	545	1,025	35,181	100

Sources and assumptions

Coffee: Data from the Coffee Produce Board. The two crop years are weighted 1/4 and 3/4 according to number of months in the calendar year.

Sisal: Data from the Sisal Produce Board.

Tea: Data from the Tea Produce Board.

Cashew: All cashew in Kenya is grown in the Coast province according to land use statistics (Statistical Abstract, 1971).

Wattle: Economic Review of Agriculture, Vol. 3, No 4, 1971, p. 32.

Coconuts: All coconuts are grown in the Coast province according to land use statistics (Statistical Abstract, 1971).

Fruit: In this category are included only fruit from permanent crops. There are no data on production by province. Therefore the acreage on small farm and large farm under these crops has been calculated (small farm survey 1969/70, large farm survey 1971. See Statistical Abstract, 1976). The large farm acreage constituted only about 3.4 per cent of the total acreage, but an informed guess from the Horticultural Crops Development Authority says that the share of large farms in marketed output may be about twenty per cent. I have therefore distributed eighty per cent of total production according to small farm acreage and twenty per cent according to large farm acreage.

Table VII.1.2:5
Livestock and related products
Gross marketed production by province (K£'000)

	Cattle	Sheep	Pigs	Poultry	Wool	Hides	Dairy	Total	Per cent
Nairobi	52	4	40	5	1	3	-	105	0.40
Central	143	31	226	96	9	9	2,200	2,714	10.42
Coast	802	24	-	97	8	51	79	1,061	4.07
Eastern	2,274	103	-	261	31	143	199	3,011	11.56
North Eastern	2,185	50	-	-	15	138	-	2,388	9.17
Nyanza	40	-	-	291	-	3	42	376	1.44
Rift Valley	7,834	521	316	83	156	494	6,780	16,184	62.13
Western	-	-	11	199	-	-	-	210	0.81
TOTAL	13,330	733	593	1,032	220	841	9,300	26,049	100

Sources and assumptions

Cattle: Distributed according to provincial breakdown of number of heads delivered to Kenya Meat Commissions factories in Athi River, Mombasa, Ngong, and Nakuru. Data from Kenya Meat Commission (KMC).

<u>Sheep & Goats</u>: Distributed according to origin of deliveries to KMC in 1972 (1971 unobtainable), Economic Review of Kenya Agriculture, 1972, vol. 4, No 4, p. 15.

<u>Pigs</u>: The origin of total pig purchases (Uplands) July - Dec. 1971. Economic Review of Agriculture, Vol. 3, Nos 3-4, 1971.

<u>Poultry and eggs</u>: Estimates of number of poultry by district 1970, Statistical Abstract 1976, p. 127. This survey seems more complete than the one for 1971/72.

<u>Wool</u>: Distributed in the same proportions as production of sheep etc.

<u>Hides</u>: Distributed in the same proportions as production of cattle.

<u>Dairy</u>: Distributed according to data on deliveries to Kenya Cooperative Creameries in 1974 (earlier years unobtainable). Deliveries are given by factories only; in some cases adjustments have therefore been made. Deliveries to Nyahururu is assumed to be split fifty-fifty between Rift Valley and Central; six per cent of deliveries to Sotik were assumed to come from Nyanza (6/94 is the proportion of cattle on large farms in Kisii and Kericho); nine per cent of total deliveries to Central province creameries were assumed to come from Meru in Eastern province (9/91 is the proportion of cattle on large farms in Eastern and Central).

Table VII.1.2:6
Unrecorded marketed production (K£'000)

		Per cent
Nairobi	1	0.04
Central	1,309	34.98
Coast	254	6.79
Eastern	373	9.98
North Eastern	-	-
Nyanza	444	11.87
Rift Valley	1,178	31.49
Western	182	4.87
TOTAL	3,741	100

Sources and assumptions

The unrecorded marketed agricultural production covers crops not registered elsewhere, and it is distributed among provinces in the same proportions as total gross marketed production of crops.

Table VII.1.2:7
Forestry
Gross domestic product by province (K£'000)

		Per cent
Nairobi	715	16.0
Central	894	20.0
Coast	179	4.0
Eastern	224	5.0
North Eastern	-	-
Nyanza	89	2.0
Rift Valley	2,280	51.0
Western	89	2.0
TOTAL	4,470	100

Sources and assumptions

Data on labour costs from the Forest Department are used to calculate the percentages.

Table VII.1.2:8
Fishing
Gross domestic product by province (K£'000)

		Per cent
Coast	497	40.74
Nyanza	647	53.03
Rift Valley	76	6.23
TOTAL	1,220	100

Sources and assumptions

The total production figure given in the national accounts is distributed according to how the value of fish landed in 1971 is distributed. River fish - six per cent of the total is excluded (Statistical Abstract, 1976, p. 146).

Table VI.1.2:9
Total
Modern agriculture, forestry and fishing

	Cereals	Temporary	Other temp.	Permanent	Livestock	Unrecorded
Nairobi	-	-	22	2	105	1
Central	1,324	1,004	732	16,844	2,714	1,309
Coast	-	649	615	2,603	1,061	254
Eastern	591	366	991	3,729	3,011	373
North Eastern	-	-	-	-	2,388	-

Table VII.1.2:9 cont.

	Cereals	Temporary	Other temp.	Permanent	Livestock	Unrecorded
Nyanza	342	4,710	408	1,282	376	444
Rift Valley	6,742	356	392	10,427	16,184	1,178
Western	1,747	396	337	294	210	189
TOTAL	10,746	7,481	3,497	35,181	26,049	3,741

	Total gmp in agric.	Value added Agric.	Forestry	Fishing	Total	Per cent
Nairobi	129	108	715	-	823	1.06
Central	23,793	19,840	894	-	20,734	26.76
Coast	5,151	4,295	179	497	4,971	6.41
Eastern	8,993	7,499	224	-	7,723	9.97
North Eastern	2,372	1,978	-	-	1,978	2.55
Nyanza	7,520	6,270	89	647	7,006	9.04
Rift Valley	35,001	29,185	2,280	76	31,541	40.70
Western	3,149	2,626	89	-	2,715	3.51
TOTAL	86,108	71,801	4,470	1,220	77,491	100

Sources and assumptions

It is assumed that value added in agriculture is distributed as gross marketed production (gmp), even if there should be some differences among products in the share of value added in output. The figure for Nairobi may be a bit too low. According to the survey of employment and earnings there is more employment in Nairobi within this sector than what my estimate suggests. By only looking at where the crops are grown, some administrative units in Nairobi are probably neglected.

Table VII.1.3
Mining
Value added by province (K£'000)

		Per cent
Nairobi	533	18.19
Central	4	0.13
Coast	725	24.74
Eastern	82	2.81
North Eastern	-	-
Nyanza	443	15.12
Rift Valley	1,142	38.96
Western	1	0.05
TOTAL	2,930	100

Sources and assumptions

The production of Nairobi and the Coast is shown in Surveys of Industrial Production 1968-71, p. 28. The gross product of the remaining provinces, which is not shown separately, is distributed according to the respective provincial shares in sector earnings in 1971 (Employment and Earnings, 1971). Note that the survey covers only firms with at least fifty employees. This might give a bias, if small firms are distributed differently.

Table VII.1.4
Manufacturing
Value added by province (K£'000)

		Per cent
Nairobi	38,207	53.89
Central	5,863	8.27
Coast	15,080	21.27
Eastern	2,375	3.35
North Eastern	-	-
Nyanza	2,609	3.68
Rift Valley	6,665	9.40
Western	99	0.14
TOTAL	70,898	100

Sources and assumptions

Data on gross product are provided in Surveys of Industrial Production 1968-71, p. 28, for each province, except that the Eastern and North Eastern are not separated; I therefore distribute the sum between the two provinces according to their share in sector earnings. Since this is zero in the North Eastern province, the entire sum is allocated to the Eastern province. Also in this case only firms with more than fifty employees are covered in the survey, but the percentages obtained are used to calculate the distribution of total value added; the fact that this does not lead to any large biases is shown in appendix VII.A in Bigsten (1978).

Table VII.1.5
Building and construction
Value added by province (K£'000)

		Per cent
Nairobi	20,822	89.79
Central	475	2.05
Coast	928	4.00
Eastern	46	0.20
North Eastern	7	0.03
Nyanza	42	0.18
Rift Valley	846	3.65
Western	23	0.10
TOTAL	23,189	100

Sources and assumptions

Percentages for Nairobi, Central, Coast, and Rift Valley as given in Surveys of Industrial Production 1968-71, p. 28. The rest of gross product is distributed among the remaining provinces as sectoral earnings. Only firms with more than fifty employees are covered, and the percentages obtained are used to calculate distribution of value added.

Table VII.1.6
Electricity and water
Value added by province (K£'000)

		Per cent
Nairobi	4,836	58.94
Central	400	4.88
Coast	1,485	18.10
Eastern	354	4.31
North Eastern	-	-
Nyanza	344	4.19
Rift Valley	717	8.74
Western	69	0.84
TOTAL	8,205	100

Sources and assumptions

For this sector it is assumed that production is distributed among provinces as earnings - with some adjustments. Nairobi's share in earnings seems to be bigger that its share in production, since e.g. some workers working outside Nairobi are paid by the city. Complementary information from the Central Bureau of Statistics suggests that Nairobi's share could be about ten per cent lower than what the earnings estimate suggests. I therefore deduct ten per cent from Nairobi and add 1.5 per cent to the Coast and Nyanza provinces, and 3.5 per cent to the Eastern and Rift Valley provinces.

Table VII.1.7
Commerce
Value added by province (K£'000)

	Labour income	Capital income Com	Fin.	Total	Per cent
Nairobi	21,915	12,658	8,864	43,437	58.10
Central	1,022	2,646	1,174	4,842	6.48
Coast	5,467	5,301	2,015	12,783	17.10
Eastern	509	1,727	340	2,576	3.45
North Eastern	13	18	-	31	0.04
Nyanza	1,055	1,358	826	3,239	4.33
Rift Valley	2,569	2,857	1,077	6,503	8.70
Western	306	893	147	1,346	1.80
TOTAL	32,856	27,458	14,443	74,757	100

Sources and assumptions

Labour income is distributed among provinces in the same proportions as modern sector earnings are distributed among provinces (Employment and Earnings, 1971). The distribution of capital income is calculated separately for distribution and financial services. Distribution: Urban capital income (about eighty-two per cent of the total) is distributed among provinces in the proportions that net profits are distributed according to the Survey of Distribution, 1971). The remaining eighteen per cent are distributed among provinces in the same proportions as the production which is excluded from the survey, i.e. rural distribution and the produce boards. In the survey only an aggregate figure is given for rural output. This is distributed among provinces in proportion to the regional shares in earnings of non-agricultural enterprises in rural areas 1969. This survey covered activities with a fixed place of work, such as market stalls in market places. The differences between 51.15 million, shown in the national accounts as output of the sector, and the 49.46 million, shown in the survey, is referred to the produce boards. Of this sum ninety per cent are allocated to Nairobi, five per cent to Rift Valley, five per cent to the Central province. When this is done, eighteen per cent of capital income are distributed among provinces as the sum of output from rural distribution and produce boards.

Financial services: Only the most important part, banking activity, is covered. It seems fairly reasonable to assume that insurance and real estate activities show a similar pattern.

The banking sector is divided in two parts. The three big, country-wide banks (about two-thirds of the sector) and the smaller banks with branches in Nairobi, Mombasa, Nakuru, Kisumu, and Thika plus the more dispersed cooperative bank. Profits are assumed to be distributed as deposits. Separate estimates of these have been made for the two categories, based on information from local bankers. These two estimates have then been weighted together to get the total provincial distribution of deposits. The profits of the sector have then been distributed among provinces as deposits.

Table VII.1.8
Transport
Value added by province (K£'000)

		Per cent
Nairobi	20,328	47.12
Central	639	1.48
Coast	16,337	37.87
Eastern	1,035	2.40
North Eastern	73	0.17
Nyanza	1,337	3.10
Rift Valley	3,205	7.43
Western	186	0.43
TOTAL	43,140	100

Sources and assumptions

Because no survey is available, I have had to assume that production is distributed among provinces in the same proportions as earnings. It is not self evident that the share of profits in incomes is the same in different provinces, but there is no basis for a better assumption than this one.

Table VII.1.9
Services
Table VII.1.9:1
Restaurants and hotels
Value added by province (K£'000)

		Per cent
Nairobi	3,740	47.88
Central	580	7.42
Coast	1,929	24.69
Eastern	367	4.70
North Eastern	-	-
Nyanza	240	3.07
Rift Valley	942	12.06
Western	14	0.18
TOTAL	7,812	100

Sources and assumptions

Percentage of turnover for hotels and restaurants in 1966 are calculated from Survey of Services, 1966 (p. A32). The number of bed-nights per province in 1966 was estimated (Statistical Abstract, 1976, p. 34), and the provincial ratios turnover/bed-nights were calculated; then the number of bed-nights by province in 1971 was calculated. These figures were then multiplied by the ratios estimated for 1966 for each province. After a proportional adjustment of this to make it add up to the 1971 total had been made, an estimate of the percentage turnover for 1971 was obtained. It was then finally assumed that value added was distributed among provinces as turnover.

Table VII.1.9:2
Ownership of dwellings
Value added by province (K£'000)

		Per cent
Nairobi	12,801	52.01
Central	1,049	4.26
Coast	5,691	23.12
Eastern	711	2.89
North Eastern	-	-
Nyanza	1,243	5.05
Rift Valley	2,855	11.60
Western	263	1.07
TOTAL	24,613	100

Sources and assumptions

Sector value added is distributed among provinces in proportion to the estimated urban population of 1971 (Interpolation between 1969 census and estimates for 1975). The population figure for Nairobi (and thus its share in value added) was inflated by twenty-five per cent in order to take the high rents in Nairobi into account.

Table VII.1.9:3
Miscellaneous services
Value added by province (K£'000)

		Per cent
Nairobi	11,627	74.87
Central	722	4.65
Coast	1,556	10.02
Eastern	116	0.75
North Eastern	-	-
Nyanza	497	3.20
Rift Valley	904	5.82
Western	107	0.69
TOTAL	15,529	100

Sources and assumptions

The percentage figures are based on the Survey of Services, 1966 (p. A32). These percentages have then been applied to the sum of value added in 1971 as shown in the input-output table.

Table VII.1.9:4
Public services
Value added by province (K£'000)

		Per cent
Nairobi	34,442	34.97
Central	14,281	14.50
Coast	10,903	11.07
Eastern	10,430	10.59
North Eastern	689	0.70
Nyanza	6,353	6.45
Rift Valley	16,517	16.77
Western	4,875	4.95
TOTAL	98,490	100

Sources and assumptions

The percentage distribution of recurrent expenditures is calculated for the budget year 1973/74; it is assumed that the same distribution prevailed in 1971. The reason for choosing 1973/74 is that in most of the first round district development plans there are data on recurrent expenditures by district and ministry for that year.

For the Eastern, Nyanza, and Western provinces there were complete data for all districts.

For the Coast the data were complete, except that expenditures on police were not included. Of the total national allocation to police the Coast was therefore given a share equal to its share in population.

For the Central province there were complete data for Kiambu and Nyeri. For Muranga there were data for some ministries, while they were incomplete for others. Therefore the average expenditure per capita in Kiambu and Nyeri on administration, health, information and broadcasting, and cooperatives was assumed to prevail also in Muranga. The estimated population in Muranga was therefore multiplied by the average of the per capita estimates for Kiambu and Nyeri to get expenditures in Muranga in these fields. In education, which constitutes more than fifty per cent of recurrent expenditures in Muranga, it was assumed that the average of expenditures per pupil in primary school in Kiambu and Nyeri was valid for Muranga. This figure was then multiplied by the number of pupils (the average for 1973 and 1974) to get an estimate of educational expenditures. Of course, there are other types of education than primary, but it is assumed that the development of primary education can serve as a proxy for the entire educational sector.

For Nyandarua and Kirinyaga the expenditures on administration, education and health were estimated in the same manner; it was assumed that these sectors constituted the same share in total recurrent expenditures as in Muranga, Nyeri, and Kiambu put together (that is 67.2 per cent), which made it possible to obtain an estimate of total recurrent expenditures in these two districts.

For the North Eastern province, there are only rough figures for the time when the plans are written. An estimate based on these figures is made and then reduced by one-third to take the growth of recurrent expenditures between 73/74 and this time into account. Data for administration are missing; I therefore assume that the share of administration in total recurrent expenditures in the North Eastern province is the same as the average for the provinces discussed above. This makes it possible to obtain an estimate also for this category of expenditure. Then total expenditures can be estimated.

For Rift Valley there are no data presented in the district development plans, and as far as Nairobi is concerned a plan does not even exist. These two provinces are therefore dealt with in a very crude manner. I simply split what is left of total recurrent expenditures after the above mentioned six provinces have got their shares according to the share of Nairobi and Rift Valley in total public service earnings for 1974 (Employment and Earnings, 1974).

To determine expenditures residually for these two provinces is not a very satisfactory method, since all the faults that may exist in my previous estimates may be added together and give a biased picture. The use of earnings as a proxy may also give a certain bias, even if the differences between shares in earnings and my estimates for the six previously discussed provinces in most cases are limited.

It should be noted that in the input-output table some private enterprises supplying health and education have been included in this category. It has not been possible to adjust the estimates for this, which means that there could be a slight bias. One might, for example, assume that the share of Nairobi is underestimated.

Table VII.1.9:5
Total
Services
Value added by province (K£'000)

	Rest.& hotels	Dwell- ings	Miscella- neous	Public	Total	Per cent
Nairobi	3,740	12,801	11,627	34,442	62,610	42.75
Central	580	1,049	722	14,281	16,632	11.36
Coast	1,929	5,691	1,556	10,903	20,079	13.71
Eastern	367	711	116	10,430	11,624	7.94
North Eastern	-	-	-	689	689	0.47
Nyanza	240	1,243	497	6,353	8,333	5.69
Rift Valley	942	2,855	904	16,517	21,218	14.49
Western	14	263	107	4,875	5,259	3.59
TOTAL	7,812	24,613	15,529	98,490	146,444	100

As to the following table, Production by province and sector, the most striking aspect of the figures is, of course, the tremendous dominance of Nairobi. Per capita incomes there are more than four times higher than in the next richest province, that is, the Coast province. The position of the Coast is to a very large extent dependent on the fact that Mombasa, the second most important city in Kenya, is located there. Per capita incomes in the poor North Eastern and Western provinces are less than 1/20 of what they are in Nairobi.

In agriculture, one would expect large differences in the structure of production among different areas due to the fact that the geographical conditions differ very much over space. The areas around the Arberdare Range and Mount Kenya contain some of the best land in Kenya with good volcanic soils and reliable rainfall. The second most important area is the Lake Region, which also has a high, reliable rainfall and good soils.

Much of the existing differences among areas in agricultural production are due to the cleavage between large and small farm areas. There has been little equalization between these two types of production since Independence. The large farms were mostly kept intact, except for the mixed farms which were subdivided into settlement schemes.

There are also large differences between small farmers in high-potential and other areas. Even between separate fertile areas differences have emerged e.g. between Nyanza and the Central province. Moreover, due to the shortage of land some people have been forced to move to the marginal areas, which hardly are suitable for crop production. In some areas, seven years out of ten are complete failures, and famine is becoming prevalent there.

Of course, the fertility of the land is only one factor determining productivity; the quality of the labour force, access to markets, de-

Table VII.2
Production by province and sector, 1971 (K£'000)

Sector	Nairobi	Central	Coast	Eastern	North Eastern	Nyanza	Rift Valley	Western	Total
Subsistence	-	25,488	4,571	22,671	1,347	34,211	22,091	13,170	123,549
Modern agricult.	823	20,734	4,971	7,723	1,978	7,006	31,541	2,715	77,491
Mining	533	4	725	82	-	443	1,142	1	2,930
Manufacturing	38,207	5,863	15,080	2,375	-	2,609	6,665	99	70,898
Construction	20,822	475	928	46	7	42	846	23	23,189
El & water	4,836	400	1,485	354	-	344	717	69	8,205
Commerce	43,437	4,842	12,783	2,576	31	3,239	6,503	1,346	74,757
Transport	20,328	639	16,337	1,035	73	1,337	3,205	186	43,140
Services	62,610	16,632	20,079	11,624	689	8,333	21,218	5,259	146,444
Total provincial production	191,596	75,077	76,959	48,486	4,125	57,564	93,928	22,868	570,603
Per capita income (K£)	338.4	41.8	75.9	24.1	16.4	24.9	40.4	15.9	48.7
Index	100	12.4	22.4	7.1	4.8	7.4	11.9	4.7	

Source: See table VII.1

velopment of infrastructure and supporting services also play a vital role. The latter are particularly important as determinants of the pace of development towards a commercial, i.e. monetized agriculture. Obviously, there has been, and still is, an overemphasis on the high potential areas, which has meant that already developed areas have been able to retain their position of advantage.

Thus, in terms of commercial agriculture, the Rift Valley and Central provinces are today the most developed ones; this is due to the fact that they still comprise many large commercial farms or plantations, good soils, and a developed infrastructure. In the Central province much of the commercial output originates from the small farmers. The process of commercialization which has been going on during the last decades is most advanced there.

Also subsistence production (that is, production which is own-consumed or sold on local markets) is developed in the Central province, but in this respect also Nyanza is well developed. Nyanza has, however, not been able to move very far towards increased commercialization of agriculture, which partly is due to the fact that the natural conditions there for production of the most important export crops, tea and coffee, are not very good. Nyanza is also lagging behind in the development of infrastructure, and relatively few government resources have been channeled to the area.

The development of mining, which at present is a very insignificant industry in Kenya, is mainly determined by the location of natural resources. At present, few deposits worth exploiting are known, but if, for example, the search for oil is successful, there may be drastic changes.

In terms of manufacturing, the dominance of Nairobi is overwhelming, but the size of the manufacturing sector in the Coast (of which ninety-eight per cent is to be found in Mombasa) is also considerable. In the more peripheral areas like the Nyanza, Western, North Eastern, and Eastern provinces there is very little manufacturing industry. A central location is of great importance to this industry, since it supplies and uses a large amount of intermediate goods. In 1971, the manufacturing sector delivered as much as seventy-six million pounds worth of intermediate inputs and received as much as seventy-three million pounds worth of inputs. This should be compared to the total domestic intermediate deliveries in Kenya, which, in 1971, were worth 279 million. The location of a firm may be assumed to be much affected by the location of receivers and sellers of inputs, and by locating in Nairobi it is thus possible for manufacturing firms to take advantage of agglomeration economies. Moreover, because of this sector's strong linkage effects on the growth of other sectors, a larger manufacturing sector also attracts other industries.

Very important for location decisions is also the fact that there is a very large service sector in Nairobi. Particularly business services etc. (see miscellaneous services in table VII.1) are concentrated there. Manufacturers frequently have to deal with public officials on matters such as exchange control, licences, tariff protection, tenders etc. and the government officials in charge of these matters are usually to be found in Nairobi (Wescott, 1977).

Industries locating in Nairobi are moverover close to high income earners, wholesale traders and government purchasing agents. Thus both final demand and input-output relationships and the concentration of the infrastructure tend to breed concentration.

According to these estimates, construction is more concentrated in Nairobi than any other industry. To some extent the concentration is exaggerated by the urban bias in the statistical coverage, but the high figures mostly reflect the very high growth rate of Nairobi both in terms of population and production. Just as for the utilities sector its size is to a large extent determined by the degree of urbanization in the various provinces.

That commercial and financial activities are more concentrated in the main economic centres than total production is not surprising. These sectors depend very much on the availability of a well developed infrastructure and are therefore concentrated to the urban areas. Moreover, commercial activities in the rural areas are not included in the production estimates. Their concentration is therefore exaggerated.

Transport shows a similar pattern, but here the location of Kenya's main harbour in Mombasa means that the Coast has a very large share of this sector's output. The advantageous position of the Coast in terms of communication has, however, not lead to so much industrial growth as one might have guessed. The share of the Coast in e.g. manufacturing has been approximately constant.

Finally, as far as the service sector is concerned it must be admitted that government services are more spread out that other non-agricultural activities and thus have a certain equalizing effect. Still, in terms of per capita expenditures, Nairobi is well ahead of everyone else (see Chapter XI).

Although the provinces are the basic units of analysis in this study, it should be pointed out that, in terms of economic structure, there are considerable differences between different parts of these basic units. The highest percentages of the labour force employed within the modern sector are found in Nairobi, Mombasa, Nakuru, Laikipia, Trans Nzoia, and Uasin Gishu. As expected, these districts consist of, or incorporate, important cities, that is, Nairobi, Mombasa, Nakuru, Nanyuki, Kitale, and Eldoret. The four last districts also have a sizeable large farm sector. The important cities Kisumu and Thika (forth and fifth in population) are found in the districts Kisumu and Kiambu, which also record fairly high percentages. In the agricultural districts Nyandarua, Kericho, and Nandi, there is also considerable employment in the modern sector. Thus, modern sector employment is obviously concentrated in urban areas, and areas with much employment in large scale farming.

It should here be noted that the railway has been of great importance to the location of industry and the growth of industrial towns. Of the thirteen leading industrial towns (which according to Ogendo, 1972, p.12, are Mombasa and Malindi in the Coast province, Athi River and Machakos in Eastern province, Thika and Nyeri in Central province, Kisimu in Nyanza, Eldoret, Kitale, Naivasha and Nanyuki in Rift Valley, and Nairobi) only Machakos and Malindi are located away from the railway. The importance of the communication system is obvious.

VII.2 THE PRODUCTION RELATIONS IN THE MODEL

In the previous chapter I described how the vector Z is obtained, that is final demand by region and sector. We now use the interregional input-output table constructed according to the procedure described in Chapter V, to calculate gross output by sector and region from final demand.

$$X = (1 - A)^{-1}Z \qquad \text{(VII.1)}$$

Gross output is here equal to the sum of domestic and imported intermediate inputs, consumption, investment, government consumption, and exports less competitive imports. This is transformed to value added with the help of value added coefficients $(VACO_i)$, estimated from the 1971 input-output table.

Assuming that the national value added coefficients are valid for all provinces, value added by sector and province then becomes

$$VA_i^r = VACO_i \cdot X_i^r \qquad \text{(VII.2)}$$

By using this formula for 1971 the matrix in table VII.2 is obtained. It is assumed that the coefficients are stable over time.

When X has been calculated, it is also possible to calculate non-competitive imports (MNC), which I for the sake of simplicity assume to be a constant fraction of sector gross outputs (calculated on the basis of the 1971 input-output table). Imported intermediate goods are thus treated as a shadow factor, which expands with output. Imported intermediate inputs are most important in manufacturing, where they constitute thirty per cent of gross output.

Non-competitive imports are then calculated by

$$MNC_i = MNCCO_i \cdot X_i \qquad \text{(VII.3)}$$

Now it is possible to calculate the resulting external balance. The balance on current account (TBAL) then becomes

$$TBAL = \sum_i E_i - \sum_i MC_i - \sum_i MNC_i + \sum_i (MDUTCO_i \cdot M_i) \qquad \text{(VII.4)}$$

The inclusion of the last term is due to the fact that import duties are included in both MC and MNC, and these, of course, do not constitute any burden on the external balance.

Because of the way in which the model is formulated, the current account balance has no effect on the further development of the economy. It is implicitly assumed that deficits on the current account balance are covered by capital inflows from abroad, and the foreign exchange reserves thus are kept constant. This assumption was realistic for Kenya at least until the mid-seventies, but the balance of payments constraint may come to play a more important role in the future. A great deficit may make the realisation of the production determined by the final demand impossible. Dwindling foreign reserves may e.g. force the government to sharpen the import restrictions and thus curtail some production plans.

VIII Employment

VIII.1 CHARACTERISTICS OF THE LABOUR MARKET IN KENYA

The labour market in Kenya is far from integrated. It is segmented into different parts by region, sector, and different types of production. The roots of the segmentation of the labour market in Kenya are to be found in the colonial period (Henley, 1973), when a systematic policy of discrimination was pursued and when the present disintegrated economic structure was created. This segementation has continued since Independence, although the lines of demarcation are to a lesser extent drawn according to race. In the following discussion four different categories of employment will be discussed: 1) Formal (modern), 2) informal, 3) wage employment on small farms and 4) subsistence or small farm self-employment.

The economically most favoured part of the labour market is the formal or modern labour market, that is, the employment in the modern or formal sector, which is protected through tariffs and other measures. In the surveys of the modern sector made by the Central Bureau of Statistics, data are collected from firms with a fixed location or postal address. To get an analytically more satisfying distinction, data should be collected according to some other criteria, but I have had to accept this definition, since these are the only data available at present. The jobs in this sector are thus in larger or established firms (often urban) and with the government. They usually yield better incomes than other types of employment, while they, at the same time, offer possibilities of promotion as well as better and more stable working conditions.

It has even been suggested (Mazumdar, 1975) that the defining characteristic of employment in the formal sector is that it is 'in some sense or senses protected so that the wage level and working conditions in the sector are not available, in general, to the job seekers in the market, unless they manage to cross the barrier of entry somehow'. This kind of 'protection may arise from the action of trade unions, of government, or of both acting together'. The protected character of these jobs together with the insecurity and low incomes in alternative employments explain why the rate of labour turnover within the sector is so low (Henley, 1973, p. 578). Incomes in the formal sector are generally high compared to incomes in the rest of the economy. Since there is a large surplus of labourers willing to work in the sector at the going wages, this wage rate cannot be considered to be a market clearing wage.

Given that the wage levels to a large extent are institutionally determined and that they are rigid (House, Rempel, 1975), there is thus little competition in the labour market. Instead there is job competition, that is, a large number of workers queue for the jobs generated by the modern sector. The establishments in the sector need not raise wages to attract more labour when they want to expand. They can recruit as many as they need at the going wage.

The supply side is thus not important for the determination of the employment level on this market. It is the demand side that determines the number of new jobs created, and thus how quickly modern employment may expand. The amount of labour needed is determined by the technological requirements of the firms and the demand for their output.

What determines the rate of growth of employment in this sector then is the rate at which the demand curve is shifted outwards and to some extent the wage level. There is probably some elasticity of demand for labour, so that demand would actually be somewhat lower, if wages were higher, but the elasticity is certainly low. Still, given that the wage level is more or less fixed, the employment level is determined by the above mentioned factors.

The need for labour is thus filled from the existing queue. The employer uses different sorts of screening devices to choose among the labourers willing to work, and, of course, he tries to choose those whom he believes to be most adaptable to the job. The fact that he chooses the more skilled rather than the less skilled to fill the vacancies does thus generally not mean that he has to pay a higher wage.

Of course, the majority of the labour force in Kenya still remains on the small farms, and far from all of those who leave them are absorbed by the modern sector. Many have to look for other sources of income. For those who fail to get a job in the modern sector, there is a possibility of making a living in the so-called informal sector. Jobs there are, in contrast to formal sector jobs, characterized by low wages and unstable working patterns. People in this sector are discriminated against and sometimes actively harassed. This sector receives protection from neither the government nor the unions; producers therefore have to accept the prices that result from the free play of market forces. On this submarket it would thus be more reasonable to assume that wages are determined by the interaction of supply and demand in the ordinary way. This also implies that the wages or incomes here usually are considerably lower than those in the formal sector. Still, they may often be higher than the alternative rural income.

For the purpose of this study I have to use the definition of the informal sector chosen by the Central Bureau of Statistics, since it is their data which will have to be used in the model. This means that in some cases firms with common characteristics may be classified as formal or informal, depending on the surveys by which they are covered - which as far as analysis is concerned is unfortunate. Nevertheless, there seems to be no realistic way out of this dilemma.

The narrow definition used by the CBS covers people working in working places, which are provisional or without postal address, that is, e.g. street vendors, hawkers, newspaper sellers and shoeshine boys. The CBS makes street counts of the people attached to clearly visible establishments of this nature.

The informal sector may be considered to stand in a dependency relation to the formal sector (see ILO, 1972, Singer, Jolly, 1973, Child, 1976, p. 52, World Bank, 1975, p. 19). It is the growth of the formal sector that generates the market for the informal sector as well as scrap that can be used as raw material, etc. The informal sector serves primarily the low income earners.

In the main, one should therefore regard the informal sector as complementary to the formal sector, even if there are cases of competition, like e.g. in furniture making. The growth of informal employment should, in some way, be related to either modern sector production or modern sector employment.

The majority of the population, however, still must seek its livelihood within small scale agriculture. Most of these work on the farm belonging to their family, but there is also a considerable number of labourers who are wage employed on the small farms. This is a consequence of the increasing monetization of the small farm sector in Kenya. This sector is in a transition period on the road to a commercial type of agriculture.

To sum up we can distinguish four types of employment

1) Formal
2) Informal
3) Wage employment on small farms
4) Subsistence or small farm self-employment

For formal sector employment, informal employment, and small farm wage employment there are some data. For the majority of the labour force which is self-employed on small family farms there is little data. To be able to get an estimate of the number of workers of this category one is forced to find some estimate of the labour force.

Of course, there is also a group which is part of the labour force, but without jobs, i.e. the unemployed. The question is whether one can say anything meaningful in quantitative terms about unemployment in Kenya. The problem of using the concept of unemployment in analyses of underdeveloped countries has long been recognized (Myrdal, 1968, Weeks, 1973, ILO, 1972). The concept has its roots in the capitalistic mode of production, where 'unemployed means to be denied individual access to the resources complementary to human labour which are necesrary to enable the gaining of a livelihood' (Weeks, 1973, p. 4).

In a traditional subsistence economy without private ownership of land unemployment is impossible, and even if the land is owned by families, as is the rule in the Kenyan small farm sector, no family member is denied the right to earn a living. It is therefore difficult to talk about unemployment among this category of people.

The development of a monetary economy and land adjudication has begun to change the situation, but most people still retain some ties to the land. Elkan (1976), for example, argues that a real proletariate which has severed its ties with the land has still not emerged in Nairobi. The large sums remitted to the rural areas from the city also indicate that there still is a close relation between townspeople and those remaining in the countryside (Johnson and Whitelaw, 1974). If someone fails to find a job in town the possibility of going back to the rural areas usually exists.

It is probably impossible to find many people, who are truly unemployed in the rural areas. In the urban areas, on the other hand, there obviously are people who are truly unemployed in the sense that they have no job, while they, at the same time, actively are seeking one. Still, many of those who fail to get a formal sector job manage to make a living by some type of informal activity, and these should not be considered unemployed.

It is not possible (at present, at least) to measure unemployment with any precision. It is difficult to make a clear distinction between employed and unemployed. Because of these problems, it is better to concentrate on analysing the structure of employment and the incomes that it generates.

VIII.2 THE STRUCTURE OF EMPLOYMENT

The distinction between different categories of employment identified here does unfortunately not exactly match the sectoral disaggregation above, because of the fact that the category of subsistence employed also produce some output for the market and that this output is registered as originating in modern agriculture. The monetary economy is therefore somewhat larger in terms of labour input than what the distribution of labour among categories leads us to believe.

To get some idea about the distribution of labour among different types of employment, it is necessary to estimate the size of the labour force, even if the estimate necessarily may be far from exact.

To date, no comprehensive labour force survey has been made in Kenya. (The first one will be finished in 1980.) The size of the labour force must therefore be estimated on the basis of the limited information available.

The labour force participation rates are calculated as follows. First, the participation rates for men 1970 estimated by the ILO are used. For rural women, participation rates based on the estimates made by Anker and Knowles (1978) are used. These estimates cover only married women between fifteen and forty-nine years of age, but this should not imply any serious bias, since almost all women in this age group are married. A sort of weighting procedure was used by Anker and Knowles to add categories which have replied that they have been working every year, almost every year, most years, etc. This factor (and the exclusion of unmarried women) could lead to a certain bias, but the figures match well with Tanzanian data (ILO, 1975, p. 14). They may therefore be assumed to be of the correct magnitude. Since Anker's and Knowles' figures cover only ages fifteen to forty-nine years, the Tanzanian figures are used for the remaining age groups. Finally, since the female participation rates are much lower in the urban areas, it is assumed that the female participation rate there is only one-third of what it is in the rural areas for the same groups.

In the model, however, population is not disaggregated by sex and age. Only the aggregate figure is given for each province and each year. An average labour force participation rate for each province must therefore be calculated and this is then assumed to remain constant throughout. The average labour force participation rate for Kenya is estimated at 44.19 per cent.

There are some differences between provinces in the labour force participation rates. The high figure for Nairobi (47.11 per cent) is caused by the high male/female ratio, which outweighs the negative impact of the low participation rates of women. The low figure for the Central province (42.02) is due to the heavy emigration of men, which has led to a low male/female ratio, etc. Of course, as the process of urbanization and migration goes on and the population, on the average, gets older, these figures will change, but it may be sufficient to assume that they are constant for the period considered.

Table VIII.1
Percentage of labour force in modern sector wage Employment by province

	1963	1964	1965	1966	1967	1968	1969
Nairobi	83.5	82.8	78.4	75.1	76.3	72.2	68.2
Central	13.2	14.2	14.6	15.2	13.3	13.2	13.3
Coast	19.4	21.0	20.1	19.6	19.1	19.5	19.3
Eastern	4.7	5.1	5.1	4.5	4.6	4.4	4.7
North Eastern	1.4	1.9	1.7	1.7	1.9	2.1	2.2
Nyanza	5.7	5.4	5.3	5.0	5.0	4.7	4.9
Rift Valley	19.1	19.6	19.0	18.1	17.8	17.7	17.8
Western	3.3	3.3	3.2	3.1	3.5	3.3	3.4

	1970	1971	1972	1973	1974	1975	1976
Nairobi	64.8	66.8	68.4	68.6	72.6	66.3	66.2
Central	13.5	15.0	14.9	15.1	15.9	14.3	14.9
Coast	19.1	19.2	18.5	17.8	19.3	18.8	18.9
Eastern	4.8	5.1	5.3	5.5	6.1	6.3	6.5
North Eastern	2.4	2.5	2.4	2.7	3.0	3.3	3.7
Nyanza	4.8	4.8	4.9	4.7	5.2	5.1	5.0
Rift Valley	17.9	18.1	18.1	19.3	18.2	17.9	18.0
Western	3.4	3.5	3.5	3.8	5.1	5.2	4.9

Sources

The data on modern sector employment come from the annual Employment and Earnings in the Modern Sector. The modern sector is defined as the entire urban sector (excluding what is covered by the informal sector survey), the entire public sector, large scale farms and other large scale enterprises such as sawmills and mines, located outside towns. The establishments covered are basically those with identifiable business premises. In the report of 1974 (p. ii) it is stated that some attempts have been made to include also informal sector activities within urban areas. The coverage is, however, far from complete and the main part of informal activities may be assumed to be covered by the informal sector survey. Over time the coverage may thus have changed somewhat.

As can be seen from table VIII.1 there have been no drastic changes in the degree to which the modern sector has been able to provide employment in most provinces. The most striking change, of course, is the decline of the percentage for Nairobi, which indicates that an increasing percentage of the population of Nairobi has had to find other means of support than earnings from the modern sector. The population of Nairobi is increasing at a rate which is much higher than the rate of job-creation within the modern sector, but due to the high incomes in Nairobi relative to the rest of the country and due to income opportunities outside the modern sector, there has been a high rate of migration into the capital.

Since only urban informal employment is considered and since the degree of urbanization is generally low, this sector plays a role mainly in the capital Nairobi (8.5 per cent of the labour force) and to some extent in the Coast with the big city Mombasa (two per cent).

Wage employment on small farms is of considerable importance to the traditional small farming areas of the Central, Eastern, Nyanza, and Western provinces. In these provinces this type of employment amounted to 8.9, 8.1, 10.3 and 29.9 per cent of the labour force in 1971. The figure for the Western province is very high for 1971, and a threefold increase in one year might indicate that there is some bias. Anyway, these figures indicate that for the Eastern, Nyanza and Western provinces this type of employment is more important in terms of number employed than modern sector employment.

To be able to say anything about employment for the remaining categories and years one has to introduce certain assumptions. This will be done in the model solution; the discussion of the total picture will therefore be left to the next section.

VIII.3 THE EMPLOYMENT RELATIONS OF THE MODEL

At this stage of the model analysis we have data on output by sector and region, and from this information the level of employment must be calculated. In Chapter III I gave the reasons for choosing to estimate employment by the relatively simple approach of labour productivity functions. The data base is too weak to allow reliable estimates of production functions.

As no explicit analysis by means of production functions is made, substitution cannot be dealt with separately. It is only possible to calculate the increase in labour productivity by sector. For limited time periods this may be sufficient. I assume that employment (EMP) can be estimated by the relation

$$EMP_{i,t} = e_{i,t} \cdot VA_{i,t} \qquad \text{(VIII.1)}$$

where $e_{i,t}$ is a sector employment/output or labour productivity ratio at time t and $VA_{i,t}$ is value added in sector i at time t. I assume that there is Harrod neutral labour augmenting technical progress (α_i) in all sectors, which implies that one worker in sector i now can do the work of $1 + \alpha_i$ workers in the previous period. It is assumed that the employment/output ratio decreases through time according to

$$e_{i,t} = e_{i,0} (1 + \alpha_i)^{-t} \quad \text{(VIII.2)}$$

The supply restrictions that may exist in the labour market are disregarded by the procedure used. For most categories of employees this is an acceptable simplification. As was argued in section VIII.1 there is a surplus of most labour categories at going wages.

As has been pointed out above, I distinguish between four types of employment, namely

1) Formal (modern) employment
2) Informal employment
3) Wage employment on small farms
4) Subsistence or small farm self-employment

For the first category the data availability is good. In the second category only urban informal employment is included, and similar activities going on in the rural areas thus have to be included in the fourth residual category, here called subsistence employment. The non-modern rural employment category which is considered separately is wage employment on small farms. This category includes regular as well as casual workers, and the degree of uncertainty in the estimates is large. The fourth category then is everything that is not included in the three first categories, i.e. primarily the people working on small scale farms owned by their own families but also a spectrum of non-agricultural rural activities that are not included in any of the surveys. Also those who are unemployed are included in this category.

The problem then is to determine how much employment the estimated production generates in the various categories. If we first disregard the residual category, which is called subsistence employment, employment in the remaining sectors may be divided into three categories, namely formal employment, informal employment, and wage employment on small farms. In sector 2, modern agriculture, there is modern employment and small farm wage employment; in sector 3 (mining), 5 (construction), and 6 (utilities) there is only modern employment, and in sector 4 (manufacturing), 7 (commerce), 8 (transport), and 9 (services) there is both modern and informal employment.

To establish a relation between formal production and formal employment along the lines indicated above, is no big problem, but to do the same for informal production is very problematic, since the national accounts disregard informal sector production. (This means that GDP is slightly underestimated.) It is therefore not possible to use functions relating employment to output for both formal and informal employment. Some simplified procedure must be followed.

First, the level of formal employment by sector and region is estimated, then informal and small farm wage employment; finally, these categories are deducted from the labour force estimate, which gives us a residual which I call subsistence employment (even if it also includes some people who produce non-subsistence goods, or are unemployed).

I assume that modern sector employment is a function of value added according to the formula

$$EMPM^r_{i,t} = EMPMCO^r_i \cdot VA^r_{i,t} \cdot (1 + \alpha_i)^{-t} \qquad \text{(VIII.3)}$$

that is modern sector employment in sector i and region r in year t ($EMPM^r_{i,t}$) is related to value added in the same regional sector ($VA^r_{i,t}$) through a modern employment coefficient that is differentiated by sector and region ($EMPMCO^r_i$) . It corresponds to $e_{i,0}$ in formula VIII.2. These coefficients are calculated from the data for the initial year 1971. Due to the growth in productivity the employment/output coefficient must be assumed to decrease through time, as was pointed out above. This correction is made by dividing the expression by $(1+\alpha_i)^t$, where α_i is the annual growth rate of labour productivity in sector i . Employment is thus growing at a rate slower than production, provided there is a positive development of productivity.

In the modern sector employed category I here include wage employed, self-employed and unpaid family workers. Even if the data for the two latter categories are very unreliable it is still desirable to include them. It gives a more accurate picture of how large a share of the labour force that is engaged in the modern sector. Moreover, the residual category (subsistence) would be larger, if they were excluded.

The estimates for the growth rate of labour productivity by sector used in the simulations are based on data from a very short period of time; they are therefore not so reliable as one would like them to be. The confidence level for some of the estimates is very low. The estimates are given in Chapter XI, where these estimates are compared to the realized values for the period 1971-6.

Modern employment by region and sector for the initial year 1971 is shown in table VIII.2.

As was pointed out in the previous section, the informal sector stands in some form of dependency relationship to the modern sector. It can thus be assumed that it is modern sector production which constitutes the basis for the growth of the informal sector. Of course, there are also other factors which, to some extent, are important, for example the development of the small farm sector. When income opportunities there deteriorate, an increasing number of people may be forced to look for jobs in the informal sector. The magnitude of this effect is, however, difficult to quantify. It is therefore accepted that it is a market constraint that determines the rate of growth of this type of production.

Table VIII.2
Modern employment by region and sector, 1971

	Nairobi	Central	Coast	Eastern	North Eastern	Nyanza	Rift Valley	Western	Total
Modern agriculture	5,178	56,728	11,302	14,887	-	9,782	134,579	4,056	236,512
Mining	886	83	456	133	-	725	819	3	3,105
Manufacturing	38,406	14,935	19,588	4,545	3	8,664	15,435	1,488	103,064
Construction	19,859	2,965	3,417	1,765	116	2,241	4,391	599	35,353
Utilities	2,384	447	1,434	68	-	237	470	117	5,157
Commerce	32,796	5,217	12,708	2,947	88	5,870	9,645	2,565	71,836
Transport	19,008	1,643	17,125	1,012	31	2,331	4,602	515	46,267
Services	72,491	41,456	31,228	25,605	2,741	25,383	44,461	14,510	257,875
TOTAL	191,008	123,474	97,258	50,962	2,979	55,233	214,402	23,853	759,169

Total in Kenya 759,169

Sources: In this table all those employed are included, thus wage employed, self-employed, and unpaid family workers. See tables 8-10 in Employment and Earnings, 1971.

The problem is then to calculate the coefficients relating informal urban employment to modern production. Since the degree of urbanization and other factors such as sectoral structure differ among provinces, it is reasonable to differentiate the coefficients by province. This implies that there are only five observations for each province (Surveys of the Informal Urban Sector, 1972-6), which, in turn, means that it does not make much sense to estimate any functions econometrically. There are large variations between the years. Instead, the average for the period 1972-6 of the ratio informal employment/modern production is calculated for each province. The sectoral distribution within each province of the aggregate for informal employees obtained in this way, is determined in the same manner from the average distribution over the period for which there are such data: 1974-6. The size of informal employment by region and sector is then determined according to the following formula

$$EMPIU_i^r = EMPIUCO^r \cdot EMPIUSCO_i^r \cdot \sum_{i=2}^{9} VA_i^r \qquad (VIII.4)$$

$EMPIU_i^r$ is urban informal employment by region and sector, $EMPIUCO^r$ is a coefficient determining how much informal employment within the region a certain level of modern sector production generates, and $EMPIUSCO_i^r$ is a coefficient determining how this informal employment within each region is distributed among different production sectors.

The figures estimated for small farm wage employment in the three surveys 1969-71/72 may be considerably biased (Statistical Abstract, 1974, pp. 280-2). It is therefore of interest to compare them to figures from the Integrated Rural Survey for 1974/75. Since the IRS is a much bigger survey, the data from it should be much more reliable than the data from the earlier employment survey. The differences may of course be due to changes over time, but to get a reasonable estimate of the regional distribution of small farm employment in 1971, which can be used in the model, only a weighted average of the four surveys is calculated. The weights are 1/6, 1/6, 1/6 and 1/2. The average number of employed in the three surveys is then distributed among the provinces according to the percentages obtained.

The development over time should then preferably be related to the state of small holder agriculture in some way, but there is not sufficient empirical evidence to specify any sophisticated employment function. The problem here is that the production of small farm agriculture for the market (outside local markets) is aggregated with the output from large farms in the model, and there is no statistical basis for separating this output into two categories. Still, if it is assumed that the shares of small and large scale agriculture in the output from modern agriculture remain the same, it may be acceptable to relate small farm employment to modern agricultural production. The coefficient must then, however, be different for different provinces, since the mix is different.

The small farm wage employment ($EMPSF_2^r$) is then determined with the help of the coefficient $EMPSFCO^r$ ($= EMPSF^r_{2,1971}/VA^r_{2,1971}$) according to the formula

$$EMPSF_2^r = EMPSFCO^r \cdot VA_2^r \qquad (VIII.5)$$

When we have come this far, we have estimates of all the three different types of wage employment considered in the model. Total wage employment by sector and region (that is, the part of it that is covered in the statistics) can then be calculated.

$$EMPW_i^r = EMPM_i^r + EMPIU_i^r + EMPSF_i^r \qquad (VIII.6)$$

As was explained above, all those who are in the labour force and who are not included in any of the three categories which here constitute wage employment are grouped together in one category called subsistence employment. Thus, in this category there are people working on small farms, some rural informal employment, some unemployed and those that may have escaped enumeration. The size of this category is determined residually on the basis of the labour force estimate presented above. The formula used is

$$EMPSUB^r = LFPR^r \cdot POP^r - EMPW^r \qquad (VIII.7)$$

That is, subsistence employment in a region is equal to the size of the labour force (labour force participation rate times population) less total wage employment in the region.

After this all of the labour force has been divided into the categories used in this analysis, and it is therefore possible to present the estimated total employment picture for 1971 by region and production sector (see table VIII.3).

Table VIII.3
Total employment by region and sector, 1971, ($EMPTOT_i^r$)

	Nairobi	Central	Coast	Eastern	North Eastern	Nyanza	Rift Valley	Western	Total
Subsistence	58,104	544,073	337,655	751,659	118,505	882,538	782,153	506,643	3981,329
Modern agriculture	5,172	138,693	37,326	98,810	-	79,442	186,600	72,452	618,496
Mining	863	83	443	130	-	704	795	6	3,023
Manufacturing	40,722	15,616	20,914	5,020	-	9,772	16,754	1,760	110,558
Construction	19,859	2,965	3,413	1,765	116	2,241	4,391	599	35,349
Utilities	2,386	453	1,433	70	-	238	469	117	5,165
Commerce	45,074	8,434	18,317	4,072	85	13,027	15,653	4,807	109,469
Transport	19,085	1,683	17,258	1,015	31	2,404	4,666	535	46,677
Services	75,474	42,257	32,075	26,081	2,729	26,332	45,547	14,794	265,298
TOTAL	266,738	754,257	468,834	888,622	121,466	1016,698	1057,028	601,713	5175,355

IX Population and migration

In this step of the model the size of the provincial populations are determined for each year of the analysis. There are two factors which together determine how fast the population within a province will grow, namely the intrinsic rate of population growth and migration.

IX.1 REGIONAL DISTRIBUTION OF POPULATION

There are considerable problems with demographic estimates in underdeveloped countries. Still, the censuses of 1962 and 1969 are not too bad. I am here interested in the spatial distribution of population, and I shall first present some data for the period 1962-9. Kenya's internal boundaries were radically redrawn in 1963, but a rough estimate of the population adjusted for 1963 provinces and districts is presented in the first report on the 1962 census. The figures should be interpreted with caution; it should also be noted that some minor adjustments of borders have been made after 1963. Furthermore, the 1969 figures relate to the de facto population of the whole country, while the 1962 census of a few districts was conducted on a de jure (usual abode) basis (Kenya Population Census, 1969, vol. 1).

Kenya has a very uneven distribution of population as can be seen from the density figures. There are three main clusters: 1) Around Lake Victoria extending north to the southern slopes of Mount Elgon, 2) around Mount Kenya and the Arberdare Range extending southwards to Nairobi and eastwards into the Machakos district, 3) around Mombasa at the coast. Northern Kenya, the Masai land in the south, and the coastal hinterland are very sparsely populated.

Table IX.1
Percentage of total population by province, 1962 and 1969, and population density, 1969 (persons per square kilometer)

	1962	1969	Density 1969
Nairobi	4.0	4.7	734
Central	15.3	15.3	127
Coast	8.6	8.6	11
Eastern	18.0	17.4	12
North Eastern	3.1	2.2	2
Nyanza	18.9	19.4	168
Rift Valley	20.3	20.2	12
Western	11.7	12.1	161
TOTAL			19

Sources: Kenya Population Census, 1962, Advance Report, vols I-II, p. 4, Kenya Population Census, 1969, vol. I, p. 1

The regional problems in Kenya also have an ethnic dimension. There are four main tribal groups in Kenya. The Kikuyu is the largest group (population in 1969: 2,201,632) followed by the Luo (1,521,595), the Luhya (1,453,802) and the Kamba (1,197,712). The Kikuyu and the Kamba are located in the centre of the country, while the Luo and the Luhya live in the west. These four tribes account for almost sixty per cent of the population, and thirty-seven small tribes make up the rest. The tribal homogeneity differs very much between provinces, while the districts usually are fairly homogeneous. The exception is Nairobi, which, because it is the capital, has a very heterogeneous population.

Differences in the development and opportunities between regions also mean differences between tribes, since the majority of their members live in one specific area. This problem cannot be neglected by any government aiming at national integration and stability. That tensions exist between different tribes in Kenya is obvious (Rotschild, 1969). Politically, it is one of the most burning issues.

It is no coincidence that the Kikuyu is the most dispersed of the major tribes (twenty-seven per cent outside Central province). It is of course partly a consequence of the development during the colonial period, when the Kikuyu together with the Luo were the tribes most involved in wage labour in white areas. The pressure on the land in the Central province has also forced many Kikuyus to look elsewhere for income opportunities. Lastly, the both economically and politically dominating role played by the Kikuyus since Independence has created particularly good opportunities for members of this tribe also outside the home province.

Also the Luo (thirteen per cent outside home province), the Luhya (twenty per cent) and the Kamba (thirteen per cent) have a considerable portion of their population outside the home province, and also here the main cause is the search for better income opportunities. Yet, today there are tribal barriers to movement, and most tribes have more than ninety per cent of their population in the home province, and as many as twenty-five tribes have more than ninety-five per cent.

IX.2 THE INTRINSIC RATE OF POPULATION GROWTH

It is, of course, evident that the rate of population growth is the outcome of processes and interactions within the socio-economic system, but it is beyond the scope of this analysis to go into this in any depth. It is simply assumed to be exogenously given. The problem is then reduced to finding reasonably reliable estimates of the intrinsic population growth rate by province.

The simplest way would be to assume that the intrinsic population growth rate, that is, the difference between fertility and mortality, is in all provinces equal to the national figure, and then to conclude that the recorded differences in population growth among provinces is due to migration. This is, however, not an acceptable simplification in Kenya. Already in Brass et al (1968, pp. 170-4) large inter-provincial differences in fertility and mortality are reported, and in the 1969 population census further evidence of this is given. Separate estimates of fertility and mortality and thus intrinsic population growth must therefore be made for each province. One simplifying assumption made here is that these rates do not change over time. I believe this to be an acceptable simplification for analysis over a limited time period in Kenya. The Kenyan population growth rate is now one of the highest in the world, and it seems unlikely that it will become much higher.

The estimates of provincial fertility and mortality rates made in this section are based on the figures reported in the 1969 Population Census (vol. 4), in which data are disaggregated by sex and age. No such disaggregation of population is made in my model; I have therefore had to calculate aggregate fertility and mortality rates by province. This, of course, implies that the effects of a changing composition of population cannot be taken into account, and as time goes by, the bias in the estimates will increase. For the time period considered in this context this simplified procedure may, however, be acceptable. The fertility and mortality measures calculated are the crude birth rate and the crude death rate, that is the number of births and deaths respectively per 1,000 total population.

First, the crude birth rates are calculated. They are obtained by multiplying the age-specific provincial fertility rates by the number of women in each age group, after which the total number of births is divided by the provincial populations.

The national crude birth rate according to these estimates is fifty per thousand. This is not an exact estimate. Different estimates are obtained if other demographic models are applied (1969 Population Census, vol. 4, p. 38), but they are all around fifty per thousand. The highest rates according to these estimates are to be found in the Western (57.6), Central (56.3), and Eastern (55.7) provinces, while the lowest are found in the North Eastern (37.5) and Coast (41.1) provinces.

On the basis of estimated age-specific provincial mortality rates (1969 Population Census, vol. 4, table 5.16) and information about provincial population by age and sex a crude death rate for each province is calculated. The national rate is found to be 16.4.

Mortality is found to be highest in Nyanza province (22.4) followed by Western (18.4) and Coast (18.0) provinces. In the study by Anker and Knowles (1977) it is shown that the regional differences in mortality are related to differences in disease prevalence. Particularly for areas where malaria is endemic, the survival rates are significantly lower (p. 26). They also find some evidence that a high socioeconomic status tends to increase the survival rates. There is not much information on this in the census, but it is at least pointed out (vol. 4, p. 45) that there is a consistent fall in infant mortality with the educational attainment of the mother. The high rates for the Nyanza, Western, and Coast provinces seem plausible, since these provinces are relatively poor (excluding Mombasa from the Coast) at the same time as they are situated in low, hot, and unhealthy areas. The low rate for North Eastern is surprising, but it may well be due to an underestimate as is hinted in the census.

With the crude birth and death rates given, it is possible to calculate the intrinsic population growth rate for each province. Since these rates give a national growth rate which is slightly below the most recent estimate, they are adjusted upwards (see table IX.2).

Table IX.2
Intrinsic population growth rate by province ($IPOPGR^r$)

	CBR-CDR	ADJUSTED
Nairobi	33.83	34.98
Central	42.74	43.89
Coast	23.10	24.25
Eastern	39.60	40.75
North Eastern	22.69	23.84
Nyanza	25.35	26.50
Rift Valley	31.50	32.65
Western	39.21	40.36
TOTAL	33.59	34.74

Sources: The unadjusted rates are simply the difference between the crude birth rate and the crude death rate. To get a national growth rate equal to the most recent estimate of the population growth rate since 1969 (Kenya Statistical Digest, Sep., 1976) each provincial growth rate is increased by 1.15.

From the table we see that it is the Central, Eastern, and Western provinces that have an intrinsic growth rate considerably above the national average, while the North Eastern, Coast, and Nyanza provinces end up in the bottom. The low rate of Nyanza is to a large extent due to the very high mortality rate there.

IX.3 MIGRATION

A comparison of the censuses from the 60's shows considerable differences in the rate of population growth in the various regions between 1962 and 1969. Six provinces had growth rates between 3.1 per cent and 3.9 per cent per year, while Nairobi's population grew by 5.6 per cent and North Eastern by only 1.6 per cent. The differences were partly due to differences in the intrinsic rates of population growth, but migration was also a vital determinant.

Interregional migration in Kenya has been analysed in a number of studies. See e.g. Wasow (1973), House and Rempel (1976b), Knowles and Anker (1975), Rempel (1974a), Migot-Adholla (1977) and Godfrey (1975). I tried the different explanatory variables suggested in a stepwise regression, with net migration into a district in relation to its population as the dependent variable (Bigsten, 1978). Some broad and very tentative conclusions were reached from this analysis. First, a large proportion of the population in wage employment attracts people to a region. It is in such regions that it may pay to go looking for income opportunities of various kinds. Secondly, a high educational level induces emigration. Thirdly, the availability of good agricultural land attracts migrants. These are thus the kind of variables which one would like to take into account when determining the provincial migration in the model analysis. The problems related to the specification of the function determining migration in the model will be discussed in the following section.

IX.4 DETERMINATION OF PROVINCIAL POPULATION IN THE MODEL

I shall now show how migration is determined in the model. As indicated above, the data available on migration in the population census are in many cases dubious. The changes in provincial populations that have occurred both between 1962 and 1969 (see the censuses) and during the period after 1969 (see Kenya Statistical Digest, Sep. 1976) are not consistent with the migration figures given in the 1969 census. (I.e. if the migration rates specified are applied, the provincial distribution of population would be much different from the estimate based directly on the censuses.)

Therefore, I assume that the population growth figures given in the censuses and in later estimates are more reliable, and from these estimates and my estimates of intrinsic population growth rates derive the net migration into all regions. For each province I thus start with the estimate of the annual change in provincial population. From this estimate I then deduct the change due to the intrinsic population growth as estimated in section IX.2. The residual then is the change in provincial population due to migration. If it is positive, there is net migration into the province; if it is negative, there is emigration.

In most cases the figures seem plausible, but the figure for Nyanza seems to be much too high (annual net immigration 39,000). It is a province with considerable scarcity of land and relatively slow economic development. Either the estimate of total change in provincial population or the estimate of the rate of intrinsic population growth are wrong, or there may be some to me unknown factor(s) which attract(s) people to the province. Still, I shall base my migration function on these figures since I believe that they for most provinces are at least better than any estimate based on the survey on 'place of birth' in the census.

There are very strong restrictions on the kind of function that may be used in this context. First, as I have just pointed out, the data restriction is severe. Since I have only been able to get estimates of the annual change in provincial populations due to migration, it is not possible to analyse how migrants move between the regions. Only a function indicating net gain or loss can be constructed. Secondly, when estimating such a function, there are further very strong restrictions. There are only eight observations, which makes the statistical basis very weak. To include more than one explanatory variable is practically impossible. Moreover, since the function is to be used in the model, the choice of independent variable is restricted to those that appear explicitly in the model.

Given that we accept that the factors indicated in the regression experiment mentioned above are the correct ones, the level of wage employment is the obvious choice. Neither land pressure nor education appear explicitly in the model. The following function was estimated.

$$\frac{MIG^r_t}{POP_{t-1}} = - 0.0051 + 0.0711 \frac{EMPM^r_{t-1}}{POP_{t-1}} \qquad R^2 = 0.33 \qquad (IX.2)$$

This function relates the change in population in year t relative to the population in year t-1 to the level of modern sector employment in the region in year t-1 . We see that the explanatory power of the relation is not so strong, which indicates that much of what is left out of this function is also important (e.g. land pressure and education). Therefore all other regional characteristics are assumed to be taken into account by a proxy-variable. To find the regional values for this variable I estimated migration 1971-2 with function IX.2 and compared the result with my previous estimate. I then calculated what the regional proxy-variables $MPROXY^r$ would have to be to make the net migration 1971-2 be what I previously had calculated it to be. Function IX.2 therefore finally becomes

$$\frac{MIG^r_t}{POP_{t-1}} = MIGCO^r = - 0.0051 + 0.0711 \frac{EMPM^r_{t-1}}{POP^r_{t-1}} + MPROXY^r \qquad (IX.3)$$

For Nairobi the function without the proxy explains migration very well, but in other cases there are considerable differences. Nyanza, of course, once again has a very high positive MPROXY (0.204), which it is difficult to explain. The other figures seem more plausible, for example the land pressure in Central province induces emigration (- 0.0087). Of course, the proxies may be seen as a measure of our ignorance of the determinants of interprovincial migration.

One final problem must be solved! By choosing this primitive way of estimating migration there is no guarantee that the sum of all in- and outmigration is equal to zero, which it must be in a closed system. Therefore, after the migration flows have been calculated for all regions I make the following adjustment. I first calculate

$$\sum_r MIGCO^r \cdot POP^r_{t-1} = A \qquad (IX.4)$$

and then take

$$\frac{A}{\sum_r POP^r_{t-1}} = B \qquad (IX.5)$$

and then finally adjust the migration coefficients to

$$MIGCO^r_{adjusted} = MIGCO^r - B \qquad (IX.6)$$

Thus, I first estimate $MIGCO^r$ according to formula IX.3, and then adjust this according to formula IX.6 to make the sums of immigration and emigration equal. When this final adjustment has been made, the provincial populations in year t are easily obtained according to the relation

$$POP_t^r = IPOPGR^r \cdot POP_{t-1}^r + MIGCO_{adjusted}^r \cdot POP_{t-1}^r \quad (IX.8)$$

The problem with this function, beside the various biases that exist, is that it is very inflexible. What is happening in the model affects the provincial populations only through its effect through modern employment on migration. Demographically, the model is thus fairly barren.

X Incomes

X.1 CHOICE OF INEQUALITY MEASURES

The choice of inequality measure has been extensively discussed in recent years. See e.g. Atkinson (1970),Sen (1973), Champernowne (1974), Pyatt (1976), Bhattacharya and Mahalanobis (1967), Theil (1967, 1972). This debate was reviewed in Bigsten (1978).

No measure has been found, which, in all respects, is preferable to the others. I therefore use three different indexes to measure inequaltiy among regions in per capita incomes, namely the coefficient of variation, the Gini-coefficient, and the Theil-index.

The two first ones are not disaggregated in any way. The Theil-index, however, can be disaggregated which is also done. If we start out by calculating the total inequality among all regional sectors, this can then be disaggregated into inequality due to differences among regional per capita incomes and differences due to differences among sectors within each region. The sum of these two types of inequality makes up total inequality as measured by the Theil-index.

The first two indexes measure inequality among regional per capita incomes. The Theil-index, however, measures inequality among incomes per employee. To be able to consider intersectoral, intraregional inequality as well it is necessary to relate income to employment when using this index.

I shall thus use these three different measures on inequality to check whether the choice of measure affects the results. The Theil-index will also be used for a partial investigation into intraregional inequality.

X.2 INCOME MEASURES USED IN THE MODEL

I this section I shall present the various income measures to be used in the study and also the distribution of income in terms of these in the initial year of 1971.

In the model, there is no distinction between labour and capital income. The interest is restricted to the question of how total income is divided among provinces (and in some instances among sectors). Of course, to some extent, this is due to the lack of information about the distribution of capital income, but it may also be argued that the question of factor income distribution is not primarily a regional problem. Still, if the information were available, it would have been included to give a more complete and accurate picture of the determinants of regional inquality.

As was mentioned in Chapter VI, there is some information about interregional remittances of income, but since it is uncertain and incomplete I have chosen not to try to make any calculation of regional disposable income here. I restrict the analysis to the question of where income is generated. Interregional differences in disposable income, is, of course, the income measure that gives the best indication of differences in standard of living, but on the other hand the measure used here is a better measure of the interprovincial differences in the level of economic activity. It is the latter differences which are focused upon in this study.

The output of the model is production by sector and region, and what is of interest here, is to relate this production to the number of employees and population. First, we can calculate average income (production) per employee for each regional sector $(AVRSINC_i^r)$ according to the formula

$$AVRSINC_i^r = VA_i^r/EMPW_i^r \qquad (X.1)$$

The results for the initial year 1971 are given in Table X.1. From this table we see that, for practically all sectors, the level of productivity is higher in Nairobi than anywhere else. This may, for example, be due to more capital per employee or other regional factors conducive to productivity, but the differences may also be due to differences in the mix of industries within the sectors used in the analysis, that is, firms from sub-sectors with high productivity may have chosen to locate in the developed areas.

A more aggregated measure, which is interesting to look at, is the average income (production) per wage employed for each region as a whole, that is without sectoral disaggregation. This is measured according to the formula

$$AVRINC^r = \sum_{i=2}^{9} VA_i^r / \sum_{i=2}^{9} EMPW_i^r \qquad (X.2)$$

The results for the initial year are given in Table X.2.

Table X.2
Regional income (production) per employee, 1971, (K£), $AVRINC^r$

Nairobi	918.0
Central	235.9
Coast	551.2
Eastern	188.6
North Eastern	(935.8)
Nyanza	173.9
Rift Valley	261.2
Western	102.2

The high figure for the North Eastern province is due to the fact that a considerable amount of total production there is registered as modern agricultural production, while at the same time no wage employment is registered in the same sector. This is a consequence of the statistical conventions in relation to small scale agriculture, which

Table X.1

Average income (value added) by region and sector, 1971 (K£), $AVRSINC_i^r$

	Nairobi	Central	Coast	Eastern	North Eastern	Nyanza	Rift Valley	Western
Modern agriculture	158.9	149.6	133.3	78.2	-	88.2	169.0	37.6
Mining	601.6	48.2	1589.8	616.5	-	611.0	1394.3	333.3
Manufacturing	938.4	375.4	720.9	473.3	-	266.9	397.8	56.3
Building	1048.4	160.2	271.6	26.1	60.3	18.7	192.7	38.4
El & Water	2028.4	894.9	1035.5	5205.6	-	1451.4	1525.6	589.7
Commerce	963.6	574.1	697.6	634.6	352.3	248.7	415.3	280.2
Transport	1062.5	376.1	943.9	1018.7	2354.6	554.9	684.8	347.4
Services	829.6	393.5	626.0	445.7	251.4	316.3	465.8	355.8

have been discussed earlier (see Chapter IV). If this sector is excluded, the figure is 209 K£ per employee, which makes more sense.

Nairobi is by far the region producing most per employee followed by the Coast province.

It may also be of some interest to see what the average production per employee is nationally. This is calculated according to formula

$$AVSINC_i = \sum_r VA_i^r / \sum_r EMPW_i^r \qquad (X.3)$$

The results for the initial year are given in table X.3.

Table X.3
Sectoral production per employee, 1971, (K£), $AVSINC_i$

Modern agriculture	125.3
Mining	942.0
Manufacturing	641.3
Building	655.9
El & water	1591.6
Commerce	682.9
Transport	921.7
Services	552.0

By calculating the ratio $AVRSINC_i^r / AVSINC_i$ we get a measure of the level of productivity in each regional sector in relation to the national average for that sector. If the ratio is above one, the productivity of the regional sector is above the national average and vice versa. See table X.4.

Of course, there are considerable biases in some of the figures in the table, but the general picture that the data gives should be correct. Nairobi has the greatest production per employee followed by the Coast province.

The last measure that is calculated is the regional per capita income, which is the measure one usually uses when discussing regional inequality. This is calculated according to formula

$$PCINC^r = \sum_i VA_i^r / POP^r \qquad (X.4)$$

The per capita income estimates for 1971 were given in table VII.3.

Table X.4

Productivity relative to the national average by regional sector, 1971 ($RELPR_i^r$)

	Nairobi	Central	Coast	Eastern	North Eastern	Nyanza	Rift Valley	Western
Subsistence	-	-	-	-	-	-	-	-
Modern agriculture	1.2683	1.1934	1.0636	0.6239	-	0.7037	1.3488	0.2998
Mining	0.6386	0.0512	1.6878	0.6545	-	0.6487	1.4802	0.3539
Manufacturing	1.4633	0.5855	1.1242	0.7380	-	0.4162	0.6202	0.0877
Construction	1.5984	0.2442	0.4140	0.0397	0.0920	0.0286	0.2937	0.0585
Utilities	1.2745	0.5622	0.6506	3.2708	-	0.9119	0.9585	0.3705
Commerce	1.4111	0.8407	1.0215	0.9293	0.5159	0.3642	0.6082	0.4104
Transport	1.1527	0.4081	1.0241	1.1053	2.5546	0.6020	0.7429	0.3769
Services	1.5029	0.7129	1.1340	0.8075	0.4554	0.5729	0.8439	0.6446

XI Basic model solution and actual development

In Chapters VI to X I described the main features of the model and the situation in terms of production and employment in the initial year 1971. In this chapter, the basic model solution for the period up to 1976 and the actual development for the period 1967-76 will be presented.

The realism of a model such as this can to some extent be checked by comparing its simulation results with the acutally observed values. This is what one might call an external validation. The internal validation should concern the plausibility of the specification, the quality of the data base, estimation techniques, and the degree of correspondence between the estimated structure and the theory. These latter aspects have already been dealt with in the previous chapters; I shall therefore confine the discussion which follows to the external validation.

Of course, it is a problem that in the real world there are cyclical fluctuations, external disturbances, and policy changes which are not considered in the model solution. The model merely generates the development pattern reflecting the assumptions of the model. Therefore one cannot reach conlusions about the usefulness of the model from a comparison with actual development alone.

We shall first look at the regional pattern of production growth generated by the model in the basic solution and compare this with the actually observed development pattern. The development of regional incomes and of the inequality measures used in the study will be presented and compared with the actual development. Then the regional employment levels generated by the model will be compared with the actual employment figures. Finally, some remarks on incomes and population as well as the feasibility of the solution will be given.

The simulation results and the results of the actual estimates are placed in different sections of this chapter. This is done in order to avoid confusing the two sets of estimates, and also because the actual estimates are of interest per se, not just as a norm of comparison. Very few estimates have been made of regional income levels and their development for underdeveloped countries.

XI.1 PRODUCTION IN THE BASIC MODEL SOLUTION

In the first table, I show production by sector and region, total regional production, regional per capita income, and an index indicating per capita income relative to that of Nairobi for the fifth and last year of the simulation. This can be compared with the initial situation given in table VII.2. We see that there are no drastic changes over the period in the relative position of the various provinces. Nairobi is way ahead of everybody else. The Coast province comes clo-

Table XI.1
Production (value added) by province and sector,
T=5, at 1971 year's prices (K£'000)

	Nairobi	Central	Coast	Eastern	North Eastern	Nyanza	Rift Valley	Western	Total sectoral prod.
Subsistence	-	28,140	5,047	25,030	1,487	37,771	24,389	14,541	136,404
Modern agriculture	1,094	28,301	6,831	10,650	2,754	9,638	43,534	3,730	106,531
Mining	788	6	1,040	121	-	644	1,662	2	4,264
Manufacturing	55,464	8,513	21,328	3,447	-	3,779	9,632	144	102,305
Building	34,073	766	1,485	79	12	68	1,347	39	37,870
El & water	6,999	586	2,184	518	-	530	1,085	109	12,011
Commerce	62,847	6,895	18,825	3,698	44	4,722	9,512	1,965	108,509
Transport	29,269	924	22,469	1,512	115	2,037	4,768	285	61,379
Services	91,319	24,762	29,600	17,343	1,039	12,260	31,269	7,832	215,424
Total provincial production	281,853	98,893	108,808	62,396	5,451	71,449	127,199	28,468	784,697
Per capita income (K£)	382.9	46.5	90.1	27.1	20.5	25.1	47.8	16.5	56.5
INDEX	100	12.14	23.53	7.09	5.35	6.54	12.49	4.30	
SRTHEIL	0.026	0.481	1.196	0.740	0.981	0.438	0.727	0.581	

sest with a per capita income about twenty-three per cent of Nairobi's, the Rift Valley and Central provinces between twelve and thirteen per cent, the Eastern and Nyanza provinces around seven, and the North Eastern and Western provinces end up at the bottom with a per capita income around five per cent of Nairobi's.

It should again be pointed out that the provinces, of course, are far from homogeneous. Particularly in the Coast province with the second city of the country, Mombasa, there are large differences. This can be seen from the measure of intraregional inequality (SRTHEIL) presented in the bottom row of each table. The Coast province has the highest degree of inequality according to this measure, which indicates that there are large differences among different economic sectors in the province. There are also considerable differences in the Eastern, North Eastern, and Rift Valley provinces according to this measure. Nairobi seems on the other hand to be a province with small intersectoral inequality. However, this measure is not really a measure of intraregional inequality, since it measures only inequality in average sector production among those that are employed. Since there is a large group of people in Nairobi, which must be considered unemployed, and there are intrasectoral differences, a more disaggregated inequality measure would show very much higher intraregional inequality in Nairobi. The measure should rather be regarded as a measure of intraregional economic integration among different economic sectors, and in this respect there are, of course, much larger differences in provinces containing both urban and rural areas and both subsistence and monetary production.

The provincial distribution of production during the five year period is shown in table XI.2. As can be seen, the shares of Nairobi and the Coast province are increasing, while the shares of all other regions are declining over the simulation period.

Table XI.2
The percentage distribution of GDP among provinces
in the basic model solution

	T=0	T=1	T=2	T=3	T=4	T=5
Nairobi	33.58	34.02	34.49	34.97	35.45	35.92
Central	13.16	13.05	12.93	12.82	12.71	12.60
Coast	13.48	13.62	13.72	13.80	13.84	13.87
Eastern	8.50	8.38	8.27	8.16	8.05	7.95
North Eastern	0.72	0.72	0.71	0.71	0.70	0.69
Nyanza	10.09	9.88	9.67	9.47	9.29	9.11
Rift Valley	16.46	16.41	16.35	16.29	16.25	16.21
Western	4.01	3.93	3.85	3.78	3.72	3.65

In terms of per capita incomes in the provinces relative to Nairobi, there are no drastic changes. The large migration into Nairobi means that Nairobi is not really improving its situation relative to the other regions in terms of per capita incomes, despite the fact that its share in national production is increasing. The Coast, North Eastern, and Rift Valley provinces have approached Nairobi, while the relative positions of the other provinces have deteriorated.

In table XI.3 we see that regional inequality is increasing slightly according to all three measures used. It is obviously immaterial which one of them is used. In the next section, where actual development of regional inequality is calculated, I have therefore calculated only one measure. I have followed tradition and chosen to use the regional coefficient of variation.

Table XI.3
Degree of regional inequality in the basic model solution

	RCOVAR	RGINI	RTHEIL
T = 0	1.379	0.439	0.534
T = 1	1.384	0.444	0.545
T = 2	1.391	0.450	0.557
T = 3	1.397	0.456	0.569
T = 4	1.404	0.461	0.580
T = 5	1.410	0.467	0.590

In table XI.4 the results of the calculations of the Theil-index are shown. TTHEIL is a measure of total inequality among regional sectors; it is equal to the sum of interregional inequality RTHEIL and intersectoral inequality STHEIL . The latter is the sum of intersectoral inequality in the respective regions, weighted by population.

Table XI.4
Decomposition of the Theil-index of inequality among regions and sectors

	RTHEIL +	STHEIL =	TTHEIL
T = 0	0.534	0.433	0.967
T = 1	0.545	0.443	0.988
T = 2	0.557	0.453	1.010
T = 3	0.569	0.462	1.030
T = 4	0.580	0.470	1.050
T = 5	0.590	0.479	1.069

We see that total inequality is increasing due to increases in both regional and sectoral inequality. If we compare tables XI.1 and VII.3 we find that it is increasing inequality within the less developed regions, in particular, which contributes to the increasing intersectoral inequality. When the modern sector starts to expand in these regions, it is, relative to the traditional sector, small but productive; inequality in these regions therefore increases with modernization.

The national growth rate is increasing slightly in the model solution. This is a consequence of the specification of the functions determining the growth of demand. The specification is made in such a way that the modern sector growth rate stays approximately constant. Since the traditional sector is assumed to grow at a rate of only two per cent per year, the fast growing modern sector gradually increases its share in output. This implies that the total growth rate approaches the growth rate of the modern sector. Since the same thing is happening in the provinces, the growth rates there are also increasing with one exception, namely the Coast province. There the growth rate has fallen between year 0 and year 5.

In table XI.5 the change in economic structure on the national level between years 0 and 5 is shown. The most drastic change is the declining share of subsistence production. Overall the share of agriculture declines from about thirty-five per cent to about thirty-one per cent. The share of services, a.o. public services, is increasing and so is the relative importance of manufacturing, building and commerce.

Table XI.5
Percentage distribution of production by sector in Kenya in the basic model solution

	T=0	T=5	Change
Subsistence	21.66	17.38	-4.28
Modern agriculture	13.59	13.58	-0.01
Mining	0.50	0.54	+0.04
Manufacturing	12.43	13.04	+0.61
Building	4.06	4.83	+0.77
El & water	1.44	1.53	+0.09
Commerce	13.10	13.83	+0.73
Transport	7.54	7.82	+0.28
Services	25.67	27.45	+1.78

The regional consequences of this process of structural change is illustrated in table XI.6.

On the regional level, the structural changes in Nairobi are the smallest, due to the fact that it has no subsistence sector. The most important change is the growth of the building industry, which, of course, is a reflection of the high growth rate in the city and the effect this has on building activity.

In the Central province, as in all provinces with both rural and urban areas, there is a drastic reduction of the relative importance of the subsistence sector in the regional product. The share of total agriculture is not decreasing as much since the share of modern agricultural production is increasing by about one per cent. This reflects the ongoing monetization of the agricultural sector. The importance of manufacturing in the Central province is also increasing a great deal, but the largest increase is in services. Mining and building grows, but their absolute size is very small.

Changes in the entire Coast province are of a less drastic nature, since it includes an important urban centre as well as rural areas. Here, the subsistence sector is also declining, while particularly the service sector is increasing in importance; that increase is, of course, due to the expansion of public services, but also tourism is of great importance. Commerce is of increasing importance here as in most provinces.

The subsistence sector in the Eastern province is very large in the initial year. Its relative share in output declines by almost seven per cent over the five year period, which means a far reaching change in the economic structure of the province. The declining share of this slow-growing sector explains the acceleration of the growth rate of the province. Part of the decline of subsistence production is

Table XI.6

Change in the percentage distribution of production by sector in the provinces in the basic model solution

	Nairobi	Central	Coast	Eastern	North Eastern	Nyanza	Rift Valley	Western
Subsistence	-	- 5.50	- 1.31	- 6.63	- 5.45	- 6.59	- 4.36	- 6.80
Modern agriculture	- 0.04	+ 0.99	- 0.19	+ 1.14	+ 2.56	+ 1.31	+ 0.63	+ 1.12
Mining	+ 0.01	-	+ 0.04	+ 0.03	-	+ 0.15	+ 0.13	-
Manufacturing	- 0.27	+ 0.80	- 0.01	+ 0.62	-	+ 0.76	+ 0.47	+ 0.07
Building	+ 1.22	+ 0.14	+ 0.16	+ 0.04	+ 0.04	+ 0.03	+ 0.16	+ 0.04
El & water	- 0.05	+ 0.05	+ 0.08	+ 0.08	-	+ 0.14	+ 0.09	+ 0.08
Commerce	- 0.38	+ 0.52	+ 0.68	+ 0.60	+ 0.09	+ 0.98	+ 0.55	+ 0.97
Transport	- 0.21	+ 0.09	- 0.54	+ 0.29	+ 0.33	+ 0.53	+ 0.35	+ 0.19
Services	- 0.29	+ 2.89	+ 1.08	+ 3.82	+ 2.41	+ 2.69	+ 1.98	+ 4.34

caused by the monetization of agriculture, which is reflected in the expansion of modern agriculture. The largest increase is in services, which mainly is due to the expansion of public services.

In the North Eastern province the relative importance of modern agriculture, that is sales of cattle, is increasing according to the model solution, while the importance of subsistence production, that is own-consumption and local sales of cattle, is decreasing. Also here services expand, while little else is happening. The model analysis is, however, hardly relevant for this province. The problems of the pastoralists need to be analysed by other methods.

The Nyanza and Western provinces have a similar pattern of structural change. In agriculture, the relative importance of modern agriculture is increasing, and the importance of subsistence production is decreasing. In total, however, the relative importance of agriculture in the regional product is decreasing. The growth occurs mainly in the tertiary sector, which in both provinces increases its share considerably. This is the typical pattern of growth in an area with little industrialization.

The pattern in the Rift Valley province is similar, but here there is also some growth of the secondary sector.

In the basic solution the regional growth rates are, to a large extent, determined by the relative sizes of fast and slow growing sectors in the regions. The interregional differences in sectoral growth rates are relatively small. In a region, where fast growing sectors dominate, such as Nairobi, the growth rate is bound to be high. Still, within the regions, there are considerable changes in the relative sizes of the sectors, due to the fact that they grow at varying rates as shown above. The growth rates of the regions thus change over time mainly due to changes in the sector composition of output.

In manufacturing, particularly Nairobi, and to some extent the Central province, are winning market shares at the expense of the Coast province. This is mainly due to the fact that the location of the Coast province is unfavourable in relation to the fast growing regions of the country. I have to admit that the specification of transport costs used in the analysis is crude; it does not take into account that Mombasa is the main export harbour of Kenya, and that it has good communication links with Nairobi; it is therefore probable that the disadvantage of locating in the Coast province is exaggerated in the model. There are, however, difficulties in finding a reasonable way of correcting the geographical distance, in order to get a good measure of social distance. The quality of the main roads in Kenya, with exception of the northern part of the country, are generally good; it is therefore difficult to differentiate by the quality of roads. One might, of course, try to get some measure of trip frequency, but also that is difficult. Moreover, the sizes of selling and buying sectors in the regions of origin and destination are taken into account, so, to some extent, this factor is already included in the functions determining the flows. This problem will therefore be left to the policy analysis.

There are relatively small changes in the regional distribution of manufacturing production. The same holds true for the other sectors. For the resource oriented sectors, agriculture and mining, the changes should be small, since the resources have a given location and are known.

The remaining sectors are in the model characterized as sectors which sell most of their output in the home region or in the surrounding regions. The output of these sectors is supposed to be sensitive to distance, that is, it is supposed to have a high distance elasticity. This means that it is the size and growth of local demand and demand in surrounding regions that determines the growth of these sectors. We have seen that the growth rates of the total modern sector do not differ very much among regions; the regional demands for the tertiary sector output should therefore also grow at similar rates in the basic solution.

The end result of these changes is that the Nairobi and Coast provinces are increasing their shares in total output, while the shares of the rest are decreasing. The growth rate of the Coast province is, however, decreasing over the period of analysis, mainly due to its peripheral location, while the growth rate of Nairobi is increasing. The growth rate of the remaining regions is increasing, mainly due to the decreasing relative importance of the slow growing subsistence sector.

XI.2 AN ESTIMATE OF THE ACTUAL DEVELOPMENT OF PROVINCIAL PRODUCTION BETWEEN 1967 AND 1976

As mentioned at the beginning of this chapter, it is of some interest to compare the development pattern generated by the model with the actual development (the estimates were first presented in Bigsten, 1977), but these estimates are also of interest in themselves since very few calculations of the development of regional inequality over time have been made for underdeveloped countries. The estimates made for the period 1967-76 are therefore presented here in full. The data base is too weak for estimates covering the period before 1967.

The basic procedure by which the estimates are made was presented in section VII.1. Further information is given in the notes to the following table.

The calculations presented in tables XI.7-9 are made in terms of current prices; thus, they reflect the distribution of purchasing power in the respective years. The development of a regional inequality measure is shown in table XI.10.

However, the development of regional production according to these estimates reflects both the influence of price changes and changes in actual production. It is of interest to single out the effects of these two influences. Moreover, the model used in the analysis is a constant price model; thus, it makes more sense to compare its results with the development at constant prices than with the development at current prices. Estimates at constant prices also make it possible to calculate regional growth rates. For these reasons, I have recalculated the figures in table XI.7 at constant 1971 prices (see table XI.11).

To be able to draw definite conclusions about the interregional differences in standard of living one should ideally adjust these estimates for interregional differences in the price level. For goods traded among regions, there should be a tendency towards price equalization, possibly with some differences due to transport costs. In a country like Kenya, however, there are market imperfections that may lead to considerable differences also for these goods. The differences in goods not traded, e.g. houses, are probably even more important since those markets really do not have to tend towards price equalization. The cost of accomodation in Nairobi is obviously considerably higher than what it is elsewhere, and it may safely be said that the cost of living, in general, is considerably higher in Nairobi than in most other areas.

This means that the superiority of Nairobi in terms of standard of living is exaggerated by the estimates shown here. Still, there is so little reliable information on the existing price differences that there is no basis for making a reasonable adjustment to the estimates. The reader will therefore have to be satisfied with this note of caution.

Table XI.7
Percentage distribution of production by province and sector at current prices, 1967-1976

Table XI.7.1
Subsistence production

Nairobi	-
Central	20.63
Coast	3.70
Eastern	18.35
North Eastern	1.09
Nyanza	27.69
Rift Valley	17.88
Western	10.66

Gross domestic product at factor cost (K£'000)

1967	106,970
1968	109.070
1969	114,740
1970	119,630
1971	125,950
1972	146,570
1973	156,480
1974	175,930
1975	232,560
1976	258,620

Sources: The percentage distribution of subsistence output has had to be assumed to be constant over the period, since there are no time series data available. See table VII.1 for calculation of the percentages.

Table XI.7.2
Modern agriculture, forestry, and fishing

	1967	1968	1969	1970	1971
Nairobi	0.80	0.88	0.88	0.95	1.06
Central	25.88	21.65	25.63	27.79	26.76
Coast	5.32	5.26	5.48	6.27	6.41
Eastern	10.31	10.80	10.56	10.87	9.97
North Eastern	2.50	2.08	2.24	2.45	2.55
Nyanza	9.12	9.37	8.23	8.49	9.04
Rift Valley	43.24	46.78	44.30	40.87	40.70
Western	2.83	3.18	2.68	2.31	3.50
GDP_f	59,990	64,910	68,650	77,270	78,500

	1972	1973	1974	1975	1976
Nairobi	0.72	0.84	0.76	0.75	0.54
Central	25.81	29.78	27.43	26.01	37.18
Coast	5.62	6.08	6.51	7.47	4.42
Eastern	12.82	10.22	10.08	10.29	12.89
North Eastern	2.04	0.83	0.25	0.07	0.06
Nyanza	8.74	8.95	11.17	9.69	7.87
Rift Valley	40.69	39.55	39.66	39.25	31.81
Western	3.56	3.76	4.14	6.46	5.23
GDP_f	99,170	113,040	129,950	142,970	232,230

Note: The estimates for the most important products of this sector are shown in the following tables (2.1-11). For the remaining products the following procedures were used:

Barley and other cereals: see table VII.1
Pineapples: see table VII.1
Cotton and other oil seeds: see table VII.1
Tobacco: 1967-9 - for all years in the proportions that existed in 1968 since there were no data avilable for 1967 and 1969
1970-6 - data from Economic Review of Agriculture
Pulses, potatoes, and other temporary crops: the proportions estimated for 1971 are used throughout
Coconuts: see table VII.1
Wattle: see table VII.1
Cashew nuts: see table VII.1
Fruits etc.: proportions estimated for 1971 are used throughout
Pigs: 1972-5 data from Economic Review of Agriculture. For 1967-71 the proportions of 1971 are used. For 1976 the figures for 1975 are used
Poultry: estimates for 1971 are used throughout
Wool: see table VII.1
Hides: see tableVII.1

Dairy: estimates for 1974-6 from Economic Review of Agriculture. The 1974 estimate is used for all previous years

Unrecorded marketed production: see table VII.1

Fishing: see table VII.1

Forestry: the estimate for 1971 is used throughout

The production of Nairobi is probably underestimated, since data from Employment and Earnings indicate that its share should be a few per cent. This may be due to the fact that the entire product value for each crop is distributed according to the actual place of production. This means that if e.g. head offices are located in Nairobi, incomes from these will be disregarded.

Development of gross marketed production of some agricultural products by province

2:1 Wheat	1967	1968	1969	1970	1971
Central	13.68	12.7	14.2	10.8	10.98
Eastern	4.48	7.1	7.1	8.8	10.74
Rift Valley	81.84	78.7	78.7	80.4	78.28

	1972	1973	1974	1975	1976
Central	6.6	6.4	6.5	6.5	6.5
Eastern	13.3	7.7	10.0	10.0	10.0
Rift Valley	80.1	85.9	83.5	83.5	83.5

Sources: Reports of the Wheat Board of Kenya, 1967/68-1973/74. Percentages for 1974-76 are guesses.

2:2 Maize	1967	1968	1969	1970	1971
Central	3.63	2.49	1.14	0.24	1.42
Coast	0.13	0.02	-	-	-
Eastern	1.97	4.24	6.16	2.48	2.05
Nyanza	4.25	5.96	8.66	6.41	3.12
Rift Valley	63.09	60.25	58.73	62.73	60.72
Western	26.93	27.04	25.31	28.14	32.69

	1972	1973	1974	1975	1976
Central	3.75	4.28	5.37	5.37	2.90
Coast	-	-	-	-	0.19
Eastern	5.66	4.85	1.46	1.38	1.11
Nyanza	5.67	6.17	4.14	5.39	11.50
Rift Valley	55.60	56.25	53.18	55.39	55.21
Western	29.32	28.45	35.85	32.47	29.09

Sources: Annual Reports of the Maize and Produce Board 1966/67-1976/77 plus some data from the files of the M & PB. The two crop years are weighted by the weights 7/12 and 5/12, which represent the number of crop months for each in the calendar year.

2:3 Rice	1967	1968	1969	1970	1971
Central	88.66	86.59	87.07	86.22	84.53
Coast	0.01	-	-	-	-
Eastern	0.30	0.23	0.35	-	-
Nyanza	6.37	10.20	11.94	6.72	7.77
Western	4.66	2.98	0.64	7.06	7.70
	1972	1973	1974	1975	1976
Central	82.68	85.60	88.52	86.10	83.05
Coast	-	-	-	0.05	0.13
Eastern	-	-	-	-	-
Nyanza	9.57	9.46	8.34	9.82	12.57
Western	7.75	4.94	3.14	4.03	4.25

Sources: Data from Annual Reports from the Maize and Produce Board 1966/67-1968/69, 1970/71-1975/76. Weighted averages as above (7/12, 5/12). Percentages for 1969 are from 68/69 crop year, 1970 from 70/71 crop year, and 1976 from 75/76 crop year.

2:4 Pyrethrum	1967	1968	1969	1970	1971
Central	39.94	37.50	35.00	29.18	24.97
Eastern	0.78	0.87	1.01	0.86	0.74
Nyanza	41.14	42.55	42.69	52.61	59.68
Rift Valley	18.14	19.08	21.30	17.35	14.61
Western	-	-	-	-	-
	1972	1973	1974	1975	1976
Central	26.57	23.76	11.41	16.20	14.78
Eastern	1.04	2.09	2.82	2.62	2.37
Nyanza	56.28	55.82	66.77	63.13	60.11
Rift Valley	16.07	18.22	18.85	17.91	22.60
Western	0.04	0.11	0.15	0.14	0.14

Source: See table VII.1

2:5 Sugar	1967	1968	1969	1970	1971
Coast	19.04	17.19	13.68	12.41	11.20
Nyanza	80.96	82.81	86.32	87.59	88.80
Western	-	-	-	-	-
	1972	1973	1974	1975	1976
Coast	11*	10*	9*	8*	7*
Nyanza	89*	82*	74*	66*	59*
Western	-	8*	17*	26*	34*

Source: See table VII.1. Estimates for 1972 and onwards are crude estimates based on scattered information in e.g. the Economic Survey.

2:6 Cotton	1967	1968	1969	1970	1971
Central	-	-	4.28	9.68	9.92
Coast	14.01	12.27	11.32	14.53	21.14
Eastern	17.03	30.13	33.89	17.93	3.80
Nyanza	32.86	22.61	15.75	19.58	20.87
Western	36.10	34.99	34.76	38.28	44.27
	1972	1973	1974	1975	1976
Central	11.70	17.49	18.33	9.05	4.14
Coast	26.68	24.00	19.81	20.35	21.74
Eastern	3.04	5.06	5.30	8.83	8.83
Nyanza	19.59	14.98	11.97	16.87	20.30
Western	38.99	38.47	44.59	44.90	44.99

Source: See table VII.1

2:7 Coffee	1967	1968	1969	1970	1971
Central	66.95	58.53	69.96	70.10	74.62
Coast	0.15	0.16	0.07	0.08	0.08
Eastern	20.58	25.61	18.12	18.67	15.38
Nyanza	5.36	9.45	5.51	3.90	4.07
Rift Valley	5.77	5.04	4.84	6.30	4.71
Western	1.19	1.21	1.50	0.95	1.13
	1972	1973	1974	1975	1976
Central	65.44	73.04	70.73	72.30	70.45
Coast	0.06	0.07	0.09	0.20	0.07
Eastern	23.85	18.49	20.38	18.83	17.65
Nyanza	4.83	3.15	4.25	4.76	3.69
Rift Valley	4.96	4.20	3.67	2.92	7.07
Western	0.86	1.05	0.88	1.09	1.07

Source: See table VII.1

2:8 Tea	1967	1968	1969	1970	1971
Central	1967-70: 15.01				15.46
Eastern	1967-70: 3.84				4.44
Nyanza	1967-70: 3.01				3.82
Rift Valley	1967-70: 78.14				76.28
Western	1967-70: -				-
	1972	1973	1974	1975	1976
Central	17.02	17.84	19.73	20.33	21.43
Eastern	4.69	4.97	5.90	6.02	6.88
Nyanza	4.50	4.76	5.93	6.42	6.53
Rift Valley	73.60	71.94	67.92	66.75	64.61
Western	0.19	0.49	0.52	0.48	0.55

Source: See table VII.1. No data were available for the period 1967-9; It is therefore assumed that the percentages of 1970 are valid also for these years.

2:9 Sisal	1967	1968	1969	1970	1971
Central	32.02	28.10	30.96	27.96	27.07
Coast	31.90	33.12	35.05	39.92	37.10
Eastern	3.68	5.17	5.89	7.06	6.76
Nyanza	0.90	0.05	-	-	-
Rift Valley	31.39	33.56	27.47	25.06	29.07
Western	0.11	-	0.63	-	-
	1972	1973	1974	1975	1976
Central	22.28	20.73	18.53	17.35	17.26
Coast	37.21	27.86	19.46	36.44	41.88
Eastern	10.43	9.70	10.88	4.95	5.97
Nyanza	0.49	14.20	22.39	5.08	2.53
Rift Valley	29.59	27.51	28.74	36.19	32.36
Western	-	-	-	-	-

Source: See table VII.1

2:10 Cattle	1967	1968	1969	1970	1971
Nairobi	0.18	0.29	0.31	0.51	0.39
Central	3.75	2.25	2.12	1.78	1.07
Coast	4.16	4.39	5.07	6.39	6.02
Eastern	17.18	13.90	13.58	14.32	17.06
North Eastern	14.49	12.31	13.62	15.93	16.39
Nyanza	9.10	4.94	0.36	2.27	0.30
Rift Valley	51.14	61.92	64.94	58.80	58.77
	1972	1973	1974	1975	1976
Nairobi	0.41	1.22	0.19	0.09	0.08
Central	2.82	2.54	1.93	1.41	1.63
Coast	8.40	9.39	8.78	20.18	17.86
Eastern	19.49	11.30	3.92	15.02	26.56
North Eastern	12.43	5.34	0.20	0.34	0.78
Nyanza	0.23	0.17	0.01	-	-
Rift Valley	56.22	70.04	84.97	62.96	53.09

Sources: 1971 - data from the Kenya Meat Commission, 1972-6 - data from the Economic Review of Agriculture vols 4-8. Estimates 1967-70 based on the distribution of deliveries to Athi River, Ngong, and Nakuru, and on the assumption that the percentage distribution of deliveries to the Mombasa plant for 1971 was valid also for 1967-70.

2:11 Sheep & goats	1967-72	1973	1974	1975	1976
Nairobi	0.50	0.08	0.09	-	0.24
Central	4.23	2.67	0.43	0.30	-
Coast	3.37	5.01	4.46	1.35	-
Eastern	14.03	10.87	9.19	14.21	35.67
North Eastern	6.76	10.60	22.34	3.16	-
Rift Valley	71.05	70.77	63.49	80.98	64.09
Nyanza	0.06	-	-	-	-

Sources: Data from the Economic Review of Agriculture, vols 5-8. No data were available for 1967-71, so the distribution of 1972 was assumed to be valid also for this period. In 1975 and 1976 large quantities were bought live weight; these were not distributed by district in the official statistics but I referred all of it to the Rift Valley province. This province's production probably is, therefore, somewhat overestimated for these years, while some other provinces' production consequently are underestimated.

Table XI.7.3
Mining

	1967	1968	1969	1970	1971
Nairobi	15.76	12.08	17.03	18.05	18.19
Central	0.33	2.60	1.59	2.41	0.13
Coast	25.38	25.41	22.13	26.89	24.74
Eastern	0.94	2.25	1.73	2.49	2.81
Nyanza	16.79	22.34	20.64	16.39	15.12
Rift Valley	40.80	35.32	36.88	33.69	38.96
Western	-	-	-	0.08	0.05
GDP_f	2,120	2,310	2,020	2,410	2,930
	1972	1973	1974	1975	1976
Nairobi	15.73	11.99	14.15	11.81	11.26
Central	0.24	0.02	0.07	0.02	0.38
Coast	24.69	25.55	31.78	30.52	30.72
Eastern	2.23	2.44	2.39	3.25	5.85
Nyanza	3.05	1.00	1.56	2.43	1.81
Rift Valley	53.85	58.87	49.91	51.88	49.95
Western	0.20	0.13	0.14	0.10	0.03
GDP_f	2,230	3,200	3,140	3,320	4,250

Sources: 1967-71 - Surveys of Industrial Production. Estimates for 1972-6 are based on the development of earnings. Nairobi's and the Coast's shares in earnings are adjusted according to the ratio (share in production/share in earning, 1971). For the remaining provinces the share in production is assumed to be the same as the share in earnings.

Table XI.7.4
Manufacturing

	1967	1968	1969	1970	1971
Nairobi	57.99	54.78	55.15	55.25	53.89
Central	6.45	8.91	8.73	8.31	8.27
Coast	20.53	20.72	21.35	20.11	21.27
Eastern	3.07	1.43	1.23	2.79	3.35
North Eastern	-	-	-	-	-
Nyanza	3.55	5.88	5.46	4.19	3.68
Rift Valley	8.13	8.06	7.74	8.45	9.40
Western	0.28	0.22	0.34	0.90	0.14
GDP_f	45,270	50,060	56,840	62,160	70,898

	1972	1973	1974	1975	1976
Nairobi	60.93	55.39	55.60	55.83	55.28
Central	5.81	7.54	8.11	8.18	9.32
Coast	17.15	20.61	20.45	18.86	18.77
Eastern	4.89	4.53	4.73	4.66	4.52
North Eastern	-	-	-	-	-
Nyanza	3.47	2.64	2.87	2.53	2.46
Rift Valley	7.38	8.18	6.93	7.93	7.35
Western	0.37	1.11	1.31	2.01	2.30
GDP_f	77,940	94,600	119,070	127,130	151,330

Sources: 1967-71 - Surveys of Industrial Production. Estimates for 1972-6 are based on the development of earnings. The earnings shares are adjusted according to the relation (share in production/share in earning 1967-71). For the Nairobi, Central, Coast, and Rift Valley provinces the average for the period is used, and for the Eastern, Nyanza, and Western provinces the averages for 1967 and 1971 are used.

Table XI.7.5
Construction

	1967	1968	1969	1970	1971
Nairobi	86.73	89.31	88,57	88.84	89,79
Central	1.86	0.72	0.75	0.51	2.05
Coast	5.88	5.63	6.47	5.88	4.00
Eastern	0.06	0.36	0.35	0.27	0.20
North Eastern	-	0.01	0.03	0.02	0.03
Nyanza	1.79	0.66	0.73	0.47	0.18
Rift Valley	3.68	3.15	2,88	3.85	3.65
Western	-	0.16	0.22	0.16	0.10
GDP_f	12,470	14,790	15,310	16,810	23,189
	1972	1973	1974	1975	1976
Nairobi	70.59	71.97	71.89	76.60	75.08
Central	2.92	3.74	3,58	4.01	3.71
Coast	6.57	7.74	9.24	6.31	5.69
Eastern	8.82	7.36	3.28	3.26	8.26
North Eastern	0.09	0.12	0.18	0.25	0.16
Nyanza	2.39	1.92	4.08	3.06	2.50
Rift Valley	7.45	5.29	5.46	5.69	4.04
Western	1.17	1.86	2.29	0.82	0.56
GDP_f	35,730	38,700	43,390	44,390	50,690

Sources: 1967-71 - Surveys of Industrial Production. Estimates for 1972-6 are based on the development of earnings. The shares obtained from earnings are adjusted for the Nairobi, Central, Coast, and Rift Valley provinces according to the relation (share in production/share in earnings, 1971).

Table XI.7.6
El & water

	1967	1968	1969	1970	1971
Nairobi	54.59	57.59	51.31	56.52	58.94
Central	5.37	5.64	6.51	5.85	4.88
Coast	21.53	17.32	18.10	14.85	18.10
Eastern	4.93	5.17	6.61	5.92	4.31
North Eastern	-	-	-	-	-
Nyanza	4.01	4.39	5.66	5.10	4.19
Rift Valley	8.58	9.49	11.21	10.78	8.74
Western	1.09	0.40	0.60	0.98	0.84
GDP_f	6,390	6,440	6,930	7,810	8,205

	1972	1973	1974	1975	1976
Nairobi	61.51	61.71	51.25	54.51	46.70
Central	2.42	4.33	7.03	5.65	5.18
Coast	18.66	15.14	21.40	13.77	18.39
Eastern	4.59	4.93	6.78	6.55	9.97
North Eastern	-	-	-	1.69	1.81
Nyanza	5.13	6.37	3.77	7.77	7.73
Rift Valley	7.27	6.79	9.13	8.61	8.62
Western	0.42	0.73	0.64	1.45	1.60
GDP_f	8,930	9,340	10,430	13,200	16,520

Sources: Estimates are based on earnings-figures. Adjustments have been made for the Nairobi, Coast, Eastern and Rift Valley provinces as discussed in table VII.1. For the Nairobi and Eastern provinces, however, this adjustment has gradually been reduced after 1971 to get less drastic changes in production shares than what would otherwise have been the case. It is assumed that earnings during the period give an increasingly better picture of the size of production. Still, this table may contain considerable biases.

Table XI.7.7
Commerce

	1967	1968	1969	1970	1971
Nairobi	57.57	58.84	57.74	54.75	58.10
Central	6.18	6.31	6.53	6.95	6.48
Coast	18.10	17.54	17.85	19.32	17.10
Eastern	3.40	3.87	3.91	4.17	3.45
North Eastern	0.05	0.05	0.05	0.06	0.04
Nyanza	4.39	4.30	4.45	4.78	4.33
Rift Valley	8.52	7.36	7.65	8.06	8.70
Western	1.79	1.73	1.82	1.91	1.80
GDP_f	53,260	59,350	62,300	69,740	74,757

	1972	1973	1974	1975	1976
Nairobi	59.51	59.71	58.90	58.91	58.69
Central	7.07	6.86	7.01	7.18	7.72
Coast	15.48	15.57	15.81	15.99	15.43
Eastern	3.47	3.60	3.62	3.70	3.85
North Eastern	0.04	0.03	0.03	0.03	0.03
Nyanza	4.29	4.19	4.29	4.24	4.31
Rift Valley	8.49	8.43	8.66	8.21	8.17
Western	1.65	1.61	1.68	1.74	1.80
GDP_f	97,680	115,020	162,670	176,530	207,080

Sources: 'Restaurants and hotels' and 'Business services' which up until 1972 belonged to sector nine now belong to sector seven; however, since only aggregated values are available for sector seven, it has not been possible to effect this transfer.

Four different income components were considered in the calculcation of total sectoral income. First, labour income was distributed among provinces as earnings. The share of labour in output was calculated on the basis of the 1971 estimates, one for the period 1967-71, another one for the period 1972-6 with its slightly altered sectoral composition. Capital income from distribution was for all years distributed in the same proportions as in 1971. Capital income from finance was distributed according to an estimate of the development of the provincial shares in bank deposits. Finally, for 1972-6 hotels and restaurants were included in this sector. The development of capital income from these activities was estimated on the basis of hotel bed occupancy statistics (Statistical Abstract, 1976).

Table XI.7.8
Transport

	1967	1968	1969	1970	1971
Nairobi	46.73	46.37	44.23	44.68	47.12
Central	1.94	1.99	1.53	2.09	1.48
Coast	33.85	35.30	37.10	35.56	37.87
Eastern	1.87	2.55	2.66	2.87	2.40
North Eastern	0.02	0.02	0.02	0.02	0.17
Nyanza	3.83	3.34	3.33	3.13	3.10
Rift Valley	10.82	9.63	10.19	10.64	7.43
Western	0.94	0.80	0.94	1.01	0.43
GDP_f	32,910	36,190	37,810	40,840	43,140
	1972	1973	1974	1975	1976
Nairobi	53.73	49.72	47.41	47.46	47.67
Central	1.25	1.35	2.37	1.51	1.52
Coast	35.58	39.05	36.53	40.81	41.01
Eastern	1.23	1.89	2.83	1.44	1.57
North Eastern	0.02	-	-	-	-
Nyanza	3.31	3.34	5.07	3.07	3.53
Rift Valley	4.59	4.39	5.71	5.38	4.31

	1972	1973	1974	1975	1976
Western	0.29	0.26	0.08	0.33	0.39
GDP_f	39,610	46,130	53,730	60,250	69,100

Sources: Production is assumed to be distributed as earnings.

Table IX.7.9
Services

	1967	1968	1969	1970	1971
Nairobi	46.80	45.86	45.86	45.95	42.75
Central	10.48	10.78	10.77	10.70	11.36
Coast	12.94	12.86	12.91	13.02	13.71
Eastern	7.23	7.45	7.40	7.30	7.94
North Eastern	0.43	0.45	0.44	0.44	0.47
Nyanza	5.09	5.26	5.34	5.42	5.69
Rift Valley	13.72	13.91	13.85	13.75	14.49
Western	3.31	3.43	3.43	3.41	3.59
GDP_f	86,430	99,780	111,730	122,270	146,444
	1972	1973	1974	1975	1976
Nairobi	43.02	43.45	43.06	42.83	42.75
Central	11.47	11.35	11.47	11.55	11.59
Coast	13.02	13.01	12.93	12.83	12.70
Eastern	7.94	7.77	7.82	7.83	7.81
North Eastern	0.49	0.48	0.48	0.48	0.48
Nyanza	5.94	6.09	6.32	6.56	6.80
Rift Valley	14.39	14.17	14.17	14.13	14.05
Western	3.74	3.70	3.75	3.79	3.82
GDP_f	154,210	167,250	197,990	229,220	263,540

Sources and assumptions

Restaurants and hotels: See tabel VII.1. This activity is only included in this sector between 1967-71. From 1972 and onwards it belongs to sector seven.

Dwellings: See table VII.1

Miscellaneous: It is assumed that the percentage distribution obtained in table VII.1 is valid for the entire period. Note also that individual household services are included here and distributed as micellaneous services.

Public services: Here I have been forced to assume that the percentage allocation among provinces is constant (see table VII.1). Data on employment and earnings give contradictory indications about the development before and after 1973/74. Still, there seems to be no reason to believe that there have been any drastic changes in the shares. One might guess that the largest change would have occurred between 1973 and 1974, when primary education was greatly expanded in the lagging regions. Data on earnings from services (dominated by public services) indicate a drop for the Nairobi and Central provinces and an increase of the shares of the Nyanza and Western provinces between those years. This seems fairly plausible, but that would then also indicate that the shares of the Nyanza and Western provinces would be still lower and the shares of the Nairobi and Central provinces higher in 1971 than is indicated by my estimates. However, if the distribution of the entire service sector based on my estimates for 1971 is compared with the earnings figures for 1971 the share of Central instead seems to be overestimated while the shares of the Nyanza and Western provinces seem to be underestimated. Nairobi seems, by this comparison to be correct. Thus, the evidence is contraditory, and no clear indication can be obtained without a very thorough investigation into the allocation of government expenditures. My assumption that the regional shares are approximately constant is at least not clearly disproved by the available data.

Table XI.8

Production by province and sector at current prices, 1967, 1974, and 1976 (K£'000)

Table XI.8.1

1967

	Nairobi	Central	Coast	Eastern	North Eastern	Nyanza	Rift Valley	Western	Total sectoral prod.
Subsistence	0	22,068	3,958	19,629	1,166	29,620	19,126	11,403	106,970
Modern agriculture	479	15,527	3,194	6,185	1,498	5,474	25,938	1,695	59,990
Mining	334	7	538	20	-	356	865	-	2,120
Manufacturing	26,252	2,920	9,294	1,390	-	1,607	3,680	127	45,270
Building	10,815	232	733	8	-	223	459	-	12,470
El & water	3,482	343	1,376	315	-	256	548	70	6,390
Commerce	30,662	3,291	9,640	1,811	27	2,338	4,538	953	53,260
Transport	15,379	639	11,140	615	7	1,260	3,561	309	32,910
Services	40,449	9,060	11,183	6,246	371	4,403	11,861	2,857	86,430
Total provincial production	127,852	54,087	51,056	36,219	3,069	45,537	70,576	17,414	405,810
Per capita income (K£)	280.9	34.4	57.9	20.2	12.9	23.1	34.0	14.2	39.7
INDEX	100	12.3	20.6	7.2	4.6	8.2	12.1	5.1	

Table XI.8.2
1974

	Nairobi	Central	Coast	Eastern	North Eastern	Nyanza	Rift Valley	Western	Total sectoral prod.
Subsistence	-	36,294	6,509	32,283	1,918	48,715	31,456	18,755	175,930
Modern agriculture	986	35,650	8,455	13,101	331	14,520	51,532	5,375	129,950
Mining	444	2	998	75	-	49	1,567	5	3,140
Manufacturing	66,206	9,658	24,348	5,629	-	3,423	8,248	1,558	119,070
Building	31,195	1,552	4,010	1,423	78	1,770	2,368	994	43,390
El & water	5,346	733	2,232	707	-	393	952	67	10,430
Commerce	95,813	11,403	25,718	5,889	49	6,978	14,087	2,733	162,670
Transport	25,473	1,273	19,628	1,521	-	2,724	3,068	43	53,730
Services	85,250	22,712	25,591	15,487	952	12,514	28,057	7,427	197,990
Total provincial production	310,713	119,277	117,489	76,115	3,328	91,086	141,335	36,957	896,300
Per capita income (K£)	468.1	59.9	104.2	34.8	12.8	34.7	56.2	22.9	69.1
INDEX	100	12.8	22.3	7.4	2.7	7.4	12.0	4.9	

Table XI.8.3
1976

	Nairobi	Central	Coast	Eastern	North Eastern	Nyanza	Rift Valley	Western	Total sectoral prod.
Subsistence	-	53,353	9,569	47,457	2,819	71,612	46,241	27,569	258,620
Modern agriculture	1,253	86,347	10,274	29,925	150	18,267	73,861	12,153	232,230
Mining	479	16	1,306	249	-	77	2,122	1	4,250
Manufacturing	83,655	14,104	28,404	6,840	-	3,723	11,123	3,481	151,330
Building	38,058	1,881	2,884	4,187	81	1,267	2,048	284	50,690
El & water	7,715	856	3,038	1,647	299	1,277	1,424	264	16,520
Commerce	121,536	15,987	31,952	7,973	62	8,925	16,918	3,727	207,080
Transport	32,940	1,050	28,339	1,085	-	2,439	2,978	269	69,100
Services	112,661	30,556	33,457	20,584	1,276	17,927	37,026	10,053	263,540
Total provincial production	398,297	204,150	149,223	119,947	6,487	125,514	193,741	57,801	1253,360
Per capita income (K£)	539.8	95.8	123.3	52.0	17.5	43.9	73.2	33.1	90.1
INDEX	100	17.7	22.8	9.6	3.2	8.1	13.6	6.1	

Table XI.9
The percentage distribution of GDP
at current prices among provinces, 1967-76

	1967	1968	1969	1970	1971
Nairobi	31.5	32.2	32.2	32.3	33.6
Central	13.3	12.8	13.3	13.0	13.2
Coast	12.6	12.8	13.1	13.2	13.5
Eastern	8.9	8.8	8.7	8.8	8.5
North Eastern	0.8	0.7	0.7	0.7	0.7
Nyanza	11.2	11.1	10.8	10.5	10.1
Rift Valley	17.4	17.5	17.1	16.8	16.5
Western	4.3	4.2	4.1	4.1	4.0

	1972	1973	1974	1975	1976
Nairobi	34.0	33.8	34.7	33.5	31.8
Central	13.1	13.8	13.3	13.4	16.3
Coast	11.8	12.8	13.1	12.7	11.9
Eastern	9.5	8.9	8.5	8.8	9.6
North Eastern	0.7	0.5	0.4	0.4	0.4
Nyanza	10.3	9.9	10.2	10.5	10.0
Rift Valley	16.5	16.2	15.8	15.9	15.5
Western	4.1	4.2	4.1	4.8	4.6

Source: Tables XI.7-8

Table XI.10
Degree of regional inequality 1967-76
when production is calculated at current prices
Population weighted coefficient of variation

	All provinces	All provinces excl. Nairobi
1967	1.345	0.416
1968	1.360	0.424
1969	1.344	0.447
1970	1.334	0.454
1971	1.379	0.476
1972	1.372	0.405
1973	1.355	0.456
1974	1.377	0.472
1975	1.306	0.434
1976	1.220	0.432

Source: Tables XI.7-8

If we look at the distribution of total production by province at current prices, we find that the share of Nairobi increased between 1967 and 1974 from 31.5 per cent to 34.7 per cent (see table XI.9). During the same period, the share of the Coast province increased by 0.5 per cent, while the share of the Central province was constant. The shares of all other provinces were decreasing, which means that their growth rates were below the national average.

During this time, however, there was migration, which means that these calculations do not reflect the development of per capita incomes in the provinces. They were shown in table VI.8. There is a considerable stability up to 1974, even if the drought affected the North Eastern province severely from 1973.

Regional inequality as measured by the coefficient of variation indicates that regional inequality increased between the period 1967-70 and 1971-4 (see table XI.10). In 1975 and 1976, however, regional inequality decreased considerably.

Since Nairobi weighs very heavily in the calculations, the same measure was also calculated for the provinces excluding Nairobi. As shown in the second column, this calculation gives the same result, namely that there is a tendency towards increasing inequality up to 1974 and then a decrease.

Up to 1974, migration was thus not large enough to offset the imbalances in the growth of production. Between 1974 and 1976, however, there was a considerable reduction in regional inequality. The inequality index was reduced by eleven per cent, and the share of Nairobi in total production was reduced by three per cent. To find out the degree to which these changes were due to price changes, we need to compare these figures with the production figures at constant prices (see table XI.11).

Table XI.11
The percentage distribution of GDP
at 1971 year's prices among provinces

	1967	1968	1969	1970	1971
Nairobi	33.08	33.13	32.56	32.46	33.58
Central	12.92	12.49	13.19	13.24	13.16
Coast	12.75	12.79	13.00	13.20	13.49
Eastern	8.78	8.68	8.59	8.72	8.50
North Eastern	0.78	0.72	0.72	0.77	0.72
Nyanza	10.79	10.81	10.58	10.41	10.09
Rift Valley	16.75	17.24	17.27	17.14	16.46
Western	4.16	4.15	4.09	4.08	4.01
	1972	1973	1974	1975	1976
Nairobi	34.03	34.07	33.80	33.98	34.15
Central	12.92	13.32	13.35	13.22	13.69
Coast	11.82	12.68	12.76	12.76	12.67
Eastern	9.46	8.74	8.64	8.76	9.19
North Eastern	0.67	0.48	0.41	0.40	0.40
Nyanza	10.19	9.86	10.25	10.09	9.77
Rift Valley	16.82	16.69	16.50	16.29	15.68
Western	4.10	4.16	4.30	4.51	4.46

Note: I have calculated the implicit GDP-deflators for all sectors. I have not disaggregated the sectors except agriculture, where different products have had a very different price history. The differences among products within other sectors have been less. Particularly the coffee or commodity boom in the mid-seventies affected the prices of agricultural output in different provinces differently.

The development of prices paid to producers have been used (data from Heyer et al., 1976, p. 254, and Economic Survey 1977, p. 84). There are price figures for wheat, maize, coffee, sisal, pyrethrum from 1972 and onwards. For the remaining products either the average of the whole sector has been used, or the average of the commodity group to which it belongs.

By applying the deflators calculated from these figures the figure for sector 2 in table XI.7 could be recalculated in terms of 1971 year's prices. The percentage regional distribution obtained from these (crude) calculations were then applied on the known aggregate figure for the entire sector to make the total correct.

Table XI.12
Degree of regional inequality 1967-76
when production is calculated at constant 1971 year's prices
Population weighted coefficient of variation

	All provinces	All provinces excl. Nairobi
1967	1.415	0.432
1968	1.405	0.437
1969	1.361	0.449
1970	1.342	0.456
1971	1.379	0.476
1972	1.373	0.407
1973	1.366	0.455
1974	1.339	0.452
1975	1.330	0.448
1976	1.322	0.447

We see that when we use constant prices the development pattern looks somewhat different. Instead of a weak tendency towards increasing regional inequality up to 1974, there is a weak tendency towards a reduction in inequality (at least if Nairobi is included). Since the estimate at current prices over the same period showed a tendency towards increasing inequality, we can conclude that the changes of relative prices tended to work against regional equalization up to 1974, after which the opposite happened due to the commodity boom.

Before 1971, the prices moved only slowly and there were no large intersectoral differences in the rate of price change. Between 1971 and 1974, prices in commerce, building, transport, and manufacturing increased most rapidly. These sectors are relatively more important in the most developed regions; changes in relative prices therefore tended to increase regional inequality. The domestic terms of trade thus moved in favour of the developed regions up to 1974. Between 1974 and

1976, however, the domestic terms of trade moved very much in favour of agriculture. This contributed strongly to the decrease in regional inequality at current prices, since agriculture is most important in regions other than Nairobi and the Coast province.

The coffee boom primarily benefited the Central and, to some extent, Eastern provinces. At current prices the share of the Central province in total production increased from thirteen to sixteen per cent and its share in marketed agricultural production increased from twenty-six to as much as thirty-seven per cent. Thus, the most developed agricultural area benefited the most. All provinces drew closer to Nairobi during this two year period due to higher prices of agricultural output and stagnation in urban production.

Both calculations show that Nairobi maintained its dominant position during the period, although it was slightly reduced during the two last years, due to the (temporary) increase in commodity prices. The main beneficiary of this was the Central province, but even before that it had managed to improve its relative position, e.g. in manufacturing. The Coast province, with the secondary centre of Mombasa, managed reasonably well, even if there was a slight deterioration in its relative position after 1971. The relative position of the Eastern province deteriorated slightly up until 1974, after which the coffee boom raised provincial incomes considerably. The North Eastern province was hit very hard by droughts from 1973 on, which almost wiped out the cattle sales which were flourishing before that time. The shares of both the Nyanza and Rift Valley provinces have decreased slowly throughout the period, but Rift Valley is still comparatively well off. It must be kept in mind that the Rift Valley province is far from homogeneous and that the inclusion of pastoral areas draws down the figures for the province. The Western province, finally, has improved its position in the last few years by increasing its share of both modern agricultural production and manufacturing. However, it is next to the North Eastern province, still the poorest province in Kenya.

The share of Nairobi did not decrease at all in 1975 and 1976 at constant prices. It was about half a per cent greater in 1976 than it was in 1971. The improvement of the Central province was reduced from about three per cent to about half a per cent. Thus, most of the improvement of the Central province between 1975 and 1976 was due to the coffee boom, i.e. a windfall gain. Also the deterioration of the Coast province was less at constant prices, although it was still almost one per cent betwen 1971 and 1976. For the North Eastern, Nyanza, Rift Valley, and Western provinces, the development was approximately the same at current and constant prices.

Under the conditions that existed before the oil crisis and the coffee boom there did seem to be a weak tendency towards regional equalization at constant prices. At current prices, on the other hand, there seemd to be a weak tendency towards increasing regional inequality. It is therefore difficult to categorically say anything about the development of regional inequality. Obviously, there were no great changes in the degree of regional inequality between 1967 and 1974.

The increases in commodity prices changed the picture temporarily, but as the prices of agricultural products fall to lower levels, the previous pattern of development may be expected to reoccur.

XI.3 A COMPARISON OF BASIC MODEL PRODUCTION AND ACTUAL PRODUCTION

The development of production in the basic model solution reflects the growth pattern that existed around 1971. At that time the growth rate was high and fairly stable. In reality, however, several external disturbances occurred which could not be predicted by the model: First, there was the drought in 1973-4, which affected agriculture in many parts of the country; then the 'oil crisis' and the accompanying world wide recession; finally, there was the commodity boom from 1975 on, during which particularly the coffee prices rose to unprecedented levels. All these events affected the development of the Kenyan economy to such an extent, that it is difficult to draw conclusions about the realism of the model by comparing its results with the actual development. It is, nevertheless, of interest to look at the differences between the basic model solution and the actual development and their causes.

At constant 1971 year's prices, agriculture has a larger share of GDP in 1976 than was predicted. This is mainly due to the slower than expected growth of the non-agricultural part of the modern sector. At current prices, however, the share of agriculture is much larger in 1976 than predicted due to the commodity boom.

Manufacturing is, at constant prices, slightly larger than expected, but at current prices its share is considerably less than expected.

The building industry has expanded much less than expected, which, of course, has to do with the recession.

Commerce has expanded much more rapidly than expected, while transport on the other hand, has expanded much slower than predicted. Also services have increased their share in GDP at a slower rate than expected (at constant prices).

Obviously, the pattern of structural change has differed considerably from what was predicted. The effects of the slowdown of growth have differed among regions according to the sectoral composition of the regional economies.

Looking at the distribution of GDP among provinces (tables XI.2, XI.9, XI.11) we see that the model predicts a large increase of the share of Nairobi. In reality, it increased in 1972 and 1973 at constant prices, after which it stagnated. The recession affected Nairobi severely. Manufacturing continued to expand relatively fast and increased its share in the regional product by more than two per cent; there was also some expansion of the commercial and service sectors. All other sectors, however, were stagnating. The construction sector produced less in 1976 than it did in 1972, while the model predicted that this sector would maintain the highest rate of growth. The reason was, of course, a slowdown in investment activity. Investment demand is always volatile and tends to decrease rapidly in the face of adverse business prospects. Thus, from 1973, Nairobi grew at about the same rate as the national economy.

The model predicts a slight decrease in the Central province's share of GDP. In actual fact, however, the share of the Central province increased by about one half of a per cent at constant prices. (At current prices it increased its share by three per cent due to large increases in the coffee prices.) The potential of this province thus seems to have been slightly underestimated in the model. It has done better than expected, particularly in manufacturing, building, commerce, and transport. The province has captured a larger share of the national market than was predicted in the model. This may, to some extent, be due to a misspecification of the market areas, but the relative attractiveness of the Central province may also have improved due to the rapid development of the infrastructure within this province. (See Chapter XII.)

The model predicts a slight increase in the share of the Coast province, but also that its growth rate will decrease. In reality, the share of this province decreased by as much as 0.8 per cent, which indicates that its relatively advantageous position has deteriorated more than the model predicts. Compared to the model prediction, it has lost market shares in agriculture and manufacturing as well as in commerce and services. The previously indicated fear that the locational advantage of Mombasa is underestimated in the model thus seems to be unwarranted. The Coast province is obviously not very attractive to investors. They prefer to locate closer to the rapidly developing central areas of the country.

The model predicts a decreasing share of GDP for the Eastern province, but instead there was an increase. Particularly the development of agriculture has been much better than predicted; it accounts for seventy per cent of the difference between predicted and actual output. Obviously, there have been changes on the supply side of the agricultural sector, which have not been taken into account by the model. But also manufacturing, building, utilities, and commerce have done better. This may well be due to secondary effects of the upswing in agriculture.

The case of the North Eastern province is simple. Since it was hit by the drought, the cattle sales have deteriorated catastrophically. In 1976, there were only five per cent of what they should have been according to the model prediction. Apart from this, the modern sector is dominated by the service sector, i.e. public services. There is still no manufacturing industry at all within the region.

For the Nyanza province, the model predicts a decreasing share in production; in actual fact it did decrease but less than predicted. The Nyanza province has been severely hit by the recession in modern agriculture, mining, and manufacturing; its share in output from these sectors decreased more than predicted. On the other hand, it has done better than predicted in the building, utilities, and services sectors, which has checked the decline. The region, nevertheless, seems to be an unattractive locational choice for industries selling on the national market. This may be due to the poorly developed infrastructure of the area and lack of agglomeration economies.

For the Rift Valley province the model predicts a decline in its share of GDP. In actual fact the decline was larger than predicted. The region has been loosing market shares in practically all lines of production over and above what was predicted by the model, i.e. agriculture, manufacturing, and tertiary activities. It may well be that the advantage of its location is exaggerated in the model. The low degree of concentration of production may be a drawback. It should be pointed out that large pastoral areas are included in the province and the pastoralists here have been hit just as hard as those in the North Eastern province. This explains the relatively poor development of the agricultural sector, and this also has repercussions on the important food industry in the area.

Finally, for the Western province, the model predicts stagnation, but this province has really managed to increase its share in GDP by about one half of a per cent. This positive development is primarily due to the unexpected growth of agriculture and manufacturing. Here, the active participation of the government in several ventures in the area, obviously, has had an effect. The growth of the sugar industry and also the Panafric Paper Mill in Webuye are examples of government supported initiatives which have meant much to the Western province. Regional policy may be said to have reversed a deteriorating trend in this province.

Of course, a model like the one used here produces a vast amount of figures which could be dwelled upon at length. However, I shall not prolong this discussion. From this and the two previous sections I believe the reader has got a reasonably good overall view of what the model predicts, what actually happened, and what the most interesting differences are in terms of regional production.

XI.4 A COMPARISON OF BASIC MODEL EMPLOYMENT AND ACTUAL EMPLOYMENT

As I have already pointed out, the development of employment is a reflection of the development of production. I shall therefore not dwell too long on the factors, which have already been discussed in section XI.1-3, but concentrate on other aspects.

As we remember from above, the actual national rate of growth was considerably below what was predicted, due to a number of outside shocks. This of course, implies that the predictions for employment growth are off the target.

First we look at the aggregate employment figures and see that modern employment, including self employment and unpaid family workers are predicted to increase up to 14.9 per cent of the labour force in 1976. For this year we only have the actual figure for modern wage employment, but if a reasonable estimate is made of the number of self employed and unpaid family workers, we find that employment has increased by more than what was predicted. And this in spite of the fact that production growth was less than predicted. This must imply that some factors have not developed as specified in the model (to the extent that the increase is not simply due to improved statistical coverage of the labour market). The improved statistical coverage may well explain a considerable part of the underprediction of informal sector employment. It has increased by almost 20,000 people more than predicted, which is equivalent ot 0.25 per cent more of the labour force than predicted.

There are no data available on small farm wage employment which can be used to check the estimated 1976 figure; of course, the same goes for the residual category called subsistence employment.

The fact that employment has grown more than one might expect, given the growth of production, implies that the growth of production per employee or labour productivity has increased at a slower rate than predicted. To verify this, we can investigate how labour productivity has developed in the modern sector. The sectoral estimates of the growth of labour productivity used in the model are based on data on production and modern wage employment for the period 1967-72. Similar estimates can be made from data for the period 1972-6, which then can be compared with the predicted figures. It must, however, be kept in mind that the new estimates concern the sectors according to the new classification.

Table XI.13
Actual growth of labour productivity
by sector between 1972 and 1976 (α_i)

	Actual	(R^2)	Prediction used in the model	World bank prediction
Modern agriculture	3.08	(0.61)	3.40	3.5
Mining	1.66	(0.03)	0.60	3.5
Manufacturing	2.34	(0.90)	1.53	4.5
Building	-7.79	(0.86)	4.21	6.0
El & water	-5.01	(0.05)	1.06	3.5
Commerce	-3.94	(0.70)	8.01	3.5
Transport	0.66	(0.05)	9.18	3.5
Services	-2.02	(0.81)	3.43	3.5

Sources: The actual estimates are made from data in Statistical Abstract, 1972, p. 42, Employment and Earnings, 1972-6. The World bank estimates are made by the mission to Kenya (World bank, 1975, p. 147).

Estimates made from only five observations are, of course, not very reliable. The estimated figures should only be regarded as indications of magnitudes. There have been considerable fluctuations from year to year.

The tentative conclusion that can be reached from this table is that the estimated growth rates of labour productivity for agriculture, mining, and manufacturing were reasonably close to the actual figures, while the estimates for all other sectors were much too high. For building, electricity and water, commerce, and services labour productivity actually fell.

To some extent, the poor development of prroductivity could, of course, be due to an overestimation of the level of productivity in the beginning of the period, due to a possible underestimation of the number of employees at this time. Still, this is probably not a very important factor for the employment category considered here. Instead, one might assume that the recession and other disturbances have hit many firms unexpectedly and left them with too much labour in relation to their output, i.e. with considerable excess capacity.

To sum up what has happened in the various regions one might say that in spite of the fact that production has expanded at a slower rate than predicted, total employment has expanded at about the rate expected. This means that there has been considerable divergences from the employment/production relationships assumed in the model. For example, in manufacturing employment has grown slower than the growth of production would have warranted, given the predicted level of productivity. Production per employee within this sector has thus expanded at a faster rate than expected. The opposite may be said about the tertiary sector. Here employment has expanded considerably in spite of the slow-down of production growth. This implies that the growth of production per employee has been considerably below the prediction. What has happened during this period is thus that production has grown at a slower rate, while productivity at the same time has deteriorated in many sectors; employment has therefore expanded at about the same rate as before.

To make an overall assessment of the success of the model in predicting employment levels is rather difficult, given the unstable conditions that have existed during the period. It is my belief that the approach has considerable potential. The greatest difficulty is to make reasonable predictions about the growth rate of labour productivity.

Another aspect which deserves further discussion is the model's complete reliance upon the demand side of the labour market. I believe that the arguments which I have advanced in Chapter VIII are sound, but it might be a good idea to, in the future, introduce at least some flexibility. Some sectors or categories of employment seem to expand more rapidly in the face of increasing supply pressure. I am here particularly thinking about the informal and the modern tertiary sectors, which seem to have absorbed an increasing number of people, as the pressure in the labour market increased.

XI.5 INCOMES AND POPULATION

The development of per capita incomes in the model was presented in section XI.1. Here we shall look at incomes per employee, i.e. production divided by the number of wage employed. This is not something that is wholly unproblematic, since the production and employment surveys do not always match. One obvious problem is that of modern agriculture, where a considerable amount of marketed output from small holder agriculture is included as well. The small holders are, however, not included in the employment estimate for the sector, although the wage employed on small farms are included. The productivity in the sector may be overestimated, and this bias may differ considerably among regions. A few other estimates are obviously dubious. Some tentative conclusions may nevertheless be reached.

There are only small differences among regions in the growth rates of income per employee of single sectors. This is, however, a consequence of the crude specification of the employment function and is thus not of any analytical interest. Since there are considerable differences among regions in economic structure the development of production per employee differs. Nairobi seems to have the best composition in this respect, since it had the highest percentage change in average income between T=0 and T=5 . The Eastern, Nyanza, and Western provinces had the slowest growth in average incomes.

A tentative calculation of the actual figures for 1976 at 1971 year's prices is shown in table XI.14. It should, however, be noted that the employment figures used for modern employment include only wage employment and not self-employed or unpaid family workers. The figures are therefore not directly comparable to those for 1971 in table X.1. For agriculture no figures are given at all since we have no estimate of actual small farm wage employment.

The estimates of productivity relative to the national average can, to some extent, be compared to the predicted figures, although the bias due to the exclusion of self employed and unpaid family workers may vary among regions. There are two regions which allover have a higher productivity relative to the average than predicted, namely the Central and Western provinces (except in services). I have already pointed out that these regions have increased production more than predicted, and this may thus be due to their improved productivity. Nairobi, on the other hand, has a position relative to the national average which is less advantageous than predicted. This is also in accordance with the fact that the city has grown less rapidly than predicted. The situation in the other provinces is less clear.

There are differences in productivity among regions, but the differences among sectors within regions are also very large. What is measured here is simply production per employee without any adjustment for differences in e.g. capital intensity. The figures nevertheless give an indication of the large productivity differences among sectors. The typical low productivity sector is agriculture, while productivity is high in e.g. utilities and other urban oriented sectors. I shall not go into this matter here, but simply point out that when one talks about regional inequality one must always keep in mind that there are considerable differences among sectors within regions. When old and new techniques exist at the same time, there may be large differences even in the aggregated sectors used in the analysis.

XI.6 SOME REMARKS ON FOREIGN TRADE IN THE BASIC MODEL SOLUTION

There is one aspect of the model which is not at all developed, and that is the foreign trade part. There is no adjustment mechanism specified. It is simply assumed that the deficits will somehow be covered. The problem is aggravated by the fact that the model is initiated in 1971, which was a year with an unusually large deficit.

The lack of foreign trade analysis is obviously a drawback, but I felt that this problem was not so vital to the main problem of regional inequality. Moreover, Kenya has actually been able to live with large

Table XI.14

Actual average income by region and sector at 1971 year's prices, 1976

	Nairobi	Central	Coast	Eastern	North Eastern	Nyanza	Rift Valley	Western	National Average
Mining	441.8	400.0	1,293.4	734.1	-	513.7	1,590.6	250.0	1,073.0
Manufacturing	1,086.1	495.0	934.5	1,009.3	-	322.1	403.1	521.6	802.7
Building	722.4	328.1	465.3	640.2	723.1	454.6	320.2	353.3	623.9
El & water	1,908.1	1,369.2	1,445.1	1,076.2	1,583.9	970.1	1,709.3	1,188.6	1,521.0
Commerce	944.0	613.0	735.7	671.9	647.1	289.5	469.3	255.8	710.0
Transport	987.8	417.6	782.0	511.3	-	548.6	493.5	511.8	810.8
Services	980.9	479.2	644.8	389.4	214.7	351.2	457.3	275.1	575.6

Sources: Table XI.11, Employment and Earnings, 1976, Informal Sector Survey, 1976

Table XI.15

Actual relative productivity by region and sector, 1976

	Nairobi	Central	Coast	Eastern	North Eastern	Nyanza	Rift Valley	Western
Mining	0.4117	0.3728	1.2054	0.6842	-	0.4788	1.4824	0.2330
Manufacturing	1.3531	0.6167	1.1642	1.2574	-	0.4013	0.5022	0.6498
Building	1.1579	0.5259	0.7458	1.0261	1.1590	0.7286	0.5132	0.5663
El & water	1.2545	0.9002	0.9501	0.7076	1.0414	0.6378	1.1238	0.7815
Commerce	1.3296	0.8634	1.0362	0.9463	0.9114	0.4077	0.6610	0.3603
Transport	1.2183	0.5150	0.9645	0.6306	-	0.6766	0.6087	0.6312
Services	1.7041	0.8325	1.1202	0.6765	0.3730	0.6101	0.7945	0.4779

Source: Table XI.14

current account deficits. From table XI.16 we see that, at current prices, there are considerable deficits up to 1976, when the coffee boom reversed the situation. Still, the large deficit in 1974 was due to the oil crisis, and under normal circumstances the actual deficits would have been less than the model prediction. I shall therefore not maintain that the model is well specified in this respect, but merely argue that, for my purpose, it is acceptable to abstain from penetrating into this problem as well.

Table XI.16
Balance on current account in the basic model solution and actual balance (K£ million)

	Model	Constant prices	Current prices
T = 0	-41.7	-41.7	-41.7
T = 1	-48.5	-16.1	-16.1
T = 2	-55.9	+24.4	-11.2
T = 3	-64.1	-15.6	-76.6
T = 4	-73.2	+20.5	-39.4
T = 5	-83.2	+28.2	+ 6.2

Source: Statistical Abstract, 1977, p.40

XI.7 CONCLUDING REMARKS

The basic solution growth pattern implies that production becomes increasingly concentrated to Nairobi and the Coast province, and that regional inequality increases. It should be noted that the growth rate of Nairobi is increasing while the growth rate of the Coast province is decreasing. Thus, the relative advantage of locating in Nairobi compared to locating in Mombasa is increasing according to the model. The peripheral location of Mombasa in relation to the fast growing central parts of the country seems to be a drawback. The growth rate of the remaining regions are all increasing, mainly due to the gradual decrease of the relative importance of the slow growing subsistence sector. There is thus a tendency towards convergence in the regional growth rates. If migration from poor to rich regions is sufficiently large there will eventually be convergence also in per capita incomes. The large migration into Nairobi certainly helps to reduce regional inequality in terms of per capita incomes, but at the same time the population shares of the Nyanza and Western provinces are increasing. This works in the opposite direction.

In the model, the regional growth rates are largely determined by the sectoral composition of regional output. There are no large differences between regions in the growth rate of single sectors during the period considered here; the empirical production estimates also indicate that there are no drastic changes in the regional distribution of the production of single sectors. Sectors which nationally are growing fast thus are dominating in the fast growing regions.

The actual development for the period 1967-76 has been estimated both at current and constant prices. At current prices, which gives the best indication of the distribution of purchasing power each year, there was a weak tendency towards increasing inequality up until 1975. During the two following years there was a drastic reduction in regional inequality. Thus, as long as 'normal' conditions prevailed, regional inequality did at least not decrease. The reduction in regional inequality in 1975-6 was due to the recession, which reduced growth in the urban oriented sectors, and the commodity boom, which increased incomes in the rural areas. The Central province, for example, increased its share of GDP at current prices by three per cent between 1975 and 1976.

At constant prices, on the other hand, there was a tendency towards a reduction in regional inequality. This means that prices must have moved in favour of sectors concentrated in the more developed areas. Incidentally, this is the result one might expect from an import substitution policy. In 1975-6, however, the domestic terms of trade moved strongly in favour of the agricultural sector. Since then, commodity prices have fallen and, in all probability, regional inequality has increased again.

XII Policy analysis

In this chapter I shall deal with regional policy viewed from two angels: First, there is a general discussion about the regional policy that has been pursued in Kenya so far; then follows the analysis of the actual model.

Section XII.1 contains a brief overview of the regional economic policy that Kenya has pursued since Independence; in section XII.2 I discuss regional inequality in the provision of public services - a very important policy issue which is not considered in any detail in the model itself. After this I present an anlysis of the model. It is divided into three sections, even if no clearcut division among different types of experiments can be made. The three categories considered here all teach us something about the functioning of the model. In section XII.3 I test the validity of the model by inserting realized values of final demand instead of using the final demand functions; I consider the effects of changes of a more technical nature and make parameter variations that represent changes in economic policy or development strategy. The first type of test is made to see how well the model can trace the actual regional growth pattern once the aggregate final demand estimates are correct. The second type of test is made to see how sensitive the solution is to changes in certain assumptions, that is, to provide information about how dependent the solution is on the choice of model specification or parameters. The third type of test directly seeks to represent changes in development strategy and to form the basis for an evaluation of the regional effects of various policies. The policy conclusions are given in section XII.4.

It needs to be pointed out that what can be done with a relatively aggregated model of this type is to systematically explore the effects of the implementation of certain broad development strategies. The advantage of using simulation technique to evaluate policy changes is that it also makes it possible to take indirect effects and repercussions into account, which cannot be done in partial analyses. One can, however, only draw policy conclusions of a general nature, while the detailed formulation of the regional policy to be implemented requires more detailed (and thus of necessity) partial studies.

This kind of analysis, of course, does not constitute a substitute for policy makers. They should have a knowledge about the various aspects of the institutional framework and those qualitative and political variables which have not been possible to incorporate in the model, but which need to be taken into account when the policy is to be formulated.

A study such as this should thus be regarded as the first step in a process of policy formulation. It can provide an understanding of the nature and extent of the problem and of how the economic system works and form the basis for the choice of areas of detailed investigation.

After an economy wide study has been complemented with such micro studies, it is possible for the policy makers to make those political decisions necessary for the implementation of the policy.

XII.1 REGIONAL POLICY IN KENYA

Since Independence, the Kenyan government has, in various documents, emphasized the need to distribute the fruits of development equitably. In Sessional Paper no 10 from 1965, 'African Socialism and Its Application to Planning in Kenya', the official policy objectives were stated as: Continued expansion of the economy, wider sharing of the benefits of expansion, national integration of the economy, and an attack on extreme imbalances and disparities. There was, already at this time, an awareness of the need to do something about income distribution and regional inequality; this awareness has subsequently been reflected in plans and other official documents.

In 1972, the very influential ILO-report on employment and earnings in Kenya was published. The ILO-mission found that there were three fundamental imbalances that needed to be corrected, if the economy was to be able to provide productive employment and a reasonable income for the entire population (ILO, 1972, pp. 13-14). They were:

'1) The imbalance between the rate of population growth and the nature of technology.'
'2) The imbalance between the centre and the periphery, i.e. essentially the imbalance between Nairobi and the rest of the country, between the rural and the urban areas in general, and among provinces and districts.'
'3) The imbalance between the formal and informal sectors.'

The imbalance between different regions was thus pointed out by the Mission as one fundamental aspect of the general problem of inequality in Kenya and the Mission found that the problem was growing (ILO, 1972, p. 2).

> 'The tendency of Nairobi and other urban areas to grow at the expense of the rural, of the richer regions in relation to the poorer has led to growing imbalances between regions and different groups of population.'

In the report it is furthermore pointed out (ILO, 1972, p. 301) that

> 'differential access on a regional basis to such advantages as roads, education and development projects is closely related to (family) economic disparity, and is thus a major force behind migration, both from the country to the towns and from one rural area to another. Particularly serious is the way in which regional imbalances interact with tribal fears and forces, partly as a cause and partly as a result. The Report of the National Assembley's Select Committee on Unemployment showed tribalism to be an aspect of regional and ethnic inequality with serious effects on social and economic progress: Where tribalism exists, many of the recommendations made in this report (for example, equitable distribution of development efforts geograhpically, equitable distribution of incomes, de-

centralization of industry, efficiency in Civil Service) cannot be implemented.'

In the reply of the Kenyan government to the report of the ILO-mission it accepts the central theme of the report, namely that

> 'Kenya's employment and unemployment problems are deeply embedded in the country's social and economic fabric and that these problems can be significantly alleviated only by fundamental changes in the pattern of development and in the structure of key institutions.' (Kenya, 'Sessional Paper on Employment', no 10 of 1973).

As far as regional inequality is concerned there was a declared readiness to do something about it. In the same sessional paper (paras. 242-3) it is e.g. stated that

> 'the Government is aware of the fact of regional inequalities in the distribution of welfare, services and amenities ... The Government accepts that geographic quotas are probably necessary for a variety of services, activities and programmes. ... Current planning practices and procedures will be examined with a view to introducing geographic quotas for a variety of services and amenities and for expenditures during the next Plan period.'

There thus seemed to be an acceptance of the analysis of the Mission. In the Development Plan 1974-1978 there is considerable emphasis on employment and equity objectives, and it is stated (p. 148) that improved income distribution and greater employment are the primary objectives of the plan.

However, Killick concludes from his review of official government publications (1976, p.30) that the response of the Kenya government to the ILO-mission may be characterized as a dilution; in other words, it expresses agreement in principle, but is unwilling to commit itself to any specific action.

In the report from the follow-up ILO-mission (Ghai et al., 1977, app.8) there is a comprehensive summary of the extent to which the recommendations of the ILO-mission of 1972 have been implemented. It is concluded that

> 'while it is true that many of the ILO-report's recommendations have been implemented, implementation has been distinctly patchy. Some of the measures taken are perhaps surprising in the extent to which they confront vested interest (e.g. the capital gains tax, taxation of luxury goods, abolition of investment allowance) but on the whole measures implying structural upheaval, such as land ceilings and redistribution, land tax and a freeze on the incomes of the higher paid, have been avoided.'

In an interesting paper Norcliffe (1977) reviews the industrial location policy that Kenya has followed since Independence. He finds that during the period 1963-6 there was a centralization of government to Nairobi, which also had an effect on other activities. The concentration of civil servants to Nairobi stimulated industrial growth there, and, as Norcliffe argues (p. 3), the policy of this period can be seen as 'an implicit policy of industrial concentration to Nairobi'. He notes that there are some statements about decentralization in public documents (e.g. Sessional paper no 10, 1965), but such statements are always qualified in so far as decentralization must not interfere with economic efficiency.

In the first plan (1966-70, p. 237) it is stated that

> 'the government has a strong interest in ensuring that economic development affects all parts of the country and is not unduly concentrated to Nairobi and Mombasa. Other things being equal, therefore, the government will assign a higher priority to a project that can be economically located outside the two cities. The emphasis that is being placed in the plan on the development of agricultural processing industries is motivated in part by the fact that such industries normally can be located in the areas where the products are grown. This is an effective way to achieve a wider geographical distribution of industry.'

Norcliffe comments on this (p. 5) that 'left implicit is the not unreasonable assumption that for most industries the greatest efficiency is to be achieved in Nairobi and Mombasa'. Since efficiency considerations are considered to be of overriding importance there is very little pressure for localization outside the two big cities.

A major shift in policy was, however, initiated during the period. In 1967, the president announced that greater emphasis would be placed on supporting the lagging regions. This was followed up by two different policy measures. First, between 1967-70 fifty per cent of the Graduated personal tax collected in Nairobi and Mombasa was transferred to minor or rural municipalities. Secondly, the Physical Planning Department was created with the main responsibility of devising a system of growth points.

The need for a regional policy is stressed in the second plan 1970-4 (pp.304-5). One of the stated objectives is a wider geographical dispersion of the benefits of industrialization. The main regional policy of the second plan was the design of a system of regional growth centres, which was believed to facilitate the dispersal of industrial activity. Four categories of centres were identified: First, the major cities of Nairobi and Mombasa constituted one category. They were expected to continue to grow, and due to efficiency considerations no restrictions were put on their growth. Secondly, seven major growth centres were singled out. In these the infrastructure was to be developed in order to attract industrial location. Thirdly, there were urban centres which were to serve mainly as commercial centres, but also intended to have a certain industrial role. Fourthly, there were small rural markets or local centres that would serve mainly commercial interests. The fact that such a system of centres was designed, however, seems to have had negligible effects on the government policy as far as allocation of government resources are concerned. Much remains to be done before these centres will play any effective role with regard to government policy making.

Another policy that was initiated and one which potentially could have a positive effect on regional equalization was the build up of industrial estates. By 1970, however, only the first phase of the Nairobi estate was ready. One positive policy is the small industrial scheme operated by the Industrial and Commercial Development Corporation (ICDC). This covers loans and management advice to rural areas. There also were plans to expand the Kenya Industrial Training Institute outside Nairobi and Nakuru. Overall, the second plan offers a variety of schemes designed to decentralize industry. Still, none of the plans have been mandatory, and the main thrust, the physical plan, was only indicative and could have effect only in the long run.

One positive initiative during the second plan period (in 1971), was the initiation of the Rural Industrial Development Programme (RIDP), the intent of which was to to create labour intensive, local, small scale industries in the rural areas.

In the third plan strong emphasis is put on rural development, but 'the plan is rather mute on the subject of industrial location' (Norcliffe, 1977, p. 9). The physical plan is further refined, but it still has very little effect on the course of economic policy making. There are few new initiatives, but the programme of industrial estates continues (only Nakuru and Nairobi are completed) as do the RIDP (Machakos, Kakamega, and Embu are operational) and the Special Rural Development Programme (SRDP). The latter programme is experimental, and is not directly aimed at fostering industrial development. Norcliffe (1977, p. 10) concludes that 'overall industrial location figures much less prominently in the 1974-78 plan than in the 1970-74 plan'.

In his review of the 1974-78 plan, Killick (1976, p. 17) finds little reflection of the aspirations of regional equalization. There are, for example, no quotas for government services or for government spending. Killick also points out that in the area of industrialization there seems to be a retreat from regional policy compared with the previous plan, which in fact pointed out the need for such a policy. Still, it should be observed that the increased emphasis on rural development to some extent may compensate for this as far as regional equalization of incomes is concerned.

In 1975, there was a positive initiative. Aimed at stimulating dispersion a policy of selective investment credit allowances was introduced. The allowance consisted of a twenty per cent rebate on capital outlay as a tax rebate on future profits. Originally, it was applied nationally, but from 1975 it has been denied for investment in Nairobi and Mombasa.

It is thus possible to identify three phases: From 1963 to 1967 a phase of centralization; the Administration was concentrated to Nairobi, and industrial efficiency was the only criterion of location. Between 1967 and 1974 there was a swing towards a policy of industrial dispersion. The third phase, from 1974 and onwards, Norcliffe calls a period of ambiguity. Rural development is emphasized, but it is not clear if the government is willing to pursue a policy of industrial dispersion. Norcliffe (1977, p. 10) says that 'by and large policy seems to have drifted with individual locational decisions being made on an ad hoc basis'.

The overall effect of the dispersal policies has not been large. Norcliffe (1977, pp.13-4) tries (primarily on the basis of work by Wescott) to evaluate existing policies with implications for industrial location. His findings are summarized here:

1. The industrial estates and rural industrial development centres have so far contributed very little to industrial dispersion. The Nairobi estate is by far the largest; the RIDC's work on a very small scale and can have an impact only in the very long run.
2. Minimum wage differentials may make a small contribution to decentralization, but they may also further stimulate labour migration to high wage areas. Moreover, the effect will not be large as union wages are not differentiated by region.
3. Duty remissions may be negotiated with the Industrial Protection Committee as part of a bargain by firms building new factories. Thus, the Committee can persuade a firm to locate outside Nairobi in return for a certain degree of protection. The advantage of obtaining a quasi monopoly may be large enough to outweigh the extra costs (if any) of locating outside Nairobi. Two textile mills in Nanyuki and Eldoret are cited as examples.
4. The investment credit allowance of twenty per cent is too small to have any real effect.
5. The provision of infrastructure is a necessary condition for decentralization but is in itself not sufficient.
6. Rural development will have an effect on industrial location only in the long run.

Finally, Norcliffe (1977, p. 16) gives four main reasons for the small effect of the policies which have been pursued; these are: (1) The large share of in situ expansion of existing plants, (2) the large agglomeration economies in Nairobi, (3) the large share of infrastructure investments going to Nairobi, and (4) the lack of a coherent government policy.

In this section, I have tried to summarize the evidence of the design and effects of regional policy in Kenya. In the following section I shall discuss the regional distribution of certain public services in more detail; this is of interest, not only because of its effect on the locational choice of industry, but also because of its direct impact on the welfare of people.

XII.2 REGIONAL INEQUALITY IN PUBLIC SERVICES

In the previous section we looked at the development of government regional policy. In this section we shall take a closer look at one aspect of regional policy, namely the distribution of public services. I shall concentrate on just a few types of services, namely education, health services and roads. Some comments are also made on the regional incidence of Harambee projects.

XII.2.1 Education

Colonialism had a very uneven impact on service development in different areas and once the imbalance was established there was a cumulative tendency towards increasing inequality. If an area had gone ahead in education, it could then draw on the graduates to get more teachers. Furthermore, people who received education could earn more money and contribute more to the education expenditures within the area.

As one example of the uneven impact of colonialism we can look at the level of primary education among various tribes at Independence. As Berg-Schlosser (1970, p. 40) shows, the Kikuyu were ahead of other tribes, and this headstart may, in part, explain the dominating role the Kikuyu have played since Independence.

Education is obviously a prerequisite for obtaining power, and the possession of power tends to improve the access to education and other public services. Consequently, the imbalances tend to be self-perpetuating. Today, both primary and secondary education is distributed in favour of the wealthy and politically influential areas, despite the fact that the imbalance has decreased in the last few years.

What we are interested in here is primarily regional differences. Other issues in education are not included in this study. At first, we shall take a look at primary and secondary school enrolment in 1969. One problem relating to these figures is that children migrate from the educationally advanced areas of the Central, Eastern, and Western provinces to more backward areas to get education. This may be due, a.o. to the fact that there are fewer individuals there who compete for the educational opportunities (Kinyanjui, 1974, p. 12). There may thus be some bias in the figures in table XII.1.

Table XII.1
Primary and secondary school enrolment in Kenya, 1969

	Enrolment of 5-14 year age group in primary school %	Rank order	Enrolment of 15-19 year age group in secondary school %	Rank order
Nairobi	61	2	46	1
Central	64	1	18	2
Coast	32	5	11	3
Eastern	47	3	7	5
North Eastern	4	8	1	8
Nyanza	31	6	7	5
Rift Valley	29	7	6	7
Western	40	4	8	4
KENYA	38.5		13	

Source: From Nyangira (1975, p. 144).

Nairobi and the Central province followed by the Eastern province are best provided with primary education, while the North Eastern province in particular is lagging far behind. In secondary education much larger quantitative differences are found. Here Nairobi is well ahead of all other provinces, but the Central province is also fairly well provided.

There were very large quantitative differences in enrolment between the provinces in 1969. However, a profound change occurred in 1974, when school fees were abolished for the four first years of primary school. This lead to an enormous increase in enrolment figures. As an example, Nyanza enrolment is reported to have increased from 291,000 in 1973 to 573,000 in 1974. The increase in the entire was almost one million in one year.

There has thus been a considerable equalization in primary school enrolment, but there are also qualitative differences. In the colonial days the quality of schools reflected the social stratification of the colony. The best schools were reserved for the white, the second best were for the Asians, and the third rate schools catered for the Africans. Much of the qualitative differences have been carried over to post independence Kenya. Today, the best schools are found in the cities and the centrally located areas (Kinyanjui, 1974). Data on the quality of primary school teachers confirm this, and as one might suspect, it has been difficult to recruit a sufficient number of qualified teachers to cope with the rapid increase in enrolment in primary education.

From table XII.2 we see that in Nairobi practically all primary school teachers were qualified, and in the Central province the proportion was above eighty per cent. In the remaining provinces the percentage in 1976 was between fifty and sixty per cent. The differences have increased in the last few years.

The quality of the primary education is important as the passing of the Certificate of Primary Education is very much dependent on the quality of the teaching staff, and the results obtained in East African Certificate of Education are much better in the government aided secondary schools. Children, who manage to get into schools with high quality staff, are therefore the ones with the best chance of qualifying for higher education.

Table XII.2
The quality of primary school teachers, 1974 and 1976

	Percentage of teachers who are qualified:		Rank order	
	1974	1976	1974	1976
Nairobi	97	98	1	1
Central	81	82	2	2
Coast	57	53	8	8
Eastern	61	59	6	4
North Eastern	71	61	3	3
Nyanza	64	55	4	7
Rift Valley	64	59	4	4
Western	59	57	7	6

Sources: Ministry of Education, Annual Report, 1974, p. 18, 'Education 1976: Status Report', in Social Perspectives, vol. 2, no 5, 1977.

Of course, figures on enrolment give some indication of how resources for education are distributed by province, but to find out more about the priorities of the government, it would be nice to have data on the allocation of public money. Such data are, however, difficult to come by. Nevertheless, I have been able to compile some data on the distribution of recurrent expenditures on education in 1973/74.

Table XII.3
Per capita recurrent expenditures on education by province
1973/74 (K£)

Central	4.98
Eastern	3.79
North Eastern	0.87
Nyanza	1.62
Western	2.16

Sources: District Development Plans

Since so little data on the provincial allocation of government expenditures on education are available, it may also be of some interest to see how capital expenditures are allocated (even if this type of expenditure is small compared to recurrent expenditure). Only data for secondary schools are available.

Table XII.4
Per capita development expenditures on secondary education
by province 1974-78 (K£)

Nairobi	0.31
Central	0.53
Coast	0.25
Eastern	0.20
North Eastern	0.20
Nyanza	0.15
Rift Valley	0.19
Western	0.23

Sources: Development Estimates 1975/76-1977/78. The figures for 1974/75-1976/77 concern approved expenditures; the data for 1977/78 concern estimated expenditures.

Since these data indicate where new schools are built or old ones expanded, one might expect the biggest shares to go to the provinces, where the largest increase in enrolment has occurred. The Central province had the largest increase in enrolment and also the largest share of development expenditures - actually more than twice what it would have received, if the money had been distributed according to its share of total population. Nairobi and the Coast have also obtained considerable sums, in spite of the fact that the number of pupils enrolled there has increased slowly (or not at all). This is probably due to the fact that old, established, high quality schools are well provided for. The Nyanza province gets least per capita of these types of expenditures.

The partial data presented here seem to support Nyangira's (1975) hypothesis that the money tends to flow to the most developed regions. Kinyanjui (1974, p. 39) also concludes from his study, that educational benefits are being distributed in favour of the economically and politically powerful districts and provinces in the country.

Even if the distribution of education expenditures among provinces reflects existing inequalities, they are still considerably more evenly distributed than economic activity in general. They can, therefore, to some extent, be assumed to counterbalance the regional disparities generated by the production apparatus.

XII.2.2 Health services

Health services, like education, were originally shaped according to the needs of the colonists, which is why the health services of today are highly oriented towards the urban areas. Apart from the services managed by the government, there are a number of private practitioners and missions. The activities of the missions are to some extent coordinated with the activities of the government.

Also for health services there is relatively little data, but there are some indicators that we can look at. The first table gives an indication of the development of health services in the various provinces.

Table XII.5
Health centres, hospitals, beds & cots, physicians, and attendances per million people and rank order

	Health centres	Hosp.	Beds & cots	Phys.	Attendances
Nairobi	21.4 (2)	38.6 (1)	4,500 (1)	1,451 (1)	$0.42.10^{6}$ (2)
Central	14.6 (4)	18.0 (4)	1,600 (2)	33 (4)	
Coast	6.0 (7)	18.8 (2)	1,400 (3)	128 (2)	$0.37.10^{6}$ (3)
Eastern	8.9 (6)	13.8 (5)	1,200 (4)	14 (6)	$0.44.10^{6}$ (1)
North Eastern	0 (8)	11.4 (6)	900 (7)	0 (8)	$0.32.10^{6}$ (4)
Nyanza	10.2 (5)	10.2 (8)	600 (8)	28 (3)	$0.05.10^{6}$ (7)
Rift Valley	22.5 (1)	18.6 (3)	1,200 (5)	43 (3)	$0.30.10^{6}$ (5)
Western	18.5 (3)	11.3 (7)	1,000 (6)	5 (7)	$0.14.10^{6}$ (6)
KENYA	14.1	16.0	1,300	101	

Sources: Health centres - 1975: Social Perspectives no 1, 1976, p.4
Hospitals - 1975: " "
Beds & cots - 1973/74: Economic Survey, 1976, p. 159
Physicians - 1969: Meck, 1971, table 13
Attendances - 1968: Bonte, 1974, p. 78

The health centres are the backbone of rural health services, and in 1975 there were 189 in all districts. The centres are manned by paramedical personnel and are visited occasionally by doctors. The quality of the centres, however, vary a great deal, which is why not too much importance can be attached to a comparison of their number.

In 1975, there were 215 hospitals, mostly concentrated in Nairobi and other centrally located areas. There is also an urban-rural bias that is not reflected in these figures. However, one must keep in mind that hospitals in the cities serve patients from rural areas as well.

Since the scale of hospitals differs, a better estimate of real differences is obtained if one looks at the number of beds. This may be the best estimate of differences in health services of the crude ones presented here. Of course, Nairobi dominates overwhelmingly, but this is to some extent due to the fact that hospitals in Nairobi (as well as in Mombasa) serve as referral hospitals and thus cater to patients from other areas as well. Still, Nairobi, Mombasa, and the Central province seem to be best supplied with health services, while particularly the Nyanza province is lagging behind.

The enormous bias towards Nairobi and Mombasa is even further accentuated by the distribution of qualified staff. About two thirds of all doctors are to be found in Nairobi. Data on attendance does not show any large differences except for the Nyanza and Western provinces, who are lagging behind.

The best indication of government priorities can be obtained from data on recurrent health expenditures by province. Data are available for 1973/74 for all provinces except Nairobi and Rift Valley.

Table XII.6
Per capita recurrent health expenditures by province
1973/74, (K£)

Central	0.97
Coast	0.90
Eastern	0.53
North Eastern	0.71
Nyanza	0.33
Western	0.51

Sources: District Development Plans

Of the provinces, for which data are available, the Central province comes out on top followed by the Coast. Also in this area, the Nyanza province gets the least.

In this context it may be of some interest to see if investments are allocated in such a way that the regional differences are decreased. The dominance of Nairobi (table XII.7) is due to large investments at Kenyatta National Hospital. It does not reflect the concentration of private practitioners and hospitals in the city. The North Eastern and Western provinces get relatively little resources, while the high share of the Nyanza province should indicate that its very low standard of health services is improving.

What previously was said about education may also be said about health services, namely that they are concentrated to the more developed areas, but are still more dispersed than the economic activity in general.

Table XII.7
Per capita development expenditures on curative health by province, 1974-78 (K£)

Nairobi	6.59
Central	0.50
Coast	0.97
Eastern	0.64
North Eastern	0.04
Nyanza	0.58
Rift Valley	0.34
Western	0.18

Sources: Development Estimates 1975/76-1977/78. Data for 1974/75-1976/77 concern approved amounts, data for 1977/78 concern estimated amounts.

A special problem as far as health services are concerned is the large private sector that is completely located in the urban areas; similarly, the large municipalities provide some services of their own. These factors work against the poorer areas, and the lack of comprehensive central control makes it difficult to remedy the situation. Even if funds were available there is lack of qualified people, who are willing to take jobs in the rural areas. In the mid-seventies only one-third of all doctors were in government service (Economic Survey, 1976, p. 160). The rest worked as private practitioners, who naturally chose to work where the money is, that is, primarily in Nairobi.

XII.2.3 Roads

Roads, obviously, are very important determinants of how well an area can become integrated within itself and with the rest of the country. To be able to take advantage of expanding markets elsewhere it must be possible to ship goods out of the regions without costs that are too high.

It would be of great interest to get some measure of road quality by province, that is, both quality of internal and interregional links. The problem is, that it is difficult to devise a good measure of the relative communication standard of different regions. It would be necessary to take into account their size, population density, and location in relation to all other regions, a task which would require a more thorough study than what I can do here.

Even if we have no good data on the present quality of the road system in different regions, it may be of interest to look at how the government allocates investment resources among provinces (table XII.8).

We see that there are two provinces which stand out in terms of expenditures per capita, namely the Central province at the top and Nyanza at the bottom. Among the other ones, the differences are not so large, even if the rank order approximately follows the usual pattern. Note, however, that Nairobi ends up way down the list, which is due to the fact that the Nairobi City Council looks after the city-streets.

Table XII.8
Per capita development expenditures by the central government on roads by province, 1974/78 (K£)

Nairobi	4.42
Central	9.67
Coast	6.25
Eastern	4.85
North Eastern	3.84
Nyanza	1.90
Rift Valley	5.50
Western	4.74
KENYA	5.17

Sources: Development Estimates 1974/75-1977/78. Data for 1974/75-1976/77 concern approved expenditures, data for 1977/78 estimated expenditures. Note that only expenditures which are possible to locate by province are included. Excluded are thus expenditures on rural access roads and some general expenditures. Unfortunately, the expenditures of municipalities are also excluded.

The tentative conclusion also from this section must then be that the government puts high priority on the expansion of roads within areas, where there is considerable economic development. The allocation of expenditures on roads does not seem to be a part of any conscious policy aimed at reducing regional inequality.

XII.2.4 The location of Harambee projects

Since Independence, the Harambee (self help) movement in Kenya has played a significant role in development efforts in the rural areas. The total value of self help projects in 1976 was K£ 5,141 (Economic Survey, 1977, p. 164), and the total sum contributed from the mid-sixties to the mid-seventies is around K£ 20 million (Social Perspectives, no 1, 1976, p. 2). It is estimated, that Harambee activities constitute about thirty per cent of total capital formation in rural areas (Ng'ethe, 1977, p. 3).

Education is the dominant type of expenditure within the movement. It accounts for about half of total expenditures. Apart from education, a whole range of socially or economically oriented projects are initiated. It should be pointed out, however, that projects are often started without proper planning and have to be abandoned before they are completed, or one may find out when they are finished, that there is no money to cover the expenses of running the services. There may thus be some wastage of resources.

I shall not consider the value of the Harambee movement as such, but merely take a brief look at the regional aspects of the movement. As a self help movement it is to a large extent dependent on the contributions of the people within the community, which, naturally, makes it easier to initiate Harambee projects in the economically more advanced areas. The distribution of Harambee activities may therefore be assumed to reflect existing regional inequalities. They can hardly be expected to contribute to the equalization of infrastructural availability among areas.

It may be possible that Harambee has the opposite effect. There is often a substantial amount of money coming from individuals or groups of individuals in the urban areas, and since Harambee is more common in the relatively developed areas, these flows might tend to increase the inequality among regions. Harambee projects are in some cases started on local resources only so that they later on may constitute a basis for demands for funds from the Centre. It has been pointed out that there is a tendency to initiate projects unlikely to be initiated by the government, but likely to be taken over (Mutiso and Godfrey, 1973). For example, a school may be started, and when the community cannot raise the money needed to cover the recurrent expenditures locally, it starts to pressure the government to supply the funds. The location of Harambee projects may, therefore, to some extent, determine where the government's money flows.

In this study I shall limit myself to a 'mini-investigation' of the regional distribution of the Harambee projects for 1972, which is the last year for which regional data are available (Kenya: A statistic analysis on self-help projects, 1972). The total value of the Harambee-projects for that year was K£ 3,115,933 (p. 57); the distribution among provinces of this total is shown in table XII.9.

Table XII.9
Value of self-help projects by province, 1972 (K£)

		Contributions by:			
	Total	the people	centr.gov.	local	other
Central	1,003,071	922,420	47,372	7,114	26,165
Coast	239,222	180,098	32,937	368	25,819
Eastern	483,998	419,523	40,336	2,859	21,244
North Eastern	63,887	40,351	20,009	1,676	1,851
Nyanza	459,245	407,165	25,385	1,320	25,375
Rift Valley	635,923	550,670	38,289	8,051	38,913
Western	230,577	186,852	3,745	10,291	43,725

Source: A statistical analysis on self-help projects, 1972, p. 55

To get a better picture of the differences, one should look at the per capita figures instead.

Table XII.10
Value of self-help projects by province per capita 1972 (K£)

	Total	Rank order	Contributions by: the people	centr.gov.
Central	0.54	(1)	0.50	0.025
Coast	0.23	(4)	0.17	0.031
Eastern	0.23	(4)	0.20	0.019
North Eastern	0.25	(3)	0.16	0.079
Nyanza	0.19	(6)	0.17	0.011

cont. Table XII.10

	Total	Rank order	Contributions by: the people	centr.gov.
Rift Valley	0.27	(2)	0.23	0.016
Western	0.15	(7)	0.13	0.003

We see that the Central province is well ahead of the others, which is what might be expected. It is also interesting to note that the government is spending relatively large sums of money on Harambee in the lagging North Eastern province, which is positive as far as regional equalization is concerned. On the other hand, the relatively poor Western and Nyanza provinces get very little.

To get an even better picture of the differences in economic potential among areas we shall look at per capita cash contributions in each of the various areas. This may also be assumed to be a good indicator of how much money people have in the area; it is also easier to make a correct valuation of this part.

Table XII.11

Cash contributions to Harambee projects by province, 1972 (K£)

	Amount	Percentage of all contri-butions	K£ per capita	Rank order
Central	517,773	56	0.28	(1)
Coast	68,986	38	0.07	(5)
Eastern	204,507	49	0.10	(3)
North Eastern	13,669	34	0.05	(6)
Nyanza	141,640	35	0.06	(4)
Rift Valley	304,212	55	0.13	(2)
Western	230,577	37	0.05	(6)

Sources: A statistical analysis of self-help projects, 1972

This table underlines the fact that it is communities within the Central province that most easily can raise cash. This should indicate that the people there (or at least some of them) are better off than those in the other provinces.

Of course, no definite conclusion can be drawn from this small investigation. It is not quite clear whether Harambee contributes to increasing inequalities, or if it just is a manifestation of those that exist. To be able to say anything definite, it is necessary to look more carefully at those who contribute to the projects, and where they come from. If, for example, well-to-do people living in Nairobi primarily contribute to the Central and Rift Valley provinces, one might argue that the Harambee movement creates or sustains regional inequalities. An equitable distribution would be more likely with a system of taxation and a conscious regional distribution of infrastructure investments by the government.

XII.2.5 Concluding remarks on public resource allocation

In his study of public resource allocation in Kenya, Nyangira finds support for his hypothesis that the higher the level of modernization the larger the resources allocated to the area. More developed areas tend to get more public resources than poorer ones. He also finds that political influence also (of course) affects the allocation of government money, but, interestingly enough, he finds that it is secondary to economic forces in explaining the regional allocation of public resources. By using factor analysis only very tentative conclusions can be reached, but his findings still support the hypothesis that economic forces are fundamental determinants of the development of regional inequality in this respect as well. Once an area has gone ahead, it tends to maintain its advantage.

Amsden (1974) and Bienen (1974) both emphasize the fact that ethnic politics are important in this context. Bienen (p. 130) argues that the politics of distribution in Kenya is perceived by the actors primarily in ethnic terms. There is the tradition of the 'big man', who can provide patronage and protection for his clients. This implies that there are few attempts to seek support across tribal barriers. Instead rich and poor within the same area work together to get public money for the area.

An estimate of the provincial allocation of recurrent expenditures was presented in Chapter VII. Total recurrent expenditures per capita by province are shown below.

Table XII.12

Per capita recurrent expenditures by province 1973/74 (K£)

Nairobi	70.76
Central	9.69
Coast	13.07
Eastern	6.42
North Eastern	3.54
Nyanza	3.28
Rift Valley	8.84
Western	4.09

Source: See table VII.1

The dominance of Nairobi is enormous, which, of course, to a large extent is due to the fact that central government authorities are located there. These, of course, cater to the entire country. Still, it certainly is true that Nairobi and Mombasa are well cared for in terms of public services. Among the other provinces the Central province gets the most money followed by the Rift Valley, while the Western, North Eastern and Nyanza provinces get least per capita. These overall figures support the tentative conclusion drawn from the analysis of individual services that the most developed regions get the largest share of public resources.

A similar conclusion is drawn in the World Bank report (1975, p. 22), where it is stated that the 'direct impact (of the public sector) on the problems of income distribution has certainly been largely negative'. This, of course, also has to do with the type of development strategy, that has been followed. To make industrialization possible, the government has been forced to provide the modern sector in the more developed regions with an infrastructure. A change in the allocation of public services might be difficult to accomplish, if the development strategy is not changed.

XII.3 SIMULATION EXPERIMENTS

I shall here provide a brief description of the technical details of the various simulation experiments. However, only the main results are presented. For a full presentation the reader is referred to Bigsten (1978). In this section I briefly present the various experiments that have been performed. The main conclusions that can be drawn from them are presented in section XII.4.

I first make a further attempt to validate the model. I insert actually realized figures for the period 1972-76 on total demand for modern sector consumption, modern sector investment, government consumption, and exports at constant prices, as well as the actual figures for sectoral labour productivity growth and subsistence production. I then compare the regional pattern of development which the model generates with this data input with the realized pattern.

Of course, the comparison is problematic. One should not expect the model to work too well, since the economic scene was very different from what was presupposed in the model specification. It is for example not well adapted to take the effects of large variations in the growth rate into account. Still, the comparison should give at least a partial insight.

However, it is not possible to determine the validity of the model, or its similarity to reality, merely by regarding it as a 'black box' and judging it by its output. One should also try to determine whether or not its internal structure is valid or plausible. One obvious drawback of the model, a drawback that makes it difficult for it to trace the pattern of development for the period considered here, is the fact that price changes are not taken into account. The relative prices have changed considerably during the period, and because of this the purchasing power of different groups or regions has not developed at the same rate as real output. This problems is intrinsic to any model formulated in real terms.

The model was designed to simulate development over time and under 'normal' conditions, and to test the effects of policy changes under these conditions. That there are certain deviations in a situation, which must be considered far from normal, is therefore not reason enough to consider the model invalid.

Table XII.13
List of model validation tests

SA 1: Realized final demand at constant prices
SA 2: Realized final demand at constant prices, with the relative sizes of the different demand categories determined from the current prices estimates

I next test some alternative specifications of the model. These tests are made to check how dependent the results are on certain assumptions or parameters. The test of the first alternative (SA 3) is done by assuming that the share of each region in the national CDIN-demand pool for each sector remains constant throughout, instead of using the delta procedure. This assumption implies that it does not matter in what region demand grows.

The next experiment (SA 4) is to assume that communication capacity remains unchanged, instead of increasing by five per cent per year, as is the case in the basic solution.

In (SA 5) it is assumed, that there is no migration of people among regions; this is done in order to see how important migration is to the development of regional inequality.

After this I test the effect of assuming that there are no earnings remitted among provinces (SA 6).

Finally, in (SA 7) I test the effect of using the Engel elasticities derived from the Kenyan input-output tables (1967, 1971), instead of using those of the basic model.

Table XII.14
List of sensitivity analyses

SA 3: Constant regional shares in the sectoral national demand
SA 4: Constant communication capacity
SA 5: No migration
SA 6: No remittances
SA 7: Alternative consumption expenditure elasticities

Next, I consider the effects of variations which reflect certain development strategies or policies.

When simulating policy variations one alternative is to let the choice among policy alternatives be made once and for all at the beginning of the period. A more ambitious alternative would be to let the choice among policy alternatives be made in each year on the basis of the behaviour of the model up to that time. I have chosen the first alternative, since the second alternative requires a more sophisticated type of model. Besides, one advantage of the first alternative is that it gives more clearcut answers.

First, I test the effects of increasing agricultural exports, (SA 8, SA 9), which may be assumed to be the result of an export promotion policy or changes in foreign markets. Next, I test the consequences of a policy of import substitution in the manufacturing sector (SA 10). After this, I consider the effects of expansion of infrastructure as an inducement to industrial relocation (SA 11). Lastly, I test an alternative which reflects a policy of investment control (SA 12).

Table XII.15
List of policy experiments

SA 8: Increasing agricultural exports (ten per cent more rapid growth of agricultural exports. No decrease in the growth of other production.)
SA 9: Shift from manufacturing exports to agricultural exports
SA 10: Import substitution in manufacturing (Reduction of competitive imports.)
SA 11: Infrastructure investments (Decentralization of government activity with an assumed effect on other production activities, particularly manufacturing.)
SA 12: Investment control (favouring less developed regions)

XII.4 POLICY CONCLUSIONS

In the previous section I described the experiments in which I tested the model's sensitivity to certain changes in the model specification and to parameter variations. The outcomes of these variations are compared with the basic solution described in Chapter XI. I shall try to sum up some of the conclusions which may be reached on the basis of the analysis; I shall also point to certain limitations of the results.

First, I let the realized (national) final demand figures replace the ones generated from the final demand functions of the model. This was done in order to test how well the model represents the actually realized regional pattern of production, once the development of national final demand is known. I found that the divergence between the realized regional production figures and those generated by the model was reduced considerally compared to the basic solution. It also became clear from this simulation that an important factor working against regional inequality (which existed during some years in the mid-seventies) is stagnation in the modern parts of the economy. It implies that the relative share of the subsistence sector in output increases; this improves the relative position of the poorer regions.

After this validation test was made, I tested some alternative model specifications. The first one illustrated the fact that it is not so important to take the shape of market areas into account, as long as the modern sector grows at similar rates in all regions. Thus, the result of the basic simulation does not differ much from the results obtained from a simpler specification, e.g. that the share of each region in the national demand pool remains constant for each sector. If the modern sector growth rates differ, the location of the market areas becomes important. It is vital for regional growth to be located close to regions with rapid economic growth.

If communication capacity is scarce, it becomes more important to be located close to the markets, or to have cheap access to them. In the

Table XII.16
Average growth rates of regional incomes in the simulation experiments

	Rea-lized	BS	SA1	SA2	SA3	SA4	SA5	SA6	SA7	SA8	SA9	SA10	SA11	SA12
Nairobi	5.20	8.03	3.17	5.39	8.04	8.02	8.03	8.11	7.47	8.78	7.96	9.00	7.07	7.59
Central	5.68	5.67	2.66	4.59	5.67	5.69	5.67	5.59	5.62	8.11	7.03	6.18	5.58	5.56
Coast	3.65	7.19	3.45	6.20	7.16	6.71	7.19	7.29	6.40	7.96	7.14	7.91	6.92	6.73
Eastern	6.76	5.17	2.50	3.73	5.17	5.22	5.17	5.07	5.04	6.64	5.89	5.60	5.55	5.61
North Eastern	-6.35	5.77	2.79	5.51	5.75	5.80	5.77	5.77	5.82	7.91	6.80	6.47	6.66	5.57
Nyanza	4.21	4.43	2.23	3.07	4.40	4.59	4.43	4.30	4.33	5.02	4.55	4.83	5.34	5.80
Rift Valley	3.87	6.27	2.83	4.48	6.27	6.50	6.27	6.24	6.27	7.32	6.43	7.07	6.30	6.23
Western	7.07	4.60	2.28	2.88	4.62	4.68	4.60	4.42	4.46	5.36	4.88	4.93	5.68	6.40
KENYA	4.83	6.59	2.89	4.77	6.59	6.59	6.59	6.59	6.25	7.86	6.84	7.31	6.37	6.59
RCOVAR	1.322	1.410	1.322	1.345	1.411	1.409	1.491	1.416	1.393	1.385	1.385	1.425	1.358	1.376
RGINI	-	0.467	0.444	0.456	-	-	0.473	0.469	0.462	0.464	0.462	0.472	0.452	0.452
RTHEIL	-	0.590	0.546	0.538	-	-	0.594	0.593	0.585	0.567	0.577	0.587	0.569	0.571

Table XI.17
Regional percentage distribution of production in some simulation alternatives, T=5

	Rea-lized	BS	SA1	SA2	SA6	SA7	SA8	SA10	SA11	SA12
Nairobi	34.15	35.92	33.96	34.49	36.04	35.55	35.36	36.30	34.69	35.20
Central	13.69	12.60	13.03	13.06	12.56	12.78	13.44	12.48	12.68	12.54
Coast	12.67	13.87	13.83	14.36	13.93	13.57	13.67	13.86	13.83	13.57
Eastern	9.19	7.95	8.36	8.11	7.91	8.03	8.11	7.84	8.18	8.12
North Eastern	0.40	0.69	0.72	0.72	0.69	0.71	0.73	0.69	0.73	0.69
Nyanza	9.77	9.11	9.79	9.33	9.05	9.21	8.91	8.97	9.61	9.72
Rift Valley	15.68	16.21	16.42	16.24	16.19	16.48	16.19	16.27	16.40	16.19
Western	4.46	3.65	3.90	3.68	3.62	3.68	3.60	3.59	3.88	3.98

Table XII.18

Regional per capita incomes relative to Nairobi's in some simulation alternatives, T=5

	Rea-lized	BS	SA1	SA2	SA5	SA7	SA8	SA9	SA10	SA11	SA12
Nairobi	100	100	100	100	100	100	100	100	100	100	100
Central	13.9	12.14	13.30	13.21	10.60	12.42	13.14	12.97	11.92	12.63	12.32
Coast	22.6	23.53	24.84	25.54	22.72	23.26	23.58	23.54	23.32	24.27	23.48
Eastern	8.6	7.09	7.89	7.60	6.05	7.22	7.34	7.35	6.93	7.56	7.37
North Eastern	3.2	5.35	5.86	5.86	4.59	5.50	5.72	5.63	5.30	5.86	5.40
Nyanza	7.4	6.54	7.45	7.05	6.47	6.68	6.52	6.60	6.40	7.14	7.12
Rift Valley	12.8	12.49	13.41	13.14	11.11	12.81	12.68	12.63	12.43	13.08	12.71
Western	5.5	4.30	4.86	4.55	3.90	4.38	4.31	4.37	4.19	4.73	4.76

simulations no differentiation was made between different communication links, but in a real economy the quality of these vary. Even if the quality of roads may be similar, the frequency of contact may differ. The overall view given by the model on this matter should therefore be complemented by detailed studies of the qualitative differences of the communication links.

I also tested how important migration is for the reduction of regional inequality, and in the case of Kenya it is obviously most important. Regional inequality (as measured by the coefficient of variation) increased three times as fast without migration as it did with migration. It was also found that intraregional inequality increased when migration ceased. This conclusion, however, rests on the assumption that, if there is no migration, the subsistence sector will swell by a number of people equal to the number that would have left the region (net) in the migration case. This is not self-evident, but given the character of the economy it is not inconceivable. Even if the poorest people are not the ones who move, the slots left higher up in the hierarchy will be filled from below; the changing distribution of labour among activities will therefore show up at the bottom.

I then tested the effect of omitting the remittances of earnings. The effect on the regional distribution of production was limited. But if we look at the regional distribution of consumption, we find that the equalizing effect is considerable. The remittances thus help raising the consumption standards in the poorer regions, and we might guess that, to a large extent, the money flows to the really poor groups within the regions. The remittances are thus very important for the equalization of welfare.

Subsequently, I tested another set of consumption expenditure elasticities to see how sensitive the solution is to the choice of these. It was found that the degree of regional inequality becomes slightly lower with the alternative set. Since the elasticity in this set was higher for agricultural output and lower for some tertiary sectors, the relative positions of Nairobi and the Coast province deteriorated, while the position of the other regions improved.

Thus, the pattern of demand has an effect. One may for example assume, that, if incomes are redistributed from the richer groups in society towards the poorer, demand for food will increase, and this will thus help the poorest regions (as well as the poorest groups within these). Thus, the general direction of development is of importance for regional inequality. Redistribution towards the poorer groups in the society helps people engaged in production in low productivity sectors.

Next, I tested two alternatives with expansion of agricultural exports. In the first one I let agricultural exports increase at a faster rate without any decrease in other line of production. In the second case I let agricultural exports increase at the expense of manufacturing exports.

In the first case all regions (except Nyanza) improved their position relative to the position of Nairobi. The regional inequality measures were thus reduced. Yet, one may raise certain objections. The region that benefited the most was the Central province, a region which is already fairly well developed. Also the Eastern province improved its position considerably, but the Nyanza and Western provinces which are really poor, did not benefit from this expansion of agricultural exports. They produce the wrong type of output, that is, they are dependent on the internal market for their sales.

In the second case, where we had to sacrifice some manufacturing exports to get the expansion of agricultural exports, the Central, Coast, and Rift Valley provinces did worse than in the first case. This is because of the importance of manufacturing to these regions. In this case the relative position of the Nyanza and Western provinces improved somewhat.

One may thus conclude from these simulations that the regions in Kenya that benefit most from agricultural export expansion are regions that are on an intermediate level of development. It is difficult to improve the position of the very poorest regions in Kenya on the basis of expansion of agricultural exports.

I also tested the regional consequences of an import substitution policy of traditional character. Even if the negative impact of changing domestic terms of trade on rural areas is disregarded, the model shows that such a policy primarily benefits Nairobi and thus works against regional equalization. Such an industrialization policy tends to increase the uneven impact of economic growth. Besides, there might very well be more efficient ways of using the new investment resources than for investment in manufacturing, e.g. investment in agriculture. If the resources are to be used for investment in manufacturing, some kind of public location policy would be needed, if the desired locational pattern is to be achieved.

An alternative to direct control is to try to make locating in poorer regions more attractive to investors. I have tried to simulate the effects of a policy aimed at improving the infrastructure of the regions, where it is least developed. There are difficulties in specifying the magnitude of the effect which such a policy would have on the location of industry, but there should be some effects. First, there is a direct effect on regional production since the public services, located in a region, themselves imply production. This will also have secondary effects on other sectors. The expansion of the infrastructure makes the location more attractive to investors, since it may create agglomeration economies, improve contacts with other regions etc. It also will imply an expansion of the market for output in the region, since public consumption generates incomes within the region. One may therefore be certain that there will be some effects, but predictions of their magnitude should be made with some caution.

Even if it is difficult to say anything about the magnitude of the effect which investment in infrastructure has on regional development, one may at least be sure that lack of infrastructure within a region will be an obstacle to expansion. Infrastructure development must therefore be an integral part of a policy aimed at regional equalization.

Since it is likely that investment in infrastructure is insuffcent to change the regional allocation of investment to the extent desired, such a policy should be complemented with other means. These can be of a more or less direct kind. In my last simulation I specify, a priori, a certain regional distribution of new investment in manufacturing to test how large an effect such a specification would have on regional inequality.

The reason for choosing manufacturing is that the sector contains many firms that sell on the national market, and thus are less bound to certain regions than for example services (even if some firms are resource oriented, that is, e.g. firms processing agricultural products). Another reason for choosing manufacturing is that it is a sector which is very much interdependent with the rest of the economy. One might therefore expect the secondary effect of manufacturing investments in a region to be larger than for other types of production.

To, a priori, specify a certain regional distribution of investment would naturally correspond to applying an industrial licensing policy. It is a direct policy, with which you do not have to rely on uncertain effects of incentives. Even so, it may be better to rely on indirect means such as fiscal incentives, e.g. labour subsidies. In order to apply direct control a great deal of information is required at the planning unit, and even if much effort is devoted to the task of gathering information, the planners are seldom as well informed about all aspects of the projects as the investor himself. There is therefore a considerable risk of misallocation of resources, if the central planners have the final say. The 'wrong' industries may be forced to move to locations in the less developed regions.

There is a further problem relating to the use of selective measures namely that they leave room for arbitrary decisions and corrupt practices within the administration. Political influence may become more important than objective criteria. Therefore, if the same results could be achieved by fiscal measures of a general character, they should be preferred. Richardson et al. (1977, pp.40-1) have proposed the use of labour subsidies combined with a levy on investments in Nairobi and Mombasa. The incentives scheme would be financed by the levies on investments in Nairobi and Mombasa, in other words, the scheme would operate at zero budgetary cost.

There is a further problem with the use of direct control, namely that the (private) investors may choose to abstain from making any investment at all, if they cannot invest in the area of their own choice. Particularly foreign firms may decide to invest in another country, if they are denied the freedom to choose location. This is also an argument in favour of the use of some kind of incentives scheme, since it would make the alternative locations more attractive. Such a scheme should be combined with an expansion of infrastructure in the regions or centres, where one wants investments to take place. The better the natural conditions for investments, the less fiscal incentives are required to lure investors to that particular location.

Nevertheless, it is possible that a location will remain unattractive until a certain level of economic activity and industrial tradition actually exist. In that case infrastructure and fiscal incentives may not be sufficient, but must be complemented by a policy which guarantees the establishment of some industries in the area. Even if such investments are not profitable for the private firms, their positive external effects may be so large that the government should undertake them in any case. This resembles the arguments for the balanced growth doctrine. Its main point was that one industry might be unprofitable, if located alone, while a number of industries located together might find that they can produce at a profit.

One point about decentralization should be stressed here: In the analysis I have dealt with regions. I have not discussed the pattern of location within the regions, which, of course, is a further problem. It is impossible to spread economic activity (at least non-agricultural) evenly over the landscape. The resources are limited; there must therefore be concentration within the decentralization policy. Non-agricultural investments within the regions have to be concentrated to a limited number of centres. A system of centres has been set up by the planners in Kenya. It contains centres on different levels. In Richardson et al.'s (1977) report on urban development strategy it is suggested, that even nine main growth centres, as suggested in the plan, is too much, if one is to be able to create sufficient agglomeration economies to induce large scale manufacturing industries to locate outside Nairobi to the extent desired. They therefore recommend that the main effort to create good conditions for this type of production outside Nairobi and Mombasa should be concentrated to just a few alternative growth centres, like Kisumu and Eldoret. It should, nevertheless, be possible to stimulate development of industry in other centres by decentralization of government activities, as well as support to small and medium sized consumer goods industries.

I agree with the authors of the report that resources have to be concentrated. It is not conceivable that the government should stimulate expansion in all towns given the limited resources. However, my analysis does not try to tackle the problem of intraregional planning. It simply presents the framework within which such detailed planning can be made. In the microphase of planning, one must, for example, consider the types of manufacturing activities that are to be located in a given region. It is then no longer sufficient simply to specify an aggregate figure.

The benefits of decentralization are mainly related to the issue of distribution, but it must be kept in mind that by locating economic activity within the poorer regions one attacks only one dimension of the general problem of inequality in Kenya. The regional policy needs to be set in a larger framework of distribution policy.

If a basic needs strategy is to be pursued (which has been suggested lately) regional equalization must certainly be a part of it. As far as satisfying the basic needs for goods produced directly by the government, this is obvious. In section XII.2 I pointed out the large differences that exist among different regions in terms of supply of education, health, etc. If these differences are not dealt with, it is very difficult to create a more equal distribution among different groups of people. If this type of public services does not exist in an area, people may obtain them only at a very high cost (by travelling elsewhere or buying it privately).

The other goal of the basic needs strategy is to guarantee that every family has a certain level of consumption, of certain private goods such as food, clothing, and housing. To be able to consume, a family must have income (either in kind or in cash). To decentralize economic activity means that its distribution to a larger extent will correspond to the distribution of people in the area; this will make it easier for families in peripheral regions to earn more income from modern employment. This is vital, since it is practically impossible to redistribute income through the tax system in an economy of the Kenyan type. It tends to stay where it is earned. The expansion of modern production in a region may also have very important secondary effects on small farmers. It makes it possible for them to sell more of their produce for cash, and thus possibly to expand their production, or make it more efficient.

Some investment in cheap, small industries in rural areas therefore should receive support. They should produce simple and cheap products that meet the demand of subsistence farmers; they could use some of the rural surplus labour. This description very much resembles the informal sector. When there is a certain degree of monetization the scope for this kind of production should exist also in rural areas.

The benefits of decentralization thus seem rather obvious, but there are also costs. The fact, that industrialists prefer to locate in the largest urban agglomerations imply that these are the places where they believe the costs of production to be the lowest (or the profits highest). A forced decentralization could therefore (if their belief is correct) have negative effect on the growth rate of production. It is, however, difficult to determine what the magnitude of the negative effect would be. In the model, this problem is circumvented. The problem of allocation of capital or labour is not dealt with directly. It is assumed that demand determines the location(s) at which production will expand, and that capital and labour flows there in sufficient quantities for the output to be realized. If more capital is needed per unit of output in a less developed region, decentralized growth will naturally require more capital to sustain the same national growth rate. The model simulations might therefore give a too rosy picture of the effects of regional equalization.

On the other hand, there is also the effects in the opposite direction, namely the stimulus to activities in the peripheral regions, which would not be forthcoming, if the concentrated pattern of development were continued. Particularly the monetization of small farming should be stimulated by the expansion of monetary production in poor areas. This effect should then be balanced against the negative effect of the loss of aggomeration economies.

There is also another cost of concentrated development about which the government is worried, and that is the fact that particularly Nairobi is growing at a rate, which is considered to be above what the authorities can cope with. The negative external effects of rapid urbanization are obvious.

It is not possible to perform a full fledged cost-benefit analysis at present, since so many factors are unknown. What needs to be done in the future is to try to determine the extent to which production effeciency differ among regions (and within them as well). Such studies would have to be partial, and they cannot take into account the kind of interdependencies discussed here. Information about regional productivity differentials should therefore ideally be fit into a country-wide model. It should then be easier to analyse the effect of decentralization on economic growth. There would, however, still be variables which would be difficult to model, such as the interdependence between the levels of productivity in different sectors (e.g. the possible positive effect on small farmers of modern economic growth in an area).

If regional differences in the use of capital per unit of output were better known, one could make sensible feasibility checks of the investment programme. Even if the incremental capital output ratios in an underdeveloped country remain uncertain, it should at least be possible to get some idea about the magnitude of the differences in the amount of capital which different locational patterns require. Such a feasibility check would, at present, amount to no more than pure guesswork.

XIII Concluding remarks

In this final chapter I shall briefly discuss the results of the study and the limitations of the model.

In the first chapter I presented some evidence indicating that income inequality in the long run develops with the level of per capita GDP according to an inverted 'U'. I argued that this pattern of development is occurring also with regard to regional inequality. Obviously, the degree of regional inequality in Kenya is now greater than what it was in the precolonial days; it is reasonable to expect that when the economy in the future becomes more integrated and homogeneous regional inequality will be less than what it is today. The inverted 'U' pattern is therefore valid for Kenya in the very long run.

In this study, however, I am only concerned with a limited phase of this cycle. I hypothesize that the forces working towards increasing regional inequality in Kenya are still very strong, and that the country thus for the period analysed is in the phase of increasing regional inequality.

The reason for this is the great regional differences in economic structure. Given this structure, the endogenous economic forces tend to sustain or widen regional differences. In the analysis I particularly emphasize the input-output linkages and the links between final demand and production as determinants of the location of production. Interregional flows of capital are not assumed to contribute to a reduction of regional inequality. Migration of labour, on the other hand, tends to reduce regional inequality substantially, since people normally move from poorer regions to richer.

I have empirically estimated how production by province has developed between 1967 and 1976 at both current and constant prices. At current prices there was a weak tendency towards increasing regional inequality up until 1975, but in 1975-6 it decreased drastically due to the stagnation in the urban oriented sectors and the commodity boom. At constant prices, on the other hand, there was a gradual decrease in regional inequality during most of the period. This means that up until 1975 the domestic terms of trade moved against the less developed regions.

The development strategy followed by the Kenya government since Independence, i.e. an import substitution strategy, has meant that particularly manufacturing has been favoured at the expense of agriculture. The middle class has been able to improve its economic position and this, in turn, has made possible an expansion of the production of Western consumer goods. This production has mainly been located in the most developed areas. The government has made some efforts in the direction of a regional policy, but the results are so far limited.

The model is initiated in 1971, and the growth pattern that it generates is a reflection of the conditions that existed at that time.

Cyclical fluctuations in the economic activity are disregarded, and naturally exogeneous shocks such as the 'oil crisis' and the commodity boom cannot be predicted. For these reasons the model generates a growth pattern that is somewhat different from the realized one.

In the basic solution the model generates a pattern of increasing regional inequality. An economy with the economic structure and the behavioural characteristics specified in the model thus tends to generate increasing regional inequality at this stage of development. In Kenya, it is mainly Nairobi that increases its share in GDP according to the basic simulation. At the same time, however, there is considerable migration into the capital, which keeps down inequality in regional per capita incomes. The migration is, however, not sufficiently large to completely counterbalance the increasing concentration of production.

The model used is an interregional input-output model encompassing the entire economy. To be able to apply a country-wide interregional model in a country like Kenya I have had to neglect certain aspects of the economic reality which, ideally, should have been included in the model.

The first, and most obvious, deficiency of the model is the disregard of price changes. As I have previously pointed out, changes in domestic terms of trade have been of importance. For most of the period discussed they have tended to aggravate regional inequalities.

Another deficiency is the lack of explicit consideration of regional supply restrictions. Nevertheless, the simulation starts from the actual 1971 situation, and the model is formulated in such a way that there are no radical locational changes in the short run. The location of economic activity changes gradually; one may assume that changes in the regional distribution of the magnitude contemplated here can, in most cases, be realized. The idea is that the model will allocate production increases with regard to the existing (or emerging) regional potential.

Another model imperfection is that 'urbanization economies' are not dealt with directly. No explicit distinction is made between urban and rural areas (although the city of Nairobi is treated as a separate region). Nevertheless, the size of the modern sector is vital in the model, and its size is very much correlated with the degree of urbanization in an area. Therefore, the advantages of locating close to a concentration of modern sector production is considered, while other urbanization advantages are neglected. Thus, for my analysis this deficiency may not be too serious, but it certainly has to be remedied when the detailed actual investment decisions are to be taken. Obviously, there must be a certain degree of concentration (towards urban areas) even in a policy of decentralization.

Finally, the balance of payments restriction is disregarded. This means that it is assumed that Kenya will be able to manage its balance payments. In any case, I abstain from analysing the regional consequences of a possible balance of payments crisis.

In the model, the growth of the various demand categories first determines the national sectoral growth rates. The regional distribution of government consumption and export demands can then be made directly. For consumption and investment demand less competitive imports it must, however, first be determined how much of this demand is generated in the various regions. The regionally generated demands must then be distributed among delivering regions. This is done with regard to the estimated interregional trading pattern. The growth of a region is thus determined by its own economic structure (it is advantageous to produce a lot of goods with high income elasticities) and by the rate of growth of its most important market areas. Since regions sell a considerable part of their output locally, there is a tendency for fast-growing regions to continue to grow rapidly. The relative success of a region in increasing its share of the total output of a specific sector is thus mainly determined by its access to the expanding markets.

A strong force working against increasing regional inequality in terms of per capita incomes is migration. It is assumed that the direction and magnitude of migration flows are determined by the availability of income opportunities. Of course, it is not easy to give a comprehensive description of the relative opportunities in different locations. Land pressure is, for example, an important factor which, in this study, is not explicitly taken into account.

For the purpose of reducing regional inequality, the alternative to migration is to shift income opportunities towards the less fortunate areas. This alternative has certain advantages.

A more dispersed pattern of production would, under existing circumstances, probably lead to a more even distribution of income among households. The poor households are relatively more common in poor areas, and these households' chances of earning cash incomes should improve when the economic activity in the area increases. They may also get indirect benefits through the expansion of markets for their output. Improved employment opportunities in less developed areas also reduces the need for cash migration. It should be socially beneficial for families to live together. It may also be assumed that the traditional home areas of most people provide a better environment than the sprawling slums of Nairobi. For these reasons I think that there is a need for a regional policy. 'Growth now - regional policy later' is not a dictum which I support.

If Kenya in the future is to pursue a strategy aimed at satisfying the basic needs of the population, a regional policy must be part and parcel of it. It has been shown that the allocation of public services is very unequal and that it, to a considerable degree, follows the distribution of private economic activity. One part of a strategy aimed at giving all people access to basic public services, such as health and education must be measures to bring about a regionally more even distribution of public services. The poor families also need private goods such as food, clothes, housing, etc.; to be able to obtain these they must have an income of some kind. Regional equalization in the availability of income opportunities should, to some extent, contribute to this end.

In a country like Kenya, there are still large intersectoral and interregional differences, and there is still a long way to go before these gaps will be significantly reduced. Given the limited size of the investment budget each year, it will be a long time before non-agricultural activities can absorb a substantial share of the labour force. Therefore, labour will for a long time be distributed among sectors with widely different levels of productivity and incomes. The regional incidence of these sectoral differences are, and will continue to be, markedly uneven; this means that households living in certain areas will be at a disadvantage for a long time to come.

In a policy aimed at improving the situation of the poorest households in Kenya society, the government must therefore consider (among other things) the regional aspects of resource allocation. All economic activity must be located somewhere in a geographical space, and where is not immaterial.

Bibliography

Publications from the Kenyan government are listed alphabetically under Kenya. The years to which the publications refer are given instead of the years of publication.

References to unpublished data obtained from produce boards etc. are made only in the relevant tables and not in the bibliography.

Adelman, I., Morris, C., An Anatomy of Income Distribution Patterns in Developing Nations - A Summary of Findings, mimeo, IBRD, 1971.

Adelman, I., Morris, C., Economic Growth and Social Equity in Developing Countries, Stanford University Press, Stanford 1973.

Adelman, I., Morris, C., Robinson, S., 'Policies for Equitable Growth', World Development, vol. 4, 1976.

Adelman, I., Robinson, S., Income Distribution Policy in Developing Countries. A Case Study of Korea, Oxford University Press, Oxford 1978.

Ahluwalia, M.S., 'Income Distribution and Development: Some Stylised Facts', American Economic Review, vol. 66, 1976 a.

Ahluwalia, M.S., 'Inequality, Poverty, and Development', Journal of Development Economics, vol. 3, 1976 b.

Alila, P.O., Kenyan Agricultural Policy: The Colonial Roots of African Smallholder Agricultural Policy and Services, Working Paper, no. 327, Institute for Development Studies, University of Nairobi 1977.

Allen, R.I.G., Gossling, W.F., (eds.), Estimating and Projecting Input-Output Coefficients, Input-Output Publishing Company, London 1975.

Alonso, W., 'Urban and Regional Imbalances in Economic Development', Economic Development and Cultural Change, vol. 17, 1968.

Amin, S., L'accumulation à l'échelle mondiale, Anthropos, Paris 1970.

Amsden, A.H., International Firms and Labour in Kenya: 1945-70, Frank Cass, London 1971.

Amsden, A.H., 'A Review of Kenya's Political Economy Since Independence', Journal of African Studies, vol. 1, 1974.

Andersson, Å.E., 'A Closed Nonlinear Growth Model for International and Interregional Trade and Location', Regional Science and Urban Economics, vol. 5, 1975.

Andersson, Å.E., Ohlsson, O., 'En långsiktigt balanserad sektoriell och regionalekonomisk struktur i Sverige', in SOU 1974:4, 1974.

Anker, R., 'An Analysis of Fertility Differentials in Developing Countries', The Review of Economics and Statistics, vol. 60, 1978.

Anker, R., Knowles, J., An Empirical Analysis of Mortality Differentials in Kenya at the Macro and Micro Levels, Population and Employment Working Paper, no. 60, World Employment Programme, ILO, Geneva 1977.

Anker, R., Knowles, J., A Micro-Analysis of Female Labour Force Participation in Kenya, Population and Employment Working Paper, no. 62, World Employment Programme, ILO, Geneva 1978.

Atkinson, A.B., 'On the Measurement of Inequality', Journal of Economic Theory, vol. 2, 1970.

Barber, W.J., 'Urbanization and Economic Growth: The Case of Two White Settler Territories', in Mincer, (ed), 1967.

Barlow, R., Davies, G.W., 'Policy Analysis with Disaggregated Economic-Demographic Models', Journal of Public Economics, vol. 3, 1974
Barna, T., (ed.), Structural Interdependence and Economic Development, St. Martin's Press, London 1963.
Beckerman, B.J., 'Market Share, Distance, and Potential', Regional and Urban Economics, vol. 1, 1971.
Berg-Schlosser, D., The Distribution of Income and Education in Kenya: Causes and Potential Economic Consequences, IFO-Institut für Wirtschaftsforschung, München 1970.
Bhalla, A.S., (ed.), Technology and Employment in Industry, ILO, Geneva 1975.
Bhattacharya, N., Mahalanobis, B., 'Regional Disparities in Household Consumption in India', American Statistical Association Journal, vol. 62, 1967.
Bienen, H., Kenya. The Politics of Participation and Control, Princeton University Press, Princeton, N.J., 1974.
Bigsten, A., The Spatial Economic Structure of Kenya, Memorandum no. 44, Department of Economics, University of Gothenburg 1975.
Bigsten, A., Regional Inequality in Kenya, Working Paper, no. 330, Institute for Development Studies, University of Nairobi 1977.
Bigsten, A., Regional Inequality and Development. A Case Study of Kenya, Economic Studies, no. 5, Department of Economics, University of Gothenburg 1978.
Bigsten, A. (forthcoming), 'A Note on the Estimation of Interregional Input-Output Coefficients', Regional Science and Urban Economics.
Bigsten, A., Dahlberg, L., Ekonometrisk skattning av tidsförseningsfenomen, Memorandum no. 42, Department of Economics, University of Gothenburg 1974.
Black, W.R., 'Interregional Commodity Flows: Some Experiments with the Gravity Model', Journal of Regional Science, vol. 12, 1972.
Blandy, R., Wery, R., 'Population Growth and Employment: Bachue-1', International Labour Review, vol. 107, 1973.
Blitzer, C.R., Clark, P.B., Taylor, L. (eds.), Economy-Wide Models and Development Planning, Oxford University Press, London 1975.
Bogue, Principles of Demography, Wiley, New York 1967.
Bonte, I., 'Patterns of Mortality and Morbidity', in Vogel et. al. (eds.), 1974.
Borts, G.H., 'The Equalization of Returns and Regional Economic Growth', American Economic Review, vol. 50, 1960.
Borts, G.H., Stein, J.L., Economic Growth in a Free Market, Colombia University Press, New York 1964.
Bos, H.C., Linneman, H., de Wolff, P. (eds.), Economic Structure and Development, North-Holland, Amsterdam 1973.
Boudeville, J.R., Problems of Regional Economic Planning, Edinbourgh University Press, Edinbourgh 1966.
Brass, W., et. al., The Demography of Tropical Africa, Princeton University Press, Princeton, N.J., 1968.
Brett, E.A., Colonialism and Underdevelopment in East Africa, The Politics of Economic Change 1919-1939, Heinemann, London 1973.
Brodersohn, L.S., A Multiregional Input-Output Analysis of the Argentine Economy, mimeo, Instituto Torcuato Di Tella Centro de Investigaciones Económicas 1965.
Brody, A., Carter, A.P. (eds.), Input-Output Techniques, North-Holland, Amsterdam 1972.

Brown, T.M., 'Habit Persistence and Lags in Consumer Behaviour', Econometrica, vol. 20, 1952.

Cain, G.G., 'The Challenge of Segmented Labor Market Theories to Orthodox Theory: A Survey', Journal of Economic Literature, vol. 14, 1976.

Carter, A., Structural Change in the American Economy, Harvard University Press, Cambridge, Mass. 1970.

Carter, A.P., Brody, A. (eds.), Applications of Input-Output Analysis, North-Holland, Amsterdam 1970a.

Carter, A.P., Brody, A. (eds.), Contributions to Input-Output Analysis, North-Holland, Amsterdam 1970b.

Chakravarty, S., Capital and Development Planning, MIT Press, Cambridge, Mass. 1969.

Champernowne, D.G., 'A Comparison of Measures of Inequality of Income Distribution', Economic Journal, vol. 84, 1974.

Chenery, H. (ed.), Studies in Development Planning, Harvard University Press, Cambridge, Mass. 1971.

Chenery, H., 'The Structuralist Approach to Development Policy', American Economic Review, Papers and Proceedings, vol. 65, 1975.

Chenery, H., et al., Redistribution with Growth, Oxford University Press, London 1974.

Chenery, H., Eckstein, P., 'Development Alternatives in Latin America', Journal of Political Economy, vol. 78, 1970.

Chenery, H., Syrquin, M., Patterns of Development, 1950-1970, Oxford University Press, London 1975.

Child, F.C., Employment, Technology and Growth - The Role of the Intermediate Sector in Kenya, Occasional Paper no. 19, Institute for Development Studies, University of Nairobi 1976.

Christaller, W., Central Places in Southern Germany, Englewood Cliffs, New Jersey 1966.

Cline, W.R., 'Distribution and Development: A Survey of Literature', Journal of Development Economics, vol. 1, 1975.

Colebatch, H., Institutional Forms and the Access to Services: A Kenyan Case, IDS Discussion paper no. 30, Institute of Development Studies, University of Sussex, Brighton 1973.

Colebatch, H., Government Services at the District Level in Kenya. Roads, Schools and Health Services, IDS Discussion Paper no. 38, Institute of Development Studies, University of Sussex, Brighton 1974a.

Colebatch, H., Local Service and the Governmental Process in Kenya, unpublished PhD Thesis, University of Sussex, Brighton 1974b.

Dahl, H.E., Household Demand for Consumer Goods in Kenya 1963-65. With Projections for 1966-73, Chr. Michelsen Institutt, Bergen (Pt. 1) 1969.

Damachi, U.G., Routh, G., Ali Taha, A-R.E. (eds.), Development Paths in Africa and China, Macmillan, London 1976.

Datta-Chaudhuri, M.K., 'Interindustry Planning Models for a Multiregional Economy', in Blitzer et al., (eds.), 1975.

Davidson, B., Africa in History. Themes and Outlines, Weidenfeld and Nicolson, London 1968.

Day, R.H., 'Recursive Programming Models: A Brief Introduction', in Judge, Takayama, (eds.), 1973.

Deaton, A.S., 'The Measurement of Income and Price Elasticities', European Economic Review, vol. 6, 1975.

Dervis, K., 'Planning Capital-Labour Substitution and Intertemporal Equilibrium with a Non-Linear Multi-Sectoral Growth Model', European Economic Review, vol. 6, 1975.

Dixon, R., Thirlwall, A.P., 'A Model of Regional Growth-Rate Differences on Kaldorian Lines', Oxford Economic Papers, vol. 27, 1975.

Edgren, G., Reforming the Structure of Minimum Wage Regulations in Kenya, mimeo, Nairobi 1974.

Elkan, W., 'Is there a Proletariat Emerging in Nairobi?', Economic Development and Cultural Change, vol. 24, 1976.

Engle, R.F., 'A Disequilibrium Model of Regional Investment', Journal of Regional Science, vol. 14, 1974.

Enke, S., 'Reducing Fertility to Accelerate Development', Economic Journal, vol. 84, 1974.

Faber, M., Seers, D., The Crisis in Planning, vol. 2. The Experience, Chatto & Windus, London 1972.

Fields, G.S., 'Rural-Urban Migration, Urban Unemployment and Underemployment, and Job-Search Activities in LDS's', Journal of Development Economics, vol. 2, 1975.

Fortune, J.N., 'Some Determinants of Trade in Finished Manufactures', Swedish Journal of Economics, vol. 73. 1971.

Frank, A.G., Capitalism and Underdevelopment in Latin America, Rev. ed. Modern Reader Paperbacks, New York 1969.

Friedman, J., Regional Development Policy. A Case study of Venezuela, The MIT Press, Cambridge, Mass. 1966.

Friedman, J., 'A Generalized Theory of Polarized Development', in Hansen, (ed.), 1972.

Gaude, J., 'Capital-labour substitution possibilities: a review of empirical evidence', in Bhalla, (ed.), 1975.

Georgescu-Roegen, N., The Entropy Law and Economic Process, Harvard University Press, Cambridge, Mass. 1971.

Ghai, D., 'The Machinery of Planning in Kenya', in Faber and Seers, (eds.), 1972.

Ghai, D., Stewart, F., Statistics on Income Distribution in Kenya, Staff Paper no. 25, Institute for Development Studies, University of Nairobi 1968.

Ghai, D., Thorbecke, E., Godfrey, M., Alleviating Poverty and Meeting Basic Needs in Kenya, mimeo, ILO, 1977.

Ghosh, A., in collaboration with A. Chakrabarti, Programming and Interregional Input-Output Analysis, Cambridge University Press, London 1973.

Gilbert, A., Goodman, D.E., 'Regional Income Disparities and Economic Development: A Critique', in Gilbert, Goodman, (eds.), 1976.

Gilbert, A., Goodman, D.E. (eds.), Development Planning and Spatial Structure, Wiley, New York 1976.

Godfrey, M., 'A Note on Rural-Urban Migration: An Alternative Framework of Analysis', Manpower and Unemployment Research in Africa, vol. 8, 1975.

Green, R.H., Seidman, A., Unity or Poverty? The Economics of Pan-Africanism, Penguin, Harmondsworth 1968.

Gunnarsson, J., Production Systems and Hierarchies of Centres, Nijhoff, Leiden 1977.

Gyllström, B., The Organization of Production as a Space-Modelling Mechanism in Underdeveloped Countries - The Case of Tea Production in Kenya, CWK Gleerups, Lund 1977.

Hansen, N.M. (ed.), Growth Centres in Regional Economic Development, The Free Press, New York 1972.

Haraldson, S., The Kenyan Health Service, mimeo, WHO-Kenya 1968.

Harlow, V., Chilver, E.M., History of East Africa, vol. 2, Oxford University Press, London 1965.

Harris, J.R., Todaro, H.P., 'Migration, Unemployment and Development: A Two-Sector Analysis', American Economic Review, vol. 60, 1970.

Hart, K., 'Informal Income Opportunities and Urban Unemployment in Ghana', The Journal of Modern African Studies, vol. 11, no. 1, 1973.

Henley, J.S., 'Employment Relationships and Economic Development - The Kenyan Experience', The Journal of Modern African Studies, vol. 11, no. 4, 1973.

Hermansen, T., 'Development Poles and Related Theories. A Synoptic View', in Hansen (ed.), 1972.

Heyer, J., 'Achievements, Problems and Prospects in the Agricultural Sector', in Heyer et al. (eds.), 1976.

Heyer, J., Waweru, J.K., 'The Development of Small Farm Areas', in Heyer et al. (eds.), 1976.

Heyer, J., Maitha, J.K., Senga, W.M. (eds.), Agricultural Development in Kenya. An Economic Assessment, Oxford University Press, Nairobi 1976.

Higgins, B., Economic Development, 2nd ed., Constable, London 1968.

Hirschman, A.O., The Strategy of Economic Development, Yale University Press, New Haven, Conn. 1958.

Hjalmarsson, L., 'The Size Distribution of Establishments and Firms Derived From an Optimal Process of Capacity Expansion', European Economic Review, vol. 5, 1974.

Holtham, G., Hazlewood, A., Aid and Inequality in Kenya, Overseas Development Institute, London 1976.

Hopkins, M.D., Rodgers, G.B., Wéry, R., A Structural Overview of Bachue Philippines, Population and Employment Project, Working Paper no. 20, ILO, Geneva 1975.

Hopkins, M.D., Rodgers, G.B., Wéry, R., 'Evaluating a basicneeds strategy and population policies: the BACHUE approach', International Labour Review, vol. 114, 1976.

House, W.J., Rempel, H., An Analysis of the Variation in Modern Sector Earnings Among the Districts and Major Urban Centers in Kenya, Working Paper no. 243, Institute for Development Studies, University of Nairobi 1975.

House, W.J., Rempel, H., 'The Determinants of and Changes in the Structure of Wages and Employment in the Manufacturing Sector of the Kenyan Economy, 1967-1972', Journal of Development Studies, vol. 3, 1976a.

House, W.J., Rempel, H., The Determinants of Interregional Migration in Kenya, Working Paper no. 272, Institute for Development Studies, University of Nairobi 1976b.

ILO, Labour Force Projections 1965-1985, Pt II, Geneva 1971.

ILO, Employment, Incomes and Equality. A Strategy for Increasing Productive Employment in Kenya, Geneva 1972.

ILO, Yearbook of Labour Force Statistics, Geneva 1975.

ILO, Employment, Growth and Basic Needs, Geneva 1976.

Isard, W., 'Interregional and Regional Input-Output Analysis. A Model of A Space Economy', The Review of Economics and Statistics, vol. 33, 1951.

Johansen, L., Production Functions, North Holland, Amsterdam 1972.

Johansen, L., A Multi-Sectoral Study of Economic Growth, 2nd ed., North-Holland, Amsterdam 1974.
Johnson, G.E., Whitelaw, W.E., 'Urban-Rural Income Transfers in Kenya: An Estimated Remittances Function', Economic Development and Cultural Change, vol. 22, 1974.
Judge, G.G., Takayama, T. (eds.), Studies in Economic Planning over Space and Time, North-Holland, Amsterdam 1973.
Kaldor, N., 'The Case for Regional Policy', The Scottish Journal of Political Economy, 1970.
Kaldor, N., 'The Irrelevance of Equilibrium Economics', Economic Journal, vol. 82, 1972.
Kaplinsky, R. (ed.), Readings on the Multinational Corporation in Kenya, Oxford University Press, Nairobi 1978.
Karvis, B., 'International Differences in the Distribution of Income', Review of Economics and Statistics, vol. 42, 1960.
Kenya, African Socialism and its Application to Planning in Kenya, Sessional Paper no. 10, 1965.
Kenya, Agricultural Census of Large Farms 1970 and 1971.
Kenya, Census of Industrial Production 1967.
Kenya, Development Estimates 1974/75, 1975/76, 1976/77, 1977/78.
Kenya, Development Plan 1966-1970.
Kenya, Development Plan 1970-1974.
Kenya, Development Plan 1974-1978.
Kenya, Directory of Industries 1974, 1977
Kenya, District Development Plans 1973/1974 for Kiambu, Kirinyaga, Muranga, Nyeri, Kilifi, Kwale, Lamu, Mombasa, Taita, Tana River, Embu, Isiolo, Kitui, Machakos, Marsabit, Meru, Garissa, Mandera, Wajir, Kisii, Kisumu, Siaya, South Nyanza, Kajiado, Bungoma, Busia, Kakamega.
Kenya, Economic Review of Agriculture 1969, 1970, 1971, 1972, 1973, 1974, 1975, 1976.
Kenya, Economic Survey, 1973, 1974, 1975, 1976, 1977, 1978.
Kenya, Employment and Earnings, 1963-1967, 1968-1970, 1971, 1972-1973, 1974, 1975, 1976.
Kenya, Estimates of Recurrent Expenditure, 1973/74, 1974/75, 1975/76, 1976/77, 1977/78.
Kenya, Input-Output Table, 1967, 1971.
Kenya, Integrated Rural Survey, 1974/75.
Kenya, Ministry of Education Annual Report, 1969, 1971, 1974.
Kenya, Ministry of Labour, Annual Report, 1968.
Kenya, Report of the Commission of Inquiry (Public Service Structure and Remuneration) 1970-1971.
Kenya, Population Census 1962, Advance Report of volume I & II.
Kenya, Population Census 1969, vols. 1-4.
Kenya, Road Reclassification, Ministry of Works, 1970.
Kenya, Sessional Paper on Employment, no. 10, 1973.
Kenya, Small Farm Survey 1969/70, mimeo.
Kenya, Social Perspectives, vol. 1, no. 1, 1976, vol. 2, no. 4, 1977.
Kenya, Statistical Abstract, 1972, 1973, 1974, 1975, 1976, 1977.
Kenya, Statistical Digest, June 1971, June 1972, Sept. 1972, June 1973, Sept. 1973, Sept. 1976.
Kenya, A Statistical Analysis on Self-Help Projects, 1972.
Kenya, Survey of Distribution, 1971, mimeo.
Kenya, Survey of Industrial Production, 1968-1971.
Kenya, Survey of the Informal Sector, 1972-1974, 1975, 1976.

Kenya, Survey of non-agricultural enterprises in the rural areas, 1969, mimeo.
Kenya, Survey of Services, 1966.
Kenya Wheat Board, Annual Reports, 1965/67-1973/74.
Killick, T., Strengthening Kenya's Development Strategy: Opportunities and Constraints, Discussion Paper no. 239, Institute for Development Studies, University of Nairobi 1976.
Kimani, S., Taylor, M., D.F.R., Growth Centres and Rural Development in Kenya, Thika, Kenya 1973.
Kinyanjui, K., The Distribution of Educational Resources and Opportunities in Kenya, Discussion Paper no. 208, Institute for Development Studies, University of Nairobi 1974.
Kipnis, B.A., 'Local versus National Coefficients in Constructing Regional Input-Output Tables in Small Countries: A Case Study in Northern Israel', Journal of Regional Science, vol. 16, 1976.
Knowles, J., Anker, R., Economic Determinants of Demographic Behaviour, Population and Employment Working Paper no. 28, World Employment Programme, ILO, Geneva 1975.
Knowles, J., Anker, R., Economic Determinants of Demographic Behaviour in Kenya, mimeo, ILO, 1977a.
Knowles, J., Anker, R., The Determinants of Internal Migration in Kenya: A District Level Analysis, Population and Employment Working Paper no. 56, World Employment Programme, ILO, Geneva 1977b.
Knowles, J., Anker, R., An Analysis of Income Transfers in a Developing Country: The Case of Kenya, Population and Employment Working Paper no. 59, World Employment Programme, ILO, Geneva 1977c.
Kuznets, S., 'Economic Growth and Income Inequality' American Economic Review, vol. 45, 1955.
Kuznets, S., 'Quantitative Aspects of the Growth of Nations: VII, The Share and Structure of Consumption', Economic Development and Cultural Change, vol. 10, 1962.
Kuznets, S., 'Quantitative Aspects of the Economic Growth of Nations: VIII Distribution of Income by Size', Economic Development and Cultural Change, vol. 11, 1963.
Langdon, S., Multinational Corporations in the Political Economy of Kenya, unpublished. Ph.D. thesis, University of Sussex 1975.
Laurenti, L., 'Urbanization Trends and Prospects' in Urbanization in Kenya, International Urbanization Survey, The Ford Foundation 1972.
Lefeber, L., Datta-Chaudhuri, M., Regional Development Experiences and Prospects in South and Southeast Asia, Mouton, Paris 1971.
Leontief, W., 'The Dynamic Inverse', in Carter, Brody, (eds.), 1970b.
Leontief, W., 'Explanatory Power of the Comparative Cost Theory of International Trade and Its Limits', in Bos et al. (eds.), 1973.
Leontief, W., in collaboration with Strout, A., 'Multiregional Input-Output Analysis', in Barna (ed.), 1963.
Lewis, W.A., 'Economic Development with Unlimited Supplies of Labour', Manchester School of Economic and Social Studies, vol. 22, 1954.
Lewis, W.A., 'Unlimited Labour: Further Notes', Manchester School of Economic and Social Studies, vol. 26, 1958.
Leys, C., 'Interpreting African Underdevelopment: Reflections on the ILO Report on Employment, Incomes and Equality in Kenya', African Affairs, vol. 72, no. 289, 1973.
Leys, C., Underdevelopment in Kenya. The Political Economy of Neo-Colonialism, Heinemann, London 1975.
Linnemann, H., An Econometric Study of International Trade Flows, North-Holland, Amsterdam 1966.

Little, I.M.D., Mirrlees, J.A., Manual of Industrial Project Analysis in Developing Countries, OECD, Paris 1968.

Little, I., Scitovsky, T., Scott, M., Industry and Trade in Some Developing Countries, Oxford University Press, London 1970.

Lluch, C., Powell, A., 'International Comparisons of Expenditure Patterns', European Economic Review, vol. 5, 1975.

Lösch, A., The Economics of Location, Yale University Press, New Haven, Conn. 1954.

Mabogunje, A.L., 'Urbanization in Nigeria - A Constraint on Economic Development', Economic Development and Cultural Change, vol. 13, 1965.

Mabogunje, A.L., Growth Poles and Growth Centres in the Regional Development of Nigeria, UNRISD, Geneva 1971.

Maitha, J.K., 'The Kenyan Economy', in Heyer et al. (eds.), 1976.

Maize & Produce Board, Annual Reports, 1966/67-1975/76.

Manne, A.S., 'Multi-Sectoral Models for Developing Planning - A Survey', Journal of Development Economics, vol. 1, 1974.

Manpower and Unemployment Research in Africa - A Newsletter, Special Issue from the Institute of Development Studies, University of Sussex, Centre for Developing Area Studies, McGill University, Montreal, Quebec, Canada, vol. 6, no. 2, 1973.

Marglin, S.A., Public Investment Criteria, Allen & Unwin, London 1967.

Massell, B., Heyer, J., Household Expenditure in Nairobi: a statistical analysis of consumer behaviour, Discussion Paper, no. 48, Institute for Development Studies, University of Nairobi 1967.

Mathur, P.N., 'Multi-Regional Analysis in a Dynamic Input-Output Framework', in Brody, Carter (eds.), 1972.

Mazumdar, D, Analysis of the Dual Labour Market in LDC's, mimeo, Development Economics Department, IBRD 1975.

Mazumdar, D., 'The Urban Informal Sector', World Development, vol. 4, 1976.

McKee, D., Dean, D., Leahy, W.H., Regional Economics - Theory and Practice, The Free Press, New York 1970.

McMenamin, D.G., Haring, J.E., 'An Appraisal of Non-Survey Techniques for Estimating Regional Input-Output Models', Journal of Regional Science, vol. 14, 1974.

Meck, M., Problems and Prospects of Social Services in Kenya, IFO-institut für Wirtschaftsforschung, Munich, Africa-Studienstelle 1971.

Mennes, L.B.M., Tinbergen, J., Waardenburg, J.G., The Element of Space in Development Planning, North-Holland, Amsterdam 1969.

Migot-Adholla, S., Migration and Rural Differentiation in Kenya, Ph.D. thesis, Department of Sociology, University of California, L.A., 1977.

Mincer, H. (ed.), The City in Modern Africa, Pall Mall Press, London 1967.

Morawetz, D., 'Employment Implications of Industrialization in Developing Countries: A Survey', Economic Journal, vol. 84, 1974.

Morawetz, D., 'Elasticities of Substitution in Industry: What Do We Learn From Econometric Estimates?', World Development, vol. 4, 1976.

Morrison, W.J., Smith, P., 'Non-Survey Input-Output Techniques at the Small Area Level: An Evaluation', Journal of Regional Science, vol. 14, 1974.

Mutiso, G.C.M., Godfrey, M., The Political Economy of Self-Help: Kenya's Harambee Institutes of Technology, Working Paper no. 107, Institute for Development Studies, University of Nairobi 1973.

Myrdal, G., Economic Theory and Underdeveloped Regions, Meuthen, London 1963.

Myrdal, G., Asian Drama, Pantheon, New York 1968.
Nairobi Urban Study Group, Nairobi - Metropolitan Growth Strategy, vol. 1, Main Report, Nairobi 1973.
Ng'ethe, N., Harambee and Rural Development in Kenya. Towards a Political/Administrative Reinterpretation, Working Paper no. 302, Institute for Development Studies, University of Nairobi 1977.
Nikaido, H., Introduction to Sets and Mappings in Modern Economics, North-Holland, Amsterdam 1970.
Norcliffe, G.B., Towards a Locational Policy for Manufacturing Industry in Kenya, mimeo, Ministry of Finance and Planning, 1977.
Nyangira, N., Relative Modernization and Public Resource Allocation in Kenya, East African Literature Bureau, Nairobi 1975.
Ogendo, R.B., Industrial Geography of Kenya, East African Publishing House, Nairobi 1972.
Ogot, B.A. (ed.), Zamani, A Survey of East African History, East African Publishing House, Nairobi 1973.
Ogot, B.A. (ed.), Kenya Before 1900, East African Publishing House, Nairobi 1976.
Ohtsuki, Y., 'Regional Allocation of Public Investment in an N-Region Economy', Journal of Regional Science, vol. 11, 1971.
Okoth-Ogendo, H.W.O., 'African Land Tenure Reform', in Heyer et al. (eds.), 1976.
Oliver, R., Mathew, G., History of East Africa, vol. 1, Oxford University Press, London 1963.
Olsen, E., International Trade Theory and Regional Income Differences, United States 1880-1950, North-Holland, Amsterdam 1971.
Oshima, H., 'The International Comparison of Size Distribution of Family Incomes with Special Reference to Asia', Review of Economics and Statistics, vol. 44, 1962.
Ozaki, I., 'Economies of Scale and Input-Output Coefficients', in Carter, Brody (eds.), 1970a.
Pack, H., Employment and Productivity in Kenyan Manufacturing, Discussion Paper no. 149, Institute for Development Studies, University of Nairobi 1972.
Pack, H., Employment and Production in Kenyan Manufacturing, Discussion Paper no. 196, Economic Growth Center, Yale University 1974.
Pack, H., 'The Substitution of Labour for Capital in Kenyan Manufacturing', Economic Journal, vol. 86, 1976.
Paelinck, J.H., Nijkamp, P., Operational Theory and Method in Regional Economics, Saxon House, Farnborough 1975
Paukert, F., 'Income Distribution at Different Levels of Development. A Survey of Evidence', International Labour Review, vol. 108, 1973.
Perroux, F., 'Note on the Concept of Growth Poles', reprinted in McKee et al. (eds.), 1955.
Powell, R.P., The Stock of Fixed Capital in Kenya in the Monetary Economy 1964-1971, Occasional Paper no. 9, Institute for Development Studies, University of Nairobi 1973.
Power, J.H., The Role of Protection in Industrialization Policy, Discussion Paper no. 136, Institute of Development Studies, University of Nairobi 1972.
Pyatt, G., 'On the Interpretation and Disaggregation of Gini-Coefficients', Economic Journal, vol. 86, 1976.
Rahman, A., 'Regional Allocation of Investment', Quarterly Journal of Economics, vol. 77, 1963.

Rempel, H., Urban In-migration and Urban Unemployment, mimeo, Inter Disciplinary Urban Seminar, Institute for Development Studies, University of Nairobi 1974a.

Rempel, H., An Analysis of the Information on Inter-District Migration Provided in the 1969 Kenya Census, Working Paper no. 142, Institute for Development Studies, University of Nairobi 1974b.

Rempel, H., An Estimate of Kenya's Labour Force, Working Paper no. 159, Institute for Development Studies, University of Nairobi 1974c.

Rempel, H., House, W.J., The Kenya Employment Problem. An Analysis of the Modern Sector Labour Market, ILO, Geneva (Recently published by Oxford University Press), 1975.

Richardson, H.W., Regional Economics, Weidenfeld and Nicolson, London 1969.

Richardson, H.W., Input-Output and Regional Economics, Weidenfeld and Nicolson, London 1972.

Richardson, H.W., Regional Growth Theory, MacMillan, London 1973.

Richardson, H.W., Khanna, A., Sampaio, O.A., National Urban Development Strategy, mimeo, Nairobi 1977.

Riefler, R.F., 'Interregional input-output; a state of the arts survey', in Judge, Takayama, (eds.), 1973.

Robinson, S., 'Toward an Adequate Long-Run Model of Income Distribution and Economic Development', American Economic Review, vol. 66, 1976.

Rosenstein-Rodan, P.N.,'Problems of Industrialization in Eastern and Southern Europe', Economic Journal, vol. 53, 1943.

Rosser, C., Urbanization in Tropical Africa: a demographic introduction, International Urbanization Survey, The Ford Foundation, 1972.

Rotschild, D., 'Ethnic Inequalities in Kenya', The Journal of Modern African Studies, vol. 7, no. 4, 1969.

Rundin, U., Perspectiv på Östafrika, Prisma, Stockholm 1973.

Russel, R.R., 'International Disparities in Income Elasticities', Review of Economics and Statistics, vol. 49, 1967.

Sakashita, N., 'Regional Allocation of Public Investment', Papers, Regional Science Association, vol. 19, 1967.

Schumpeter, J., The Theory of Economic Development, Oxford University Press, London 1969.

Seers, D., 'What are we trying to measure', Journal of Development Studies, vol. 8, 1972.

Seidman, A., Comparative Development Strategies in East Africa, East African Publishing House, Nairobi 1972.

Sen, A., Choice of Techniques, Basil Blackwall, Oxford 1960.

Sen, A., On Economic Inequality, Clarendon Press, Oxford 1973.

Senga, W.M., 'Kenya's Agricultural Sector', in Heyer et al. (eds.), 1976.

Sevaldson, P., 'The Stability of Input-Output Coefficients', in Carter, Brody, (eds.), 1970a.

Sharpley, J., Intersectoral Capital Flows: Evidence from Kenya, mimeo, University of Wisconsin-Madison 1976.

Siebert, H., Regional Economic Growth: Theory and Policy, International Textbook C.O., Scranton, Pa., 1969.

Silberston, A., 'Economies of Scale in Theory and Practice', Economic Journal, vol. 82, 1972.

Singer, H., Jolly, R., 'Unemployment in an African Setting. Lessons of the Employment Strategy Mission to Kenya', International Labour Review, vol. 107, 1973.

Singer, H., Reynolds, S., Aspects of the Distribution of Income and Wealth in Kenya, mimeo, UNESCO 1973.

Smith, L.D., 'An Overview of Agricultural Development Policy', in Heyer et al., (eds.), 1976.

Soja, E.W., The Geography of Modernization in Kenya. A Spatial Analysis of Social, Economic, and Political Change, Syracuse University Press, Syracuse, New York 1968

SOU 1974:4: Regionala prognoser i planeringens tjänst, Stockholm 1974.

SOU 1976:42: Långtidsutredningens modellsystem. Bilaga 8 till 1975 års långtidsutredning, Stockholm 1976.

Stewart, F., 'Kenya. Strategies for Development', in Damchi et al., (eds.), 1976.

Stone, R., Mathematical Models of the Economy and other Essays, Chapman and Hall, London 1970.

Streeten, P., The Frontiers of Development Studies, Wiley, New York 1972.

Sunkel. O., 'Transnational Capitalism and National Disintegration in Latin America', Social and Economic Studies, vol. 22, 1973.

Sutton, J.E.G., Early Trade in East Africa, East African Publishing House, Nairobi 1973.

Swainson, N., The History of Investment in Kenya Before 1945, Working Paper no. 242, Institute for Development Studies, University of Nairobi 1975.

Swainson, N., The Role of the State in Kenya's Post-War Industrialization, Working Paper no. 275, Institute for Development Studies, University of Nairobi 1976.

Taylor, L., 'Theoretical Foundations and Technical Implications', in Blitzer et al. (eds.), 1975.

Theil, H., Economics and Information Theory, North-Holland, Amsterdam 1967.

Theil, H., Statistical Decomposition Analysis, North-Holland, Amsterdam 1972.

Thorbecke, E., The Employment Problem: A Critical Evaluation of the Four ILO Comprehensive Country Reports, ILO, Geneva 1973.

Thorbecke, E., Sengupta, J.K., A Consistency Framework for Employment, Output and Income Distribution Projections Applied to Colombia, mimeo, IBRD, 1972.

Tobin, J., Input/Output Computer Programs, mimeo, Institute for Development Studies, University of Nairobi 1973a.

Tobin, J., Unofficial Addenda to Kenya Input/Output Tables 1967, mimeo, Institute for Development Studies, University of Nairobi 1973b.

Tobin, J., Estimates of Central Capital/Output Ratios for Kenya, Working Paper no. 171, Institute for Development Studies, University of Nairobi 1974.

Todaro, M.P., 'A Model of Labour Migration and Urban Unemployment in Less Developed Countries', American Economic Review, vol. 59, 1969.

Todaro, M.P., Migration and Economic Development : A Review of Theory, Evidence, Methodology and Research Priorities, Occasional Paper no. 18, Institute for Development Studies, University of Nairobi 1976.

UNRISD, Research Notes, no. 3, Geneva 1970.

van Zwanenberg, R., The Agricultural History of Kenya, East African Publishing House, Nairobi 1972.

van Zwanenberg, R., Colonial Capitalism and Labour in Kenya 1919-1939, East African Literature Bureau, Nairobi 1975.

van Zwanenberg, R., King, A., An Economic History of Kenya and Uganda 1800-1970, Macmillan, London 1975.

Vogel, L.C., et al. (eds.), Health and Disease in Kenya, East African Literature Bureau, Nairobi 1974.

Vukovich, A.M., Urban Development Strategy and Projected Population in Urban Areas in Kenya During 1969-2000, mimeo, Nairobi 1974.
Wasow, B., Regional Inequality and Migration in Kenya: Some Indirect Evidence, Working Paper no. 125, Institute of Development Studies, University of Nairobi 1973.
Wasserman. G., 'Continuity and Counter-Insurgency: The Role of Land Reform in Decolonizing Kenya, 1962-1970', The Canadian Journal of African Studies, vol. 7, 1973a.
Wasserman, G., 'The Independence Bargain: Kenya Europeans and the Land Issue 1960-1962', Journal of Commonwealth Political Studies, vol. 11, 1973b.
Wasserman, G., Politics of Decolonalization, Cambridge University Press, London 1976.
Weeks, J., 'An Exploration into the Nature of the Problem of Urban Imbalance in Africa', in Manpower and Unemployment Research in Africa, vol. 6, no. 2, 1973.
Weeks, J., 'Introduction', in Manpower and Unemployment Research in Africa, vol. 6, no. 2, 1973.
Weisskopf, R., 'Demand Elasticities for a Developing Economy: An International Comparison of Consumption Patterns', in Chenery (ed.), 1971.
Wéry, R., Some Notes on Projections of GDP, Employment and other macroeconomic variables, ILO, Geneva 1972.
Wéry, R., Technological Change in Input-Output Relationships, Population and Employment, Working Paper no. 17, ILO, Geneva 1975.
Wéry, R., Rodgers, G.B., Hopkins, M.D., Bachue-2: Version-I. A Population and Employment Model for the Phillipines, Population and Employment, Working Paper no. 5, ILO, Geneva 1974.
Wescott, C, Industrial Location and Public Policy: The Case of Kenya's Textile Industry, Working Paper no. 288, Institute for Development Studies, University of Nairobi 1976.
Wescott, C., Industrial Location and Regional Inequalities in Kenya's Formal Sector, mimeo, Nairobi 1977.
Williamson, J.G.,'Regional Inequality and the Process of National Development: A Description of the Patterns', Economic Development and Cultural Change, vol. 13, 1965.
Wolff, R.D., The Economics of Colonialism. Britain and Kenya 1870-1930, Yale University Press, New Haven 1974.
World Bank, Cost-Benefit Analysis in Education: A Case Study of Kenya, Washington D.C. 1969.
World Bank, Kenya. Into the Second Decade, The John Hopkins Press, Baltimore 1975.